Revolution in the Balance

Latin American Perspectives Series

Ronald H. Chilcote, Series Editor

†Available in hardcover and paperback

Revolution
in the Balance

Law and Society
in Contemporary Cuba

Debra Evenson

Westview Press

Boulder • San Francisco • Oxford

Latin American Perspectives Series, Number 14

Copyright © 1994 by Westview Press, Inc.

Published in 1994 in the United States of America by Westview Press, Inc., 5500 Central Avenue, Boulder, Colorado 80301-2877, and in the United Kingdom by Westview Press, 36 Lonsdale Road, Summertown, Oxford OX2 7EW

Library of Congress Cataloging-in-Publication Data
Evenson, Debra.
   Revolution in the balance : law and society in contemporary
Cuba / Debra Evenson.
      p.   cm. — (Latin American perspectives series ; no. 14)
   Includes bibliographical references and index.
   ISBN 0-8133-8466-4 — 0-8133-2146-8 (pbk.)
   1. Law—Cuba.   I. Title.   II. Series.
KGN327.E93   1994
349.7291—dc20   1000647678
[347.291]   93-44093
                                                                                              CIP

Printed and bound in the United States of America

The paper used in this publication meets the requirements
of the American National Standard for Permanence of Paper
for Printed Library Materials Z39.48-1984.

10   9   8   7   6   5   4   3   2   1

To Raúl Gómez Treto—in memoriam

Contents

Acknowledgments

This book is the product of more than four years' work, during which I received the generous help and support of many friends and colleagues both in the United States and in Cuba. I express my special gratitude to Raúl Gómez Treto and Emilio Marill Rivero for opening their libraries to me and for their valuable insights and suggestions. To the librarians at the Supreme Court of Cuba, the National Union of Cuban Jurists and the DePaul University College of Law for their help in finding materials. To the National Union of Cuban Jurists, especially Magali Rojas and Rosario Fernández, for doing so much to facilitate my research in Cuba. To my research assistants Stacy Pochis, Tracy McGonigle and Lisa Acevedo for their painstaking work tracking down information. To those who read drafts and provided critical comments, especially Jules Lobel, Carole Travis, Esther Mosak and Marc PoKempner. To Bill Montross for doing the copyediting. To DePaul University and Dean John Roberts of the College of Law for their support of this project from its inception and for providing funding for the research.

Debra Evenson

Introduction

For more than ten years I have traveled to Cuba to learn something about the concept, function and content of law in the Cuban revolution and to understand the role of jurists, in all the many facets of that term, in the process. I found, of course, that my inquiry raised many more questions than could be answered, questions that have taken on more profound meaning since 1989 when Cuba was challenged by international events to either reinvent its socialist system or give it up. As I write, Cuba has accelerated the pace of reform and experimentation under the pressures of both a dire economic situation, which is deepened by the aggressive hostility of the United States, and a natural disaster, which flooded large portions of the island in March 1993.

Speculation abounds that the Cuban economy will soon collapse, sweeping away the revolution and its leader, Fidel Castro. The assumption underlying these predictions is that the revolution is a confinable, definable object, personified by Castro himself. The premise not only dismisses more than thirty years of history, it also masks the inevitable complexities of the present situation and ignores the profound differences between the Cuban revolution and the former socialist systems of eastern Europe. Without doubt, the Cuban revolution has made a distinct imprint on Cuban society. Just as aspects of the pre-revolution social and political order continue to echo in Cuban society, the transformations and achievements of the past three decades will resonate into the future.

For those like myself who are sympathetic with the humanistic goals of the revolution, the intensity of this critical moment itself suggests that the most important question is not simply whether the system will endure under the crushing pressure of events, but rather, What has a generation of revolution accomplished? What internal contradictions and failures have impeded the effort? And what lessons and achievements become the basis for future developments in Cuba and elsewhere? This book tries to address these questions and others by looking at the development of the Cuban legal system; that is, the evolution of the framework of law and legal process that establishes and regulates the complex interrelationships between the structures of the state and the collective and its individual members.

From well before the triumphant march into Havana in January 1959, the Cuban revolution was premised on egalitarian and humanistic goals: racial and gender equality; equitable distribution of wealth including land reform; fulfillment of basic social rights to education, health care and housing; and the democratization of Cuban society. The measures employed to implement these goals were indeed radical, abruptly dismantling the structures and tenets of bourgeois capitalism and replacing them with a socialist system based on Marxist philosophy. The socialist revolution would, in the words of Ché Guevara, "create the new man."

Yet, in the early years, there was no clear ideological construct defining these decisions. Although one of the first tasks was to bring to trial the collaborators of the previous regime who were responsible for torture, assassinations and other abuses, virtually no attention at all was paid to the legal system in general except to remove obstructive justices. Lawyers were considered at best unimportant and at worst parasites. The study of law itself was deliberately permitted to atrophy. By and large, law in the first decade of the revolution consisted of major enactments and hundreds of decrees authored by the revolutionary leadership that were intended to obliterate the old order and redraw the social, economic and political landscape. These dictates were legitimized by both the moral authority of the revolution itself and the popular fervor that ratified the process by enthusiastic participation.

It was not until the early 1970s that the leadership began to elaborate a juridical basis for the revolution that would both reflect its principles and direct the evolution of socialism in Cuba. This process, frequently called the "institutionalization" of the revolution, produced the 1976 Constitution as well as new codes to replace the old pre-revolutionary laws, which had been modified piecemeal to serve the revolution's objectives. Many institutional models were adapted from the Soviet Union and other socialist countries, but the Cuban versions reflected their own national character and frequently contained important innovations. Legislation, which was often presented for discussion directly with the population through its various organized sectors, was expressly seen as the primary instrument of social change required for the achievement of socialism. Laws were adopted that governed most facets of Cuban society including family relations, labor, criminal justice, housing and property, the judicial system, legal procedure and the legal profession, as well as economic and political organization. In the early 1980s, after the institutional structure had begun to mature and the impact of previous legislation could be assessed, a series of reforms began to take place to strengthen and improve the measures undertaken in the 1970s. By this time the legal profession had been rehabilitated and was emerging as an increasingly important participant in the process.

Since 1989, the sweeping transformations in the former socialist bloc countries and their adoption of free market economies have compelled Cuba to change its commercial relations with these former trading partners and to compete in the international market. It is inevitable, as its leaders acknowledge, that Cuba continue to adapt to this new economic context. At the same time, Cuba has responded to internal needs to broaden popular participation in its political system. Moreover, pragmatism obliges the leadership to concern itself with future political transition. Reforms as well as economic pressures engender new dynamics in Cuba, but whether these forces make Cuba's reversion to a capitalist system inescapable is still open to question. At the moment Cuba resists abandoning socialist principles.

At the heart of the revolutionary effort has been the attempt to create a system that would provide economic well-being based on the equitable distribution of resources as well as conditions for social and personal development. The revolution's impressive accomplishments in universal, free education and health care, gender and racial equality and in developing popular participation were unmatched in the eastern European socialist countries and remain unmatched in most of this hemisphere. These social and economic advances have taken root in the public consciousness as fundamental rights, some more deeply than others. Ideally, expansion of democratic participation would have also progressed, but space for political exercise remains limited by the present crisis as the government strives to survive without sacrificing its social achievements.

Resolution of the tension between the collective good and individual interests is a challenge in every society. In Cuba, the revolution's accomplishments have required collective commitment and the subordination of some measure of individual autonomy and freedoms. The equation is decidedly weighted toward the collective. Though certainly limited, however, individual autonomy and freedom have not been completely subsumed by collective prerogatives. The law establishes the right to due process, which is generally respected. Moreover, the benefits of the system, particularly in education and culture, have expanded opportunities for individual growth. An assessment of the experience of the past thirty-four years, however, requires consideration of how and where the balance has been struck.

This book is not specifically about human rights in Cuba, although any treatment of law inevitably is connected to the subject of human rights. It is not my purpose to either defend or condemn. It is undeniable that there are limitations on freedom of expression and political association of those who oppose the socialist system in Cuba today. But this does not make Cuban law a sham, and it certainly does not place Cuba among the most egregious violators of human rights in the hemisphere worthy of harsh sanctions. By attempting to present a broad view of law in Cuba, I hope that this book will provide a more useful perspective on human rights in Cuba, one that is proportionate to the seriousness of the rights limitations and one that illuminates the possibilities for full enjoyment of political, civil, social, economic and cultural rights.

From January 1, 1959, until today, Cuba has lived with both direct and indirect interference from the United States. Within a very short time after the triumph of the revolutionary forces, the United States armed counter-revolutionary movements, provided a base for air attacks, and sponsored the invasion at the Bay of Pigs in April 1961. Since then, the United States has continuously strived to destabilize Cuba's socialist government. These efforts have included infiltration by U.S. agents, assassination attempts against Fidel Castro, sabotage, a near total embargo on commerce and travel between Cuba and the United States and direct interference with Cuba's economic and diplomatic relations with the rest of the world. Although U.S. hostility does not explain everything that has occurred in Cuba, it has been an ever-present factor that cannot be ignored.

The U.S. embargo is not simply unilateral. Its extra-territorial reach has and continues to deprive Cuba both of opportunities to market goods to third countries and of the ability to make purchases from capitalist countries at prevailing market prices. The continuing embargo is largely responsible for today's severe shortages of food, medicine and other necessities, endangering the very lives of Cuban citizens, and it threatens to undo the achievements of the revolution. Moreover, the relentless hostility of the United States also succeeded in maintaining varied levels of tension internally. The Institute for Economic Research of JUCEPLAN (the central planning board of Cuba) estimates that the total economic cost of the embargo for the period 1960–1990 was approximately $38 billion. However, it is impossible to calculate the cost of U.S. hostility in political terms. It is plausible to project that the Cuban revolution might have developed very differently, both economically and politically, had the United States simply been neutral toward its existence.

The inspiration for this book came as a result of my first visit to Cuba in April 1982—one month before the Reagan administration imposed restrictions on travel by U.S. citizens to Cuba. During that visit I met a number of provincial court judges as the result of a letter of introduction to Enrique Marimón, then a judge of the Cuban Supreme Court. During several hours of conversation, these judges explained the structure of the court system and patiently answered my many questions with impressive candor. One of the major concerns these judges voiced was the need to improve both the quality of Cuba's courts and the quality of its bar. In fact, they underscored the insufficient number of trained lawyers. I was intrigued by the challenge of developing an entirely new legal system to support a revolutionary agenda, and I decided to continue the inquiry.

My research has focused not only on the role of Fidel Castro but also on the many others whose work and ideas have influenced the development of law, the legal profession and legal institutions in Cuba. Fidel Castro is undoubtedly the single most important figure in the Cuban revolution, and he has exercised, and continues to exercise, considerable power and authority. Because of his stature he is often portrayed, both outside and inside Cuba, as the omnipotent leader who oversees all policy and legislative decisions. Although no major policy decision is made without Castro's approval, and he is known to sometimes intervene in even small matters, there are many individuals and institutions that have played significant roles in the development of the legal system and legislation in Cuba, and they will continue to do so in the future.

As a professional engaged in research on Cuba, I am among the few U.S. citizens exempted from the U.S. government ban on travel to Cuba, and I have taken advantage of that small opening to return to Cuba numerous times to study the transformation of the legal system. During these visits I interviewed scores of Cuban lawyers, scholars and officials and spent time studying the structure and function of Cuba's legal institutions. In addition, I attended innumerable conferences, symposia and seminars sponsored by Cuban institutions. The Cuban jurists and officials were extremely generous with their time and willingness to assist my project, and the librarians at the Library of the Supreme Court, the National Library and the National Union of Cuban Jurists offered invaluable assistance locating materials and documents.

Coincidentally, I embarked on my study at the same time that the Cuban legal system was undergoing profound reform, which enabled me to study both the changes in the law as well as the process of reform itself. Many important reforms have taken place just in the last year, including significant modifications to the 1976 Constitution. Some changes have been motivated by the pressing need to reorganize economic planning, to open up investment opportunities and to expand international trade. Others, such as the enactment of a new criminal code in 1987, are the product of several years of thoughtful analysis. Even in the midst of the current crisis, Cuba is moving toward very progressive reforms of its criminal procedure and continues to modernize its judicial system.

Because of the transformative mission of socialist law, each specific substantive area must be placed in its historic as well as its revolutionary context. Therefore, some information and concepts may be repeated to various degrees in several chapters of this book. After presenting a brief review of the legal history of Cuba prior to the revolution, the first chapter describes the transformation to socialist legality. Chapter two discusses the Cuban Constitution and the concepts of socialist democracy and individual and collective rights. Chapters three and four describe the development of the institutions and professions concerned with the implementation of law: the legal profession, the court system, the procuracy and the ministry of justice. The remaining chapters analyze specific substantive issues and areas of law: equality, family law, criminal justice, private property and economic law.

Portions of the material in this book have been published previously, but because of the pace of change the material has been substantially updated. Moreover, since developing an understanding of the Cuban system is a process in itself, I have had to revise some of the analyses as well as the conclusions drawn in these earlier writings. To be sure, changes will continue to take place, and I expect that some details in this book will also soon be outdated. It is my hope, however, that this analysis of the development of legal norms and institutions in Cuba may give some insight into the direction of the Cuban revolution, past and present.

1

Transformation
to Socialism

[A] revolution consists in the first phase in the destruction of the unjust laws of the old society; there is no doubt that our revolution has been a destroyer of laws. More just laws, the new juridical order of the new society, that is what we are trying to create now.

Fidel Castro, speech at Lomonosov University, Moscow, May 21, 1963

It was clear well before 1959 that the objectives of the Cuban revolutionary leadership went far beyond the defeat of Batista. The manifesto issued by the July 26th Movement outlined a radical social and economic program that would redistribute both wealth and power in Cuba.[1] Some have interpreted these pronouncements as reformist rather than Marxist and argue that implementation would not have required the fundamental restructuring of property ownership and political institutions in Cuba. However, the inherent contradiction between fulfillment of this program and the constraints posed by private property rights should have been apparent to any observer who took the manifesto seriously. Such far-reaching reforms would inevitably collide with vested interests in the status quo. Perhaps foreseeing these obstacles, Castro predicted in 1953 that in order to carry out a revolutionary program, the legislative, administrative and judicial powers would have to be put in the hands of the revolutionary forces: "A government acclaimed by the mass of rebel people would be vested with every power, everything necessary to proceed with the effective implementation of popular will and real justice."[2]

Indeed, once in power, the revolutionaries proceeded with breathtaking speed and determination. They promulgated hundreds of laws and decrees in the name of the masses of people who felt empowered by the victory and who cheered decisions that lowered rents, redistributed land and punished those who served the dictatorship. Within a few years, the leadership had almost completely dismantled the old economic and political order, and by the end of 1960, the socialist character of the revolution was already beginning to take shape.

The revolution dramatically affected the legal order as well. Swift, radical transformation could not be accomplished utilizing the existing law, which had served to legitimize and maintain the previous system. Similarly, since the legal profession as well as the judiciary were most likely to be aligned with the propertied interests, they were not to be trusted to support the transition. Lawyers in general were thought to be of little use, and those who had served the capitalist system were considered parasites. Moreover, the judicial system, which had changed little since independence from Spain, had never been either strong or autonomous, and it was notoriously corrupt.[3] Dishonest judges, as well as those who set themselves against the policies of the revolution, were purged. Many fled to Miami; a good number of lawyers, whose client base had vanished with the nationalization of private enterprises, joined them.

Those jurists who stayed to support the revolution, however, were not prepared to fill the juridical void and to develop a coherent legal construct for the revolution. Only a handful were schooled in Marxism/Leninism or socialist philosophy. Although courses on Marxist theory were introduced into the law school curriculum in the 1960s, very few Cubans attended law school during this period.[4] Further, most trained lawyers left legal practice for administrative positions in the government.

It is not surprising, therefore, that during most of the 1960s little attention was paid to the development of a revolutionary theory of law. Although the means of production had been converted to social property, the process of developing a juridical framework to guide the transformation of society to socialism was not initiated until the late 1960s. It has taken decades to establish a credible judicial system, to produce a generation of competent lawyers, judges and legal scholars, and to develop a coherent legal order. The evolution of law has been marked by significant gains and success, but also by reversals and failures. In sum, the construction of the "new juridical order" has proved far more difficult than the "destruction of unjust laws."

A Brief Legal History

Cuba was the first important territory colonized by Spain in the western hemisphere, and it was the last to gain its independence. After years of armed struggle, the Cubans finally won their independence in 1898, only to find themselves under the rule of the United States which imposed a military government from 1899–1902. Rather than permit the Cubans to govern themselves, the United States assigned General Leonard Wood to oversee the establishment up of a new government. As a result, Cuba's legal system has dual origins. Its primary parentage is Spanish law and the European civil law tradition, but it reflects some aspects of U.S. law as well.

Even as Cuban patriots were fighting the war of independence, Spain continued to introduce new laws and codes, some of which remained in effect until well after independence and even after the revolution of 1959. For example, the Spanish Penal Code—the substantive criminal law—remained in effect and served as the basis for the 1936 Social Defense Code, which was not repealed until 1979; the Spanish Civil Code of 1889 remained in force until 1987, although with numerous modifications. The Cuban judicial system was also modelled after the Spanish system, with one important innovation—the creation of a court of constitutional review—which reflected U.S. influence. Further, the presidential system of government and the principle of the separation of powers, which were incorporated in the first constitution of the republic adopted in 1901, were patterned after that of the United States. U.S. jurisprudence also influenced the introduction of certain elements of criminal procedure, specifically protection for the accused, such as the right not to testify.

From the time it gained its independence to the time of the revolution in 1959, Cuba adopted four constitutions: 1901, 1934, 1935 and 1940. Each of these constitutions provided for representative government and liberal protection of individual rights, but none served to establish a stable, democratic system, and they were frequently amended and/or suspended in response to political pressures. For example, the Constitution of 1901 was suspended during the U.S. military intervention from 1906 to 1909, and it was substantially amended in 1928. After the fall of the Machado dictatorship in 1933, the 1928 amendments were repealed and the 1901 Constitution reinstated. The second constitution, adopted in 1934, was amended twelve times before it was suspended in 1935 and ultimately replaced by another constitution later that same year.[5]

In 1940, as a result of public pressure, Cuba adopted yet another constitution. Hailed as one of the most progressive and modern in the hemisphere, the 1940 Constitution was drafted by a popularly elected constituent assembly that included a substantial number of delegates representing liberal and progressive constituencies, including the Communist party. Indeed, it contained provisions giving rights to Cuban workers and women that have never obtained constitutional footing in the United States.[6]

The 1940 Constitution, however, failed to fulfill the aspirations of the liberal/progressive political forces which brought it about. First, many of its provisions remained empty promises because they were not self-executing. In these instances, implementation required complementary legislation, which was never enacted by the legislature. Second, the governments elected in 1944 and 1948 were notoriously corrupt, and there was little or no public accountability. Corruption did not abate after Batista usurped power in 1952 either, and, in fact, the island became a haven for organized crime controlled by U.S. mafia figures.

Cuba's political institutions and processes, therefore, never acquired sufficient stability and legitimacy to have inspired popular respect and confidence. José Martí, the intellectual and political leader of the nineteenth century independence movement which fought for liberation from Spain, espoused democratic ideals, which included principles of political freedom as well as social and economic justice. The ideas of Martí have had, and continue to have, strong influence in Cuban philosophy. Thus, within the framework of representative government formally established by Cuba's several constitutions, the democratic impulse enjoyed its moments of expression, but it was always overpowered by either corruption or authoritative regimes. Moreover, large sectors of Cuban society never truly participated in governance or politics. They were the working poor and the unemployed who survived at the margins of the political system.

The legitimacy of Cuban governments was also undermined by frequent U.S. intrusions on Cuban national sovereignty. In the early years of the republic, the United States intervened directly in Cuban affairs as a matter of right derived from the infamous Platt Amendment.[7] Military interventions occurred in 1906, 1912 and 1917. Direct interference was less important after the repeal of the amendment in 1934 because by then both the Cuban economy and the Cuban capitalist class were dependent on the United States. In 1958, Cuban trade was completely dominated by the United States which supported the Batista regime until the eve of his defeat. Needless to say, resentment toward U.S. domination runs deep in Cuban consciousness both before and after the Cuban revolution and has been a persistent theme in Cuban politics.

One of the banners under which the revolution was fought was the fulfillment of the principles of the 1940 Constitution. In many ways, the revolution made good on this promise although it never restored the prior structure of government. For example, the 1940 Constitution prohibited both racial and gender discrimination, but former governments neither enforced these provisions nor promoted equality. Although racial discrimination was a punishable offense, whether practiced by government or private individuals,[8] employers continued to discriminate freely without reproach, and many facilities remained off-limits to non-whites. Even Batista was denied admission to certain clubs because he was mulatto. The revolution set as one of its primary goals the achievement of racial and gender equality. Described in Chapter five, the effort and results have been impressive, even if the project remains incomplete and imperfect in design. Further, the 1940 Constitution required abolition of *latifundio* (large landholding)[9] and restriction of foreign ownership of Cuban property[10] as well as efforts to improve public education[11] and to address the need for low-income housing,[12] but no action was forthcoming until after 1959.

The First Years

On January 1, 1959, neither Washington nor Cuba's propertied elite were capable of taking the lead after Batista's sudden departure, and they stood by virtually immobile as the revolutionary forces stepped into power buoyed by popular euphoria over the defeat of the dictatorship. Immediately, the revolutionary forces began to assume control of political and legal institutions. A number of liberals, including some prominent lawyers, who had supported the overthrow of Batista in hopes of establishing a bourgeois democracy, joined the new government.

As previously agreed, Castro installed Manuel Urrutia Lleo, a former judge, as president on January 2, 1959. Urrutia had been chosen because of his prestige and acceptability to both the moderate middle-class backers of the revolution and to the guerrilla forces who took part in the alliance formed in Caracas in 1958.[13] In his brief tenure as president of Cuba, Urrutia presided over a cabinet comprising both prominent members of the middle-class who were moderates and members of Castro's July 26th Movement.[14] The moderates, including Urrutia, resisted the revolutionary program for reconstructing Cuba, but they were unable to pose an alternative or to solidify a base of support of their own. Fidel Castro and the revolutionary leadership had captured the hearts of the masses. Military and police power were in the hands of the revolutionaries. Thus, those expecting that defeat of Batista's tyranny would bring bourgeois democracy to Cuba were easily brushed aside by the tide of radical change. It is not surprising, therefore, that by mid-summer of 1959, many in the original cabinet, including President Urrutia, were gone.[15]

Yet, in the first six months of 1959, many fundamental legal changes took place with the approval of Urrutia and his supporters. Within weeks of Batista's abdication, the revolutionary government introduced comprehensive changes in Cuban law that radically altered Cuban society and politics and paved the way for consolidation of power in the hands of Fidel Castro and his supporters.[16] Although it reinstated much of the 1940 Constitution, the Fundamental Law of February 7, 1959 suspended the Congress and vested all legislative authority in the new Council of Ministers, which functioned under a prime minister appointed by the Council.[17] The first prime minister, José Miró Cardona, was also a political moderate and president of the Havana Bar Association. In addition, the Fundamental Law provided for the suspension of the irremovability of ministers and the judiciary.[18] These measures were signed by Urrutia and his associates, who also went along with the postponement of elections which were to have taken place within six months.[19]

Controlled by the revolutionary leadership, the Council immediately set about transforming the social and economic order, enacting over one hundred new laws between 1959 and 1963. These laws included the first Agrarian Reform Law (May 1959), the Urban Reform Law (October 1960), the Nationalization Law (October 1960) which nationalized nearly every important private enterprise, the Nationalization of Education Law (June 1961) and the second Agrarian Reform Law (October 1963). In addition to this major legislation, the government issued hundreds of detailed decrees. In a formal sense, the government was very legalistic. No action was taken without first declaring a law, even if the law was modified numerous times as circumstances required. These decrees were in essence the dictates of a small elite, but their legitimacy emanated from the unfolding revolution which enjoyed massive popular support.

New institutional structures were established parallel to the existing ministries and the courts, giving Fidel Castro more flexibility to maneuver around both the old bureaucratic structures. The most important of these was the National Institute of Agrarian Reform (INRA) which implemented land reform and agricultural policy. INRA enjoyed autonomy from the Council of Ministers and had wide latitude for creative and flexible interpretation and application of the law. Osvaldo Dórticos Torrado, who succeeded Urrutia as president of the republic in July 1959, wrote in the first issue of *Cuba Socialista,* published in September 1961, that the INRA was created because the revolution needed a mechanism free of the obsolete, bureaucratic bottlenecks of the old system.[20]

In addition, the newly created Revolutionary Tribunals operated independently of and parallel to the ordinary courts. These special tribunals tried the hundreds of Batista collaborators who had committed acts of assassination, torture and other abuses. After July 1959, they were given jurisdiction to try those accused of counter-revolutionary activity. People's Courts were also established independent of the ordinary courts to hear local complaints and try misdemeanors. Although breaking with the pattern of existing, more traditional institutions, and infusing the system with a measure of popular justice, these innovations and others did not provide the basis for the development of an integrated, unified system of legal and government structures.

By the end of the decade the counter-revolution had been quelled and the armed attacks, terrorist bombings and other acts of sabotage no longer posed a serious threat to security. Other factors, however, were threatening the stability of the revolution: a faltering economy and a chaotic web of bureaucratic regulations and institutions. It became clear that the revolution could not simply rely on revolutionary zeal and sacrifice for its survival. The government had to define a coherent legal, economic and political framework that could provide direction and continuity for the aspiring socialist state. Further, growing dependence on the Soviet Union and Cuba's integration into the socialist market of eastern Europe governed by the Council for Mutual Economic Assistance (CMEA) necessitated the development of a centralized planning apparatus which paralleled that of its new trading partners. Among other things, this meant the construction of a new juridical base, the creation of legal institutions and the production of lawyers and jurists trained to serve the socialist state. The era of radical experimentation came to an end, and the revolution looked to eastern Europe for stable models.

Elaborating a Socialist Legal Order

In the late 1960s the Central Committee of the Communist Party established the Commission on Juridical Studies to formulate this framework. Chaired by Blas Roca Calderío, former general secretary of the pre-1959 Cuban Communist Party, this commission was composed of lawyers and academics who were trained under capitalism but who were committed to socialist doctrine. These jurists set out to rationalize the system and to create both the stable institutions and the legal tools for the transformation of society. They were also concerned with predictability and fairness in the resolution of disputes and with the necessity of educating the population to conform to the new socialist system.

Although the Cubans studied the legislation and experiences of the Soviet Union and the Eastern European countries very closely, they did not simply copy them. In its legislation, institutions and legal procedures, the Cuban legal system exhibits a distinct national imprint as well as important innovations.

Over a six-year period, the commission studied every aspect of the juridical order. As a result of its work, several fundamental bodies of legislation were adopted, including the Cuban socialist Constitution of 1976, the Law on the Organization of the Judicial System, the Code of Criminal Procedure and the Family Code. This legislation was drafted by special commissions working both in coordination with the Cuban Communist Party and in consultation with mass organizations which had been created in the early 1960s, such as the Federation of Cuban Women (FMC), the Central Organization of Cuban Workers (CTC), the National Association of Small Farmers (ANAP), and the Committees for the Defense of the Revolution (CDRs).

Laxness about compliance with law had become epidemic, and recuperation of judicial process was considered essential to instill respect for and confidence in the law. Thus, the law on the judicial system itself was the first major piece of legislation to be drafted by these commissions, and it was adopted even before the constitution. The construction of a unified court system coincided with the adoption of a new Code of Criminal Procedure in 1973. Both developments contributed to greater fairness and consistency in criminal procedure, but development of a respectable, modern judicial system would take many years.

The process of institutionalization also included the restructuring of the legislative and administrative organs of government. The proposed structure of the Cuban socialist state was approved at the First Congress of the Party in 1975, and it was established in the 1976 Constitution and subsequent legislation. The 1976 Constitution established Popular Assemblies (*Poder Popular*) at the municipal, provincial and national levels. Although only the National Assembly was given legislative authority, it was the first time since the revolution that an elected body was formally given a role in governing the country. During the 1970s the government also laid the groundwork for the development of structures for the planning and management of the economy. Cuban jurists assert that the juridical foundation for these and subsequent measures rests on the concept of socialist legality, which defines the theoretical basis for the creation of the new society in Cuba.

Socialist Legality

Far from being nihilistic or arbitrary in their attitude toward law, Cuban scholars were very concerned, on the one hand, with interpreting and enriching the ideological framework and, on the other hand, with developing legal norms and procedures that not only were consistent with that framework but would contribute to the improvement of the socialist system. Legal theory, even if applied formalistically, has been central both to shaping the content of specific laws as well as to the evolution of a coherent jurisprudential basis for the Cuban socialist state. This regard for socialist legal principle is expressly stated both in the constitution and other legislation.

Pursuant to the concept of socialist legality, law and government perform a positive, dynamic function in the creation of socialism. The objective of law is not only to regulate but to transform society. In the words of Lenin, "A law is a political instrument, it is political."[21] Thus, law is a tool to shape social behavior; it serves not to preserve the status quo but to provide the basis for the continuous evolution toward socialism.

In fulfilling its function, law must satisfy two potentially conflicting objectives essential to the transformation to socialism. Law must establish the basis for social stability, but it also must create the conditions for social development as well as for the continuous perfection of legislation itself. This dynamic quality of socialist legality represents a radical departure from the conservatism of the civil law system Cuba inherited from Spain. Civil law systems, based on detailed, lengthy codes, resist change as a matter of principle. As asserted by John H. Merryman, the civil law tradition elevated the value of certainty in the law "to the level of dogma."[22]

Even under U.S. common law tradition, in which law evolves through judicial interpretation, changes generally reflect custom or a consensus that has already emerged in society. Thus, in the United States and other industrialized countries, whose legal systems have developed gradually with the emergence of modern capitalism, law has been a stabilizing, regulating force that adjusts slowly to accommodate new circumstances. It functions both to enforce established norms and to resolve conflicts arising from these norms, but it rarely has the purpose of affirmatively changing society.

Like the evolution of common law, legislative reforms are not intended to significantly alter societal values. For example, the U.S. civil rights acts of the 1960s attempted to regulate behavior that impinged on accepted definitions of individual rights. The goal of these statutes was primarily to grant racial minorities and women the same formal rights enjoyed by white males. It was not to achieve substantive equality. Thus, in general, courts interpreted their provisions narrowly, and imposed significant barriers to litigants seeking redress for discrimination.[23] When public institutions attempted to apply affirmative measures to remedy the historic impact of racial inequality—to bring about equality of results—conservative jurists and politicians acted to prevent an interpretation that would give law such a transformative role.[24] In contrast, the objective of law in socialist Cuba has been both to regulate and to transform.

In the process of developing a methodology for the development and implementation of socialist law, Cuban jurists struggled with the definition of socialist legality, an abstract expression which appears not only in the Constitution but also in other legislation. For example, the Constitution states that one of the primary roles of the courts is to "strengthen socialist legality,"[25] and the Procuracy is assigned to "enforce socialist legality."[26] The term connotes a distinction between "socialist legality" and what might be called "capitalist legality" beyond the difference in the content of the laws of the respective systems. One such difference, of course, is the transformative function of socialist law.

One might conclude, as some Cuban jurists have, that socialist legality is coterminous with the content of socialist legislation.[27] Pursuant to such a narrow, formalistic concept, socialist legality would by definition encompass any law or regulation promulgated by the socialist government. Some theorists, however, have considered this definition too limited and static. They argue for a broader principle that embraces not only the transformative content of law but the structures of enforcement and governance as well.[28] In the mid-1980s, the meaning of socialist legality was re-examined and given an even more inclusive definition that encompassed the very process by which the socialist system continues to transform itself, thus infusing the term with a juridical-political dynamic.[29] Understood in this way, socialist legality is more than just normative law which serves as an instrument to regulate society and to transform social values. It also includes the value system according to which laws are evaluated and amended as well as the very method by which the state governs the society.

Accordingly, Cuban scholars have considered the constitution much more than a legal document. Dórticos, who became Minister of Justice in the late 1970s, asserted that socialist constitutions serve as dynamic agents in the evolution toward communism, an essential quality that differentiates them from capitalist constitutions which preserve the status quo: "The Constitution in a socialist society is not just history which has taken place, but it is history which is still taking place."[30] By establishing the juridical organization of the state and society, the constitution also creates the conditions for the development of the social relations and objectives that are expressed in it.[31] In essence, it "creates the bases to propel the socialist society into the future."[32] Thus, while the constitution is foremost a legal document that establishes the norms for law and legislation, it also assumes a transformative mission which makes it a "transcendental" political document.[33]

Although a revolution is a process, not an event, Cuba has attempted to design and implement a new legal order in less than two decades. The complex task of managing a socialist economy and mediating the social contradictions that have emerged in the process of building socialism has produced a permanent state of reassessment and reform in Cuba. In the process Cuba must solve more than one paradox. Consistent with Marxist theory and their own civil law tradition, Cuban jurists accept the belief that law has a scientific basis. Yet the challenge of creating and applying new rules in untested waters is daunting, and success requires attention to the subjective aspects of law and its social impact. Further, there is an inherent tension between the need for stability and the drive to continuously perfect, but it is one that the state must perpetually strive to manage in order to generate a new society.

The response to changing circumstances and emerging problems has resulted in minor adjustments, substantial alterations and at times complete reversal of established policy. For example, in 1987 the Cuban government substantially revised the Criminal Code it had adopted in 1979. Cuba enacted a general housing law in 1984 which it repealed and replaced with a new statute in 1988. Farmers' markets, which were permitted to open in 1980, were closed in 1986. Since 1980, Cuba has also revised other laws, such as those concerning private farms and cooperatives, and reorganized the judicial system a third time. In July 1992 significant amendments to the Constitution set the stage for further reform. Other important legislative modifications are currently under consideration including significant revisions of the Code of Criminal Procedure.

Although perhaps correcting errors as well as realizing important gains, the reforms have created great uncertainty with negative effects on compliance: If the law changes from one day to the next, how can one be sure what it is today or what it will be tomorrow? The problem was highlighted in 1985 at the

Third Party Congress, which approved a program of *rectificación* (rectification) of the errors and deficiencies in the Cuban socialist system. According to one jurist, the Cuban legislative process has suffered from lack of systemization and coherence resulting from years of too much improvisation and spontaneity and too little research, analysis and planning.[34] Aggravating the problem, the pace of change since 1989 has left little time to study and to reflect on the reverberations of the measures in society. With few appropriate models to learn from, the tension created by the need to maintain stability in the face of rapid reform complicates the possibility of sustained conformity with and movement toward socialist goals.

The fit between theory and practice is rarely perfect in any system. In Cuba the gap has been hard to narrow because the theory itself is new and unproven. Moreover, the experiments in eastern Europe, which served as a model for the Cuban system, failed and have been abandoned. In many ways the endeavor has also been impeded by the formalistic nature both of the civil law tradition Cuba inherited from Spain as well as the bureaucratic mechanisms adopted from the former Soviet Union and other eastern European countries. Despite the constraints of this legacy and the want of alternative, theoretical and practical models, however, Cuba has achieved significant progress in many areas of its legal system, and Cuban jurists have made important and interesting contributions to the development of socialist law.

In order to continue to adhere to the basic premises of socialist theory regarding social and economic welfare and the role of the state in guiding the economy Cuba must find new methods and approaches. As the economic crisis deepens, the ability to find and implement solutions that preserve its socialist principles becomes extremely difficult.

Notes

1. "Manifesto No. 1 del 26 de Julio al pueblo de Cuba," issued on August 8, 1955, from Mexico, called for the same radical reforms that Fidel Castro iterated in his famous defense speech at the 1953 Moncada trial, known as "History Will Absolve Me." These include, among other things, the outlawing of the *latifundia* and redistribution of land to small farmers and laborers, worker participation in the profits of large, commercial and mining enterprises, drastic reduction in al rents, nationalization of public services (telephone, electricity and gas), extension of education and increases in pay to public employees. The manifesto is printed in English translation in *Revolutionary Struggle* (Cambridge, Mass: The MIT Press, 1972), Rolando E. Bonachea and Nelson P. Valdés, eds., pp. 259–271.

2. Fidel Castro, *History Will Absolve Me* (New York: Center for Cuban Studies, undated), p. 25.

3. See Chapter four.

4. See Chapter three.

5. For a history and the full texts of Cuba's constitutions before 1959, see Andrés M. Lazcano y Mazón, *Las Constituciones de Cuba* (Madrid: Ediciones Cultura Hispánica, 1952).

6. For example, the 1940 Constitution prohibited gender discrimination (Art. 20) and contained a provision guaranteeing equal pay for equal work (Art. 62). It also guaranteed to each worker one month's vacation a year for each eleven months worked (Art. 67). Although extremely progressive, many of these provisions required implementing legislation which was never forthcoming.

7. The Platt Amendment was attached to the Cuban Constitution as a result of a treaty between the United States and Cuba, signed in May 1903. The withdrawal of U.S. occupational forces from the isalnd was conditioned on the Cuban acceptance of this amendment by which Cuba consented that "the United States may exercise the right to intervene for the preservation of Cuban independence, the maintenance of a government adequate for the protection of life, property, and individual liberty, and for discharging the oblgations with respect to Cuba imposed by the Treaty of Paris on the United States." The amendment also imposed limitations on the Cuban government's ability to contract debt and prohibited Cuba from permitting any foreign power from having control of any portion of Cuba or use any portion for military purposes. Treaty Between the United States and Cuba, signed in Havana May 22, 1903.

8. Constitución de la República de Cuba (1940), Art. 20.

9. Ibid., Art. 90.

10. Ibid.

11. Ibid., Art. 51.

12. Ibid., Art. 79.

13. Hugh Thomas, *Cuba: The Pursuit of Freedom* (New York: Harper & Row, 1971), p. 970. In 1957, as the presiding judge in the Santiago trial, Urrutia had dissented from the majority court decision to convict one hundred Castro supporters accused of sabotage. Urrutia argued that such actions against an unconstitutional government were justified. In December 1957, Urrutia went to Miami and joined a five-man government of Cuba in exile. Ibid., pp. 942, 970–91. Urrutia apparently was in little danger in Cuba even after voting against conviction of the rebels. Opponents of Batista had asked him to join the Miami group in November, but he stayed on until December in order to accrue his retirement benefits. Ibid.

14. Ibid., p. 1066.

15. Ibid., pp. 1232–33, 1291–92. Although many members of the legal profession left Cuba in the 1960s, many also stayed and joined the revolutionary project. They went to work for economic institutions like the National Institute of Agrarian Reform and the National Bank. Others found positions in the Ministry of the Interior, the Ministry of Justice and the courts. See Chapter three.

16. Failure to produce major institutional reform, as well as inability to wrest power from the military, led to reversal of the gains made by the provisional government which took power after Machado's fall. As a result of the liberal coalition which formed the new government, the more radical elements were isolated, and eventually the military under Fulgencio Batista re-established its control. Although some democratic reforms were instituted between 1934 and 1952, including the liberal Constitution of 1940, these were swept away by the military coup of 1952 which reinstalled Batista. Some of the rad-

ical student leaders in the 1933 revolt played important roles in the revolution which brought down Batista in 1959. For a discussion of the 1933 revolution, see Luís Aguilar, *Cuba 1933* (Ithaca, N.Y.: Cornell University Press, 1972).

17. Ley Fundamental, Art. 119, *Gaceta Oficial,* February 7, 1959.

18. Ibid., Disposiciones Transitorias Adicionales, Quinta.

19. Thomas, pp. 1084–1086.

20. Osvaldo Dórticos Torrado, "Los Cambios institucionales y políticos de la Revolución Socialista Cubana," *Cuba Socialista,* No. 1, Sept. 1961, p. 29. The Institute's initial task was to carry out land expropriations which took place between 1959 and 1963. At the end of this phase INRA was converted into a state organ in charge of organizing, promoting and overseeing agricultural production. It also promoted socialist forms of farming such as the cooperatives and peoples' farms (granjas del pueblo), and it created the National Association of Agricultural Producers (ANAP). At first INRA functioned independently, but in 1962 when Cuba adopted its first national economic plan, INRA was integrated into the economic development of the country. Ibid.

21. "La Legalidad y la Cultura Jurídica en Cuba en la Etapa Actual," *Revista Jurídica,* No. 2 (1979), p. 4 (quoting Lenin).

22. John Henry Merryman, *The Civil Law Tradition* (Stanford, Calif: Stanford University Press, 1985), p. 48.

23. Ibid.

24. See, for example, *Regents of the Univ. of California* v. *Bakke,* 438 U.S. 265 (1978)(striking down the medical school's minority admissions program); *City of Richmond* v. *Crosan,* 488 U.S. 468 (1989)(striking down a minority set-aside program to promote minority-owned business).

25. Constitución (1976), Art. 123(a).

26. Ibid., Art. 130.

27. "La Legalidad y la Cultura Jurídica en Cuba en la Etapa Actual," *Revista Jurídica,* No. 2 (1979), p. 4.

28. Julio Fernández Bulté, "El Concepto Científico Ampliado de la Nueva Sociedad," 1er. Simposio Científico Acerca de la Política y la Ideología en sus Relaciones con el Derecho (Havana: Ediciones Minjus, 1984), p. 4.

29. Ibid.

30. Osvaldo Dórticos Torrado, "Discurso Pronunciado en el Acto Central por el V Aniversario de la Constitución de la República," *Revista Cubana de Derecho,* No. 16 (1980), p. 6.

31. Ibid., p. 7.

32. Ibid.

33. Ibid.

34. Amado Guntin Guerra, "La legalidad socialista en el proceso de rectificación de errores," *Revista Cubana de Derecho,* No. 34 (1988), pp. 145, 150.

2

Democracy and Rights

The rationale currently relied upon by Cuba's detractors to justify economic strangulation of the socialist government is the lack of democracy and respect for individual rights. Much hostile propaganda produced in the 1980s portrays Cuba's socialist system as static and tyrannical. The Cuban Constitution is dismissed as not worth the paper it is printed on. For their part, Cuban officials argue that democracy in Cuba is superior to other systems and provides greater opportunities for popular participation. Further, they contend that individual rights should be understood differently in Cuba than in capitalist countries. At the core of the polemic are deep ideological differences. This chapter attempts to explore some of the key issues of debate: constitutionalism, democracy and rights.

The Cuban Socialist Constitutions

The 1976 Constitution was drafted by a commission appointed by the Party in 1974. Like the Family Code and other major legislation of the 1970s, it was circulated in draft form among all the mass organizations for discussion and recommendations. Although the changes made as a result of these discussions were minor, the process played a very important role in educating the public to the provisions and implications of the socialist order embodied in the Constitution. The Constitution was approved in a special national referendum on February 15, 1976.

The content of the Cuban Constitution is overtly ideological, but it is also juridical. It embraces the essential core of socialist legality in contemporary Cuban jurisprudence. Then Minister of Justice Osvaldo Dórticos Torrado commented on the fundamental role of the socialist constitution on the occasion of the fifth anniversary of its adoption:

> As a juridical instrument, a legal instrument, it is the principal form and source of expression of State Law. In effect, the State creates all norms basing them in the

21

Constitution, which is the juridical support of all legislation. The constitutional norms condition all drafting and realization of state legislation and condition the legitimacy of laws. The constitution also establishes the basis of the life of the state.[1]

Consistent with this view of the affirmative role of the constitution to define the objectives and character of the society, the 1976 Constitution declared Cuba to be a "socialist state" and provided that the economic system be based on the social ownership of the means of production.[2]

Central to the constitutional scheme is the state's obligation to assure the economic and social well-being of the collective. Thus, the Constitution entrusts the state with the responsibility to organize and direct the national economy.[3] By virtue of its control over economic planning and production, the state guarantees a great many positive social and economic rights to the citizens. These rights include the right to work, to leisure time and to vacations,[4] the right to social security protection,[5] the right to free health care[6] and the right to free education.[7] Thus, the state must manage economic resources to assure fulfillment of these rights and the well-being of the collective.

Since egalitarian values are at the core of Cuban socialism, the constitution also establishes both equality of rights and duties for all citizens and prohibits discrimination based on race, color, sex or national origin.[8] The state's obligation with respect to equality goes far beyond simply guaranteeing equality before the law. It must affirmatively "create all the conditions which help to make real the principle of equality" and to assure equal treatment,[9] including equal pay for equal work.[10] Special attention is given to the equality of women. Constitutional provisions accord women not only social, economic and political equality but also establish equality in family relations.[11] The Constitution also makes provision for individual liberties such as the right to freedom of speech and of the press "in keeping with the objectives of socialist society;"[12] the rights to assembly,[13] demonstration and association;[14] the right to petition authorities;[15] the right to freedom of conscience and religious belief;[16] and the rights to privacy of home and mail,[17] freedom from arbitrary arrest,[18] personal property,[19] due process of law[20] and other rights.

As the fundamental law governing society, the Constitution sets the framework for legislation that establishes the economic system and institutions as well as the governmental structure. It declares the Communist Party of Cuba "the highest leading force of the society and of the state, which organizes and guides the common effort toward the goals of the construction of socialism and the progress toward a communist society."[21] Power to legislate, however, is vested in the National Assembly[22] and its executive committee, the Council of State,[23] and administrative authority is given to the Council of Ministers.[24]

When Cuban lawyers embarked on the project of developing the juridical base for the revolution, particularly the constitutional framework, they naturally depended greatly on socialist jurisprudence, particularly the works of Soviet legal scholars. Although the content of the Cuban Constitution of 1976 does closely resemble the Soviet Constitution of 1977, sharing broad concepts and the same general structure of political institutions and the organization of the state, the Cubans did not simply imitate. Some of the methods of governance, procedures of implementation and the articulation of some rights were distinctly Cuban. For example, unlike the Soviet Constitution, the Cuban Constitution gives express recognition to the mass organizations—the Central Organization of Cuban Trade Unions (CTC), the Committees for the Defense of the Revolution (CDRs), the Federation of Cuban Women (FMC), the National Association of Small Farmers (ANAP), the Federation of University Students (FEU) and the Federation of Students of Intermediate Education (FEEM)—and grants them a role in carrying out state policy. The difference suggests that the Cubans intended at the beginning to incorporate a higher level of popular participation in the development and implementation of policy. The Cuban Constitution also contains much stronger provisions regarding the equality of women than the Soviet Constitution.

Faced with the need to integrate fully into the world market and to adjust to a new political and economic context, the Cuban government adopted significant modifications to the Constitution in July 1992. The result of more than two years of discussion and debate,[25] these amendments redefine some basic constitutional norms. Socialist ownership of property is now qualified and encompasses the "fundamental means of production" as opposed to simply "the means of production," as stated in the 1976 Constitution. The modification makes possible the introduction of economic flexibility. Further, unlike the 1976 Constitution, the 1992 revisions expressly recognize forms of non-socialist property. In addition, the revisions increase religious liberty and equality. They also expanded popular participation by permitting direct election of both the National and Provincial Assemblies. Previously, representatives to the National and Provincial Assemblies were elected by members of the municipal assemblies who had been chosen by direct elections.

Although the amendments do not represent radical reform, they have enormous transformative potential. The Cuban leadership regards them as far more than mere minor adjustments, but they contend that the charter remains fundamentally the same as the document adopted in 1976. On the other hand, observers who have characterized the changes as merely cosmetic because they did not signal rejection of socialism have missed their significance. At the very least, these amendments signal Cuba's abandonment of the Soviet model. Moreover, the alteration in the economic and political dynamic which these amendments engender creates the conditions for important changes in Cuban socialism. As Cuba follows a path of reform, the Constitution may continue to be, in the words of Dórticos, "history in the making."[26]

Specific provisions of the Constitution are discussed more fully in the following section and in subsequent chapters.

Socialist Democracy

Cuban legal scholars have shown little regard for capitalist democracy, which, in their view, is a hypocritical system: a democracy for a minority of exploiters and a form of oppression of the majority.[27] The capitalist constitution is described as a classist document that expresses the interests of the dominant class and assures its supremacy.[28] As one author has stated: "In essence the bourgeois state is the dictatorship by the bourgeoisie, but it remains democratic for the capitalists."[29] Former dean of the University of Havana's Law Faculty, Julio Fernández Bulté, recently criticized representative democracy, which he asserted was "each day less representative, and it never was democratic."[30] Certainly, although even bourgeois democracy is acknowledged to have its own dialectic that may broaden its representativeness within a range tolerable to the dominant class, the Cuban experience with it was not a happy one.

The Cuban disdain for bourgeois democracy may be partly attributed to the defense of the socialist system as a superior form of democracy, but it springs primarily from a completely different concept of democracy. Socialists argue that there is dictatorship and democracy in all systems. What characterizes "true democracy" is the measure of equality and popular participation in decision-making afforded. Thus, socialist democracy mandates the elimination of class divisions between the exploiter and the exploited, because there can never be equality between the two. Liberty for one means oppression of the other. Further, socialist democracy enhances popular participation both by creating the material conditions for education and physical health and by the eventual entrustment of governance to the masses.

Socialist democracy, which enables true equality before the law, however, requires not only the destruction of the capitalist class by eliminating the tools of domination but also the suppression of all the manifestations of the bourgeois past: individualism, egocentricity, personal greed, irresponsibility toward the collective and social property and so on. The struggle against the deformations of the past is a long-term project, not one to be accomplished overnight with the defeat of the capitalist state.[31] Thus, the transformation to socialist democracy requires repression of past values and cannot succeed without the dictatorship of the proletariat.

In addition to uprooting the corrupting vestiges of the past, the achievement of socialist democracy requires both the construction of the collective productive forces and the elevation of the political and cultural education of the masses. As a result, socialist democracy will not put the masses in charge of the organs of government from the beginning. Rather, the leaders who are the vanguard of the proletariat, will govern on behalf of and in the name of the workers on the basis of democratic centralism. To achieve full democracy, however, the political and juridical mechanisms must be developed and employed by the vanguard to promote the continuous incorporation of the workers' participation in governance. By this definition, the process is not a static one; socialist democracy creates the conditions for the progressive expansion of popular democracy.

Fundamental to socialist democracy, of course, is the collective appropriation of the means of production, which allows for both the equitable distribution of resources and the employment of resources to benefit the collective, as opposed to private interests. Education and physical and material well-being are fundamental to the development of the socialist citizen and for meaningful democratic participation. By ensuring these benefits socialism creates the material base essential to the realization of popular democracy.

Before the economic decline that began in the late 1980s, the Cuban government was able to progressively raise the educational level and provide the other material conditions necessary for meaningful democratic participation. The massive literacy campaign of 1961 sent thousands of Cuban youth into the countryside to teach reading and writing and to learn about rural life. Since then the Ministry of Education has strived to increase the national educational level to a minimum of ninth-grade achievement. Beginning in the early 1960s, the government also created vehicles for popular participation in specific areas of policy and program development and implementation, such as the mass organizations, which played an important role in the social organization of broad sectors of society.

The mass organizations, which were specifically recognized in the Constitution, were given special tasks in the development of the socialist society. Through membership in these organizations, thousands of Cubans became personally engaged in social change efforts for the first time in Cuban history. They participated in health projects, neighborhood associations, citizen militia, workplace assemblies, etc. Further, the mass organizations have had a direct influence at times on the development of legislation. At a minimum they were consulted by the Party and the assemblies on issues relevant to their concerns. For example, the FMC has frequently initiated and promoted changes in regulations affecting women in addition to participating in the drafting of the Family Code.

The system of democratic centralism, dependent on the vanguard, however, progressively limited the parameters for popular debate and channels for popular influence over national policy. As the system of government, patterned on the Soviet model, became increasingly bureaucratized, so too did the structures that had been developed to promote popular participation, including the mass organizations and the legislative assemblies. Rather than encouraging creativity and innovation in these organizations, the Party monopolized policy making and utilized the mass organizations as vehicles of implementation. The resulting formalism and dogmatic character of these institutions led to widespread criticism in the late 1980s that they were losing touch with and were not responsive to their base membership.

The failure or reluctance to broaden participation might be attributed to several different factors. The infancy of the socialist state necessitated dependence on the leadership of those who had freed themselves from bourgeois ideas and values. Moreover, the antagonistic policy of the United States toward Cuba since 1961 has constantly threatened destabilization. Limited channels of popular influence may also reflect a continuing lack of confidence on the part of the political elite in the people to steer the socialist state, as well as a simple refusal to relinquish control by those in power. Whatever the true explanation, the result over time was a tendency to entrench paternalism and to reinforce the hold of the bureaucracy rather than to extend popular democracy.

The constraints on participation and the limited boundaries of permissible debate created a fundamental contradiction: Instead of fulfilling its role of elevating the masses to a position where they could take control, the vanguard created and maintained a dichotomy between the ruling elite and the nonreliable masses. The fact that the governors may be wise, humanitarian and sensitive to the interests of the masses does not diminish the danger posed to prospects for "true democracy." To promote the progressive strengthening of socialist democracy, participation must be steadily broadened.

Recent Advances in Popular Participation

During the series of public forums leading up to the 1991 Party Congress, many Cubans severely criticized the progressive bureaucratization and formalism that had taken hold in the system. In addition, many argued for direct elections for the Provincial and National Assemblies. As a result, the proposal for direct elections was enacted as part of the 1992 constitutional amendments, and was implemented in the elections for delegates to the Provincial and National Assemblies that took place in February 1993.

The Party declared at the outset that it would not formally participate in the nomination of candidates for election. After considerable debate and discussion over how candidates would be nominated and how both regional and national representation would be accommodated, the National Assembly approved an electoral law in October 1992.[32] The law established national and provincial candidacy commissions organized to select candidates.[33] Over a three-month period, the national commission, comprising representatives from the mass organizations, received more than 60,000 nominations from their membership and the population at large, from which 589 were to be selected as candidates for the National Assembly.[34] The final selection of candidates was made in consultation with the municipal assemblies, which had been elected on December 20, 1992. The national and provincial elections were scheduled for February 24, 1993.

The electoral process gave the population the first opportunity to vote directly for its national and provincial representatives. It did not, however, provide for contested elections; nor could candidates other than those nominated by the commission be elected. Voters could either vote for all or some of the candidates selected, not vote at all, or cast a blank or defaced ballot as a way of expressing opposition to the candidates, and by extension the government. However, half the candidates for the National Assembly were to be chosen from among the delegates elected to the municipal assemblies. Since municipal delegates are nominated in open neighborhood assemblies and elected in contested elections, the population *did* have a direct say in who those potential candidates might be.

Although the electorate could not choose among competing candidates, the election was widely viewed as a means of expressing approval or disapproval with the system. Prior to the elections, Miami radio stations regularly exhorted Cubans to spoil ballots or to write "no" on the ballot as a way of expressing their opposition to the government. The Cuban government too perceived the election as a kind of referendum, and it launched a campaign to encourage voters to vote for "unity." According to official statistics, over 98 percent of the population voted. Nationally, a little over 3 percent of ballots were reported blank and 4 percent spoiled. Foreign journalists who witnessed ballot counting reported that the percentage of those voting "no" by either spoiling their ballot, leaving the ballot blank or writing an anti-government slogan varied, ranging as high as 10 to 20 percent in some voting districts.[35] In Havana, where the greatest discontent appears to be concentrated, the percentage reportedly reached 30 percent in one district. Apparently, although Cubans may have felt compelled to cast ballots to avoid the approbation of their neighbors, many did not fear reprisal for voting against the official slate. Some outside observers have characterized the new electoral process as fraudulent appeasement of internal and external pressures for democratization. The vote, however, demonstrated that, for whatever reasons, the government maintains substantial support.

Consistent with the theory of "socialist legality," these measures are viewed as steps in a continuing process, which, if allowed to continue, will create its own dynamic for further reform. Equally important, there is genuine concern in Cuba, not just among members of the leadership, but at other levels as well, that survival of the socialist system requires greater flexibility and inclusiveness in the political system. Arguing for a renewed dedication to the strengthening of popular democracy, Julio Fernández Bulté, forcefully expressed the immediacy of the task:

We are in a moment in which the falsities and errors of one model of socialist society have limited the credibility of the Marxist-Leninist project of socialism. For that reason today more than ever we Marxist-Leninists are pressed to clarify not only the theoretical bases of the socialist model but also to enrich it with real practice, so that we Cubans will enjoy the almost absolute privilege of being able to shape our own society and our own state model.

Likewise, we do not suggest abandoning electoral principles, although we do not blind ourselves with the deceptions of representative elections. To the contrary, we must perfect these models.

This will take us, together with the whole socialist project, to the full and real establishment of true human rights and their guarantee. We must work at this as we are already working, and we must reflect on all of this as, lamentably, we have not done with the necessary rigor.[36]

The introduction of direct elections for representatives to the National and Provincial Assemblies was an important step toward improving the democratic process. A substantial number of new faces appear in the National Assembly as well as in the Council of State. Only ninety-eight former delegates to the National Assembly were re-elected; more than half of the thirty-one member Council of State is new. Even if the electoral procedures employed were imperfect and the subject of controversy, the change may very well provide the basis for further expansion of participation of the electorate in the future.

Reforming the Legislature

At the same time that the new electoral process was instituted, leadership in the National Assembly began to consider measures that would begin to convert that body into a genuine deliberative legislature. The institutional structure and procedures of the National Assembly have impeded its transformation into a true legislature: The delegates have been primarily non-professionals with neither offices nor staff to assist them. Although the National Assembly organized work commissions to participate in the drafting and evaluation of legislation, the assembly itself convened only twice a year for sessions lasting only four or five days, during which it would debate and approve key pieces of legislation. However, by the time legislation reached the National Assembly it had been reviewed and discussed by Party commissions as well as by the relevant ministries, agencies and organizations, depending on the subject matter. It also had obtained the approval of the executive branch, the Council of State. Although the assembly might insert modifications or remove some provisions, all legislation submitted was eventually approved. Thus, previously, the assembly had played a mainly formal, perfunctory role of airing and then rubber stamping the decisions of the Party and the Council of State.[37]

The new electoral process has probably improved the quality of the National Assembly and the participation of the population in the selection of representatives.[38] It is essential, however, that the National Assembly also be transformed into a truly deliberative body capable of full participation, not only in the debate over present policy but also in decisions concerning the future of the socialist state including the process of renewal of the country's leadership. In early 1993, some of the proposals being considered to improve the functioning of the National Assembly included lengthening the time during which the assembly meets, strengthening the role of the work commissions and relieving some deputies of their normal work assignments so that they can devote themselves full time to legislative business.

Political Association and Pluralism

The role of the Cuban Communist Party is not clearly spelled out in the Constitution. It is designated as the "supreme leading force" of the state and society, and as such has virtual control over policy. Although the Party does not have legislative authority, it is inconceivable that legislation would be adopted which had not first met with its approval. Since 1991 there have been suggestions that Cuba may in the future consider the legitimization of other parties, but at the present no other political parties may form or participate in the political process. In response to criticism that its system does not allow for pluralism, Cuban officials suggest that democratization of the Cuban Communist Party is the best path to pluralism.

Despite its monopoly on policy initiatives, the Party itself appears to be undergoing a reassessment both of its internal make-up and its role. To begin with, participants in the pre-Congress debates almost uniformly criticized the dogma and formalism which had afflicted the Party and which stifled creativity. In addition, its membership and leadership were not representative of major segments of the population, specifically youth and religious believers. These issues were taken up at the 1991 Party Congress at which the Party statutes were amended to permit religious believers to become members and many younger members were elected to the Central Committee and the Political Bureau.[39] The resolution on the Party statutes also called on the Party to promote respect for diversity of opinion.[40] Further, internal election of leadership, at least at the lower levels has also been democratized by incorporating contested elections for leaders by secret ballot.

The Party also came under fire for the confusion that had developed between the Party and the organs of government and administration, particularly at the municipal levels. Thus, there has been an attempt to disengage the Party from administration. In addition, with respect to the recent elections the Party stepped out of the nominating process, at least formally, and yielded to the mass organizations. Although the leadership of the mass organizations is almost entirely comprised of Party members, the establishment of this role outside of formal Party control is an important step in furthering popular democracy.

In addition, mass organizations and other organizations have begun to exercise greater autonomy in recent years which enhances the potential for freeing themselves from the stifling formalism which has prevented them from developing broader perspectives on the problems facing society. This is a positive development which may lay the basis for the introduction of a new form of pluralism in the Cuban system, one which permits a diversity of points of view to bear on policy decisions. If popular democracy is to be further expanded, however, participation of the members of society in public debate, whether individually or through organizations and associations, must be encouraged and given new opportunities.

Rights and Duties of Citizens

The Cuban Constitution contains the full panoply of rights recognized in the Universal Declaration of Human Rights: those defined as economic, social and cultural rights as well as political and civil rights. Under international human rights law, these two branches of human rights are considered co-equal and interdependent. For example, the preamble to the International Covenant on Civil and Political Rights states that "the ideal of free human beings enjoying civil and political freedom and freedom from fear and want can only be achieved if conditions are created whereby everyone may enjoy his civil and political rights as well as his economic, social, and cultural rights." Similar language appears in the preambles to the International Covenant on Economic, Social, and Cultural Rights and to the American Convention on Human Rights. Articles 22–27 of the Universal Declaration set out the economic, social and cultural rights that are characterized as indispensable for human dignity and the free development of personality. These rights are to be realized not by individual autonomous action but "through national effort and international cooperation."

The Cuban Constitution recognizes both political and civil as well as economic, social and cultural rights. Article One, as revised in 1992, declares that the purpose of the Cuban socialist state is to provide "political liberty, social justice, individual and collective well-being and human solidarity." To fulfill these objectives, the Constitution contains certain material guarantees, such as the right to work, to social security, to medical care, to education and access to sports and culture.[41] In return for these rights, able adult citizens have a duty to work.[42] The Constitution also sets forth a wide range of individual rights, including the rights to due process, to personal property, to equality, to freedom of religion, to privacy and to freedom of expression. With the exception of the right to equality, to due process and certain aspects of privacy as constitutionally defined,[43] these protections are limited to the extent that they interfere with or harm the collective well-being.

In concept, the Cuban constitutional text is closer to the ideal expressed in international human rights instruments than is the U.S. Constitution. The U.S. Constitution provides very broad protection for private property, and the thrust of U.S. jurisprudence puts individual autonomy and private property rights above group rights and the collective well-being. Nevertheless, the collective good is not entirely suppressed in favor of individual liberty. Law must occasionally balance individual rights against the public interest, as when certain speech is prohibited because it is obscene or may endanger the public safety. Property uses may be regulated as well to serve the public good.

While arguably imperfect in many respects, the protection of individual liberties is more extensive in the United States than in almost any other country. In many instances, however, individual liberties, particularly property rights, are guaranteed at substantial expense to the collective. Moreover, the U.S. Constitution does not recognize economic and social rights as positive rights. Consequently, the state has no obligation to provide health care, to assure minimal nutrition, or even to provide public education. Ideologically, the system is based on the notion that greater social well-being will be derived from private competition and individual initiative than from public efforts. Yet the U.S. record with respect to tangible social and economic well-being is remarkably deficient given its wealth of resources: Access to health care is very unevenly distributed; infant mortality is higher than in most industrialized countries;[44] hundreds of thousands are homeless;[45] public education is in crisis;[46] and poverty levels are rising.[47]

Socialist legality, on the other hand, strives first and foremost to provide for the collective well-being based on egalitarian values. Cuba's achievements in the areas of free quality health care, education and social benefits have been exceptional, particularly given its economic underdevelopment.[48] Further, these advances are seen as essential to the process of democratization and full exercise of political and civil rights. These achievements, however, have been accompanied by limitations on individual liberties since the exercise of individual autonomy must always be balanced against the collective good. Such balancing, usually weighted in favor of the collective, creates inherent tensions between the two. While some commentators might minimize these contradictions because the "new citizen" would willingly sacrifice self-interest for the common good, they cannot be easily denied.

Each society must decide where the appropriate balance is to be struck based on its social and ethical values. Any resolution of the competing considerations requires concessions on one side or the other. At the extreme ends of the scale, the sacrifices of one to the benefit of the other may create conditions that will eventually destabilize the balance. In Cuba, the balance is decidedly on the side of the collective, although certain individual rights are protected, particularly in the area of equality, family law, personal property rights and criminal justice. In addition, positive rights such as health care and education benefit the individual as well. The tension between individual and societal interests is perhaps seen in highest relief in two different areas: in the treatment of persons who have tested positive for HIV and in the constitutional limitation on freedom of expression.

Health Care

The Cuban government has committed enormous resources to the development and delivery of national health care services. All Cubans have access to the full range of quality health care services, including dental care. Moreover, medical care employs first world technology and procedures. As a result of these efforts, Cuba has been able to eradicate many infectious diseases and parasites that are common in other developing countries. Not only is Cuba's system admired as a model for the developing world, but its achievements rival many industrialized countries, including the United States.[49]

The right to such quality health care, however, carries with it certain impositions on individual autonomy generally valued in U.S. society. For example, the state health system does not generally afford an individual a choice of physician or of treatment. Health workers will persist in contacting persons who miss appointments for important diagnostic testing or inoculation. For example, women will be called repeatedly if they do not appear for regular pap tests (which detect cervical cancer), and mothers of infants will be called and even visited at home if they do not bring their children in for regular examination and inoculation. Although such insistence is beneficial to both individuals and society, it might be viewed in the United States as an invasion of privacy.

In the case of AIDS, the Cuban government made the decision when the first AIDS case was diagnosed in Cuba (in 1986) to quarantine all persons who tested positive for HIV. Total quarantine was considered necessary to prevent the spread of the virus in the population. At first, the "patients," as they are called, were sent to hospital-like facilities which resembled a prison more than a sanatorium. They were virtually isolated from normal life and enjoyed few amenities. Over time, the harshness of the quarantine was tempered with the construction of attractive, comfortable sanatoriums that provide community-like surroundings equipped with recreational facilities and other amenities. Patients live in private apartments and may continue doing useful work at the sanatorium. In addition, from the outset residents of the sanatoriums have received intensive medical attention and access to the latest drug therapies, thus promoting prolongation of their lives. They also receive an enriched diet, superior to that of their friends and families on the outside. All of this requires an enormous allotment of public resources.[50]

At first, the residents were not permitted to leave the sanatorium at all, although they did receive regular visits from family and friends. Then a system of escorted furloughs was introduced, and finally, even passes for one to seven days free of supervision for those who demonstrated responsible attitudes. As the Cuban authorities continue to evaluate their policy, they are moving in the direction of reintegrating at least some of the patients into society. The distinction as to who will and who will not be reintegrated seems to depend on a person's psychological and physical health and evidence of responsible behavior.

Some have accused Cuba of "criminalizing AIDS" by its program of forced quarantine. They also criticize the premise of the policy that quarantine will control the spread of the disease. In fact, they argue, it may have the opposite effect of undermining educational efforts since people on the outside will consider themselves safe from becoming infected.

Certainly the policy imposes a profound limitation on individual autonomy, but the Cubans contend that their responsibility is both to care for those who are infected and to do everything possible to protect society and the individuals who are not infected, even if that means limiting the freedom of those who are HIV positive. Moreover, Cubans have also taken measures other than quarantine, including extensive, compulsory testing of individuals, screening the blood supply and expanding educational efforts. Most people who are at risk, which includes virtually the entire population that is sexually active, are tested routinely whenever they come into contact with the health care system. Those who travel abroad for extended periods of time are tested upon their return. Between 1986 and 1992 more than thirteen million tests were performed.[51]

As of 1992, only 892 cases had been detected, which is extremely low given the size of the population (ten million) and the fact that most adults are sexually active.[52] In contrast, in the state of Illinois, whose population size and urban/rural dispersion are comparable to Cuba, there were well over 6,000 reported cases as of 1992.[53] Some of the difference is explained by the absence of intravenous drug abuse in Cuba, a major source of HIV infection in the United States. Also, the first case in Illinois was detected in 1981,[54] five years before the first case appeared in Cuba giving the disease many more years to spread. In addition, until the mid-1980s foreign tourism was quite limited in Cuba. Still, 892 cases is very low, particularly given the potential to exposure in Southern Africa where over 50,000 Cuban troops spent tours of active duty from 1976 to 1989. Thus, widespread testing and quarantine seemingly have kept the spread of the infection in Cuba to levels significantly below those in other countries.

Yet permanent quarantine is an extreme measure. Even if those considered psychologically stable and responsible are permitted to return to their homes, some argue that forced quarantine is indefensible, both legally and morally, under any conditions. While the Cuban policy continues to evolve on the basis of internal evaluation, the Cubans are not at all apologetic about a decision they perceive as having prevented an epidemic of disastrous proportions, which would not only take the lives of thousands of citizens but would potentially bankrupt the medical system, creating other equally serious health dangers. Moreover, the current economic crisis has created dire shortages of condoms, making it difficult for individuals to protect themselves. Given this context, there is no easy solution to the equation. At the same time, however, Cuba's efforts to provide care and treatment for all those infected and its continuous re-assessment of its policy are indeed laudable.

Limitations on Freedom of Expression

The Constitution protects freedom of speech and the press but limits that freedom by the phrase "in keeping with the objectives of the socialist society."[55] Well before the 1976 Constitution was adopted, political expression had been restricted where it conflicted with state policy. In 1961 Castro issued his famous dictate: "Within the revolution everything; outside the revolution nothing."[56] The statement has generally been interpreted in Cuba to mean that everything that supports the development of socialism is permitted; efforts to oppose socialism will not be tolerated.

The definition of the boundaries of the permissible has expanded and contracted with events. In the 1960s, thousands of counter-revolutionaries were jailed for attempting to bring down the socialist government. Most were actively engaged in anti-socialist/anti-Castro conspiracies, but some got into trouble not for advocating capitalism but for criticizing the policies and methods employed to achieve socialism. Even speech meant to be supportive could arouse disapproval at times if it strayed too far from the party line. Since the 1970s, scores of intellectuals and activists have either been prosecuted or, more often, marginalized for actions in opposition to Party policy and/or to Fidel Castro. During the mid-1980s the government relaxed its attitude toward certain forms of opposition, and a small number of independent groups emerged whose activities were tolerated.

Political space narrowed again after 1989 in response to both external and internal events. Revelations of serious corruption among high level officials, including drug dealing by some military officials, rocked public confidence. These revelations were followed by the collapse of the socialist bloc, which deepened an already growing economic crisis and shook ideological faith. At the same time, the United States became increasingly aggressive in its hostility. Following the invasion of Panama, the United States initiated military maneuvers in the Caribbean that were interpreted in Cuba as rehearsals for air attacks against the island. It also took steps to tighten the embargo, and it stepped up the intensity of its international propaganda and disinformation campaign against Cuba. With some justification, Cuban officials linked all efforts to organize internal dissent either directly or by implication to the U.S. effort to destabilize the government.

With the very survival of the revolution at stake, the government has not been friendly to suggestions that it should provide room for those who they believe might be the agents of its destruction. While some leaders of the "dissident" groups have been arrested and sentenced for periods ranging from one to two years in prison, others have been subjected to harassment by organized citizens who gather to hurl insults. Official actions are generally not targeted at ordinary individuals but at groups and budding organizations, particularly those that attempt to publicize their opposition to the foreign press and embassies or to form party-like associations. Unlike the repression practiced by other regimes in Latin America, however, no dissidents have been "disappeared" or executed in Cuba, and jail sentences rarely extend beyond two years.

In general, the measures against organized opposition have not deterred individuals from expressing candid criticisms of the government both publicly and privately. For the time being, the government is trying to walk a narrow path between preventing the growth of dissident groups, whose goal is perceived to be the derailment of socialism, and broadening discussion of the economic, institutional and democratic reforms that the socialist state must undertake if it is to survive. The international context makes this path even narrower. The conclusion drawn by the Special Rapporteur appointed by the United Nations Human Rights Commission to study the situation of human rights in Cuba reflects this dilemma:

> While not overlooking the urgent need for specific measures ... any analysis concerning the situation and implementation of human rights in Cuba must, as a point of departure, accept the fact that the Government is, and has for a long time been, surrounded by an international climate extremely hostile to many of its policies and, in some cases, even to its very existence. ... [T]he abrupt breakdown in the flow of aid previously received from abroad, as well as the almost total exclusion of Cuba as a beneficiary of the multilateral financing and technical assistance agencies, have not given the Government much scope for manoeuvre in this field.[57]

The situation makes it harder to apply the theoretical model of socialist democracy, which requires, on the one hand, elimination of past deformations and, on the other, the creation of conditions for expansion of democratic participation. Use of repressive measures against political opposition carries great costs, not only in terms of international disapproval but in terms of the internal quest for solutions to the difficulties Cuba faces. At a time when the collapse of the socialist bloc demands the reevaluation of socialist doctrine and the discovery of new models for economic development, the terrain for debate needs to be broadened, not restricted. Thus, although the government contends that survival requires repression of certain forms of political expression, survival also depends on being open to new solutions. With the disappearance of accepted dogma it is increasingly difficult to define the correct line with certainty, and failure to do so will weaken the chances of success.

In areas other than political organizing and expression by opponents of the system, the scope of public debate has expanded in Cuba. Certain themes that had been discouraged, if not expressly suppressed, such as religious belief or homosexuality, have gradually found increasing acceptance both officially and socially. Academic centers, freed from dogma, are exploring new ideas and theories in a wide range of disciplines, including economics, political science, women's studies, ethics and philosophy.

In addition, despite efforts by the United States to isolate it, Cuba has never closed its borders to the outside world. To the contrary, Cuba has tried to maintain academic and cultural exchanges with other countries. After a brief opening during the Carter presidency, the Reagan/Bush administrations re-imposed travel restrictions on U.S. citizens wishing to travel to Cuba; they also prevented most academic and cultural exchanges by severely restricting visas to Cubans. Since the mid-1980s, there has been an explosion of such ex-change programs between Cuba and other countries, all of which broadens the knowledge and perspectives of Cuban artists, professionals and academics. Moreover, Cuba has hosted hundreds of international festivals and confer-ences that bring foreign intellectuals to Cuba, even those from capitalist countries (including the United States if travelers qualify under U.S. regula-tions regarding travel to Cuba).

Information, like education, is essential to a flourishing democracy. In some areas it is quite open, as in scientific and technical investigation, at least where disclosure would not compromise potential patents. However, access to government information is problematic in Cuba. High-level deliberations are generally hidden from public view, and until very recently, the govern-ment ministries kept tight control over information concerning their policies and operations.

The media in Cuba are a "mixed bag." Unfortunately, the Cuban newspa-pers rarely reflect the dynamic of research and debate that takes place in vari-ous sectors of society. The major newspapers are *Granma,* the official organ of the Party, *Juventud Rebelde,* the paper of the Union of Communist Youth (UJC), and *Trabajadores,* the paper of the CTC. *Granma* rarely presents de-bate on complex issues. Rather, it is paternalistic in tone and generally reports on official decisions only after they have been taken. Even though debates in the National Assembly will be given comprehensive coverage, rarely will vari-ous viewpoints be aired in advance to permit public response. Nor does *Granma* often report negative local news, preferring to focus on the positive.

In contrast, radio and television have improved substantially. Television broadcasts present documentaries and specials on important and complex so-cial issues. Television also offers a broad range of entertainment programs in-cluding regular screening of U.S. films, without commercial interruption.

Since 1989, Cuba has broadcast the weekly CNN Latin American report. Radio is the most dynamic forum for public debate and features popular news and information programs as well as lively, uncensored call-in shows. Of course, Cuban media are "supplemented" by U.S. radio transmissions—both the government-sponsored "Radio Martí" and private broadcasts—which regularly reach the island.[58]

Fidel Castro, famous for lengthy discourses on both the domestic economy and international economy, as well as politics, has been perhaps the richest source of information and education for the population. Few other national leaders, in Cuba or elsewhere, match his extraordinary oratorical skill. While the length of his speeches has been the brunt of innumerable jokes, Castro's vocation for thorough, coherent and comprehensible explanations of complex economic and political issues has had enormous effect. Less lengthy in their presentations, other officials such as Carlos Lage, First Secretary of the Council of Ministers, Ricardo Alarcón, former Minister of Foreign Affairs and current President of the National Assembly, and Roberto Robaina, current Minister of Foreign Affairs, have become important, articulate spokespersons for government policies. Interviews with these officials provide the population with detailed information on the economy and political and foreign policies.

Since control of information is an important source of power, all governments operate to some extent in secrecy. Secrecy may be legitimate in the early stages of policy development lest opponents derail initiatives prematurely, but it can also undermine the democratic process. If an objective of socialist legality is to strengthen socialist democracy, then the collective good depends on an informed population that can participate in the search for solutions to the problems that confront the society. As a result of government policy, the Cuban population is very well educated. Yet despite receiving increasingly comprehensive and detailed explanations of policy, at least from some quarters, the general population has not been given entree to the official discussions and debates that precede adoption of key economic and political decisions. No independent investigation apparatus or mechanism exists.

Finding the proper balance in all of these areas touching on expression and information is critical to the development of socialist democracy. The current tensions, which have been intentionally exacerbated by the aggressive policies of the United States, limit rather than create the propitious conditions for liberalization. Still, with the exception of checks on (and in some cases repression of) "dissidents" who launch frontal attacks on the legitimacy of the Party or the socialist state, there are signs that Cuba is giving more room to new ideas and debate on a broad range of economic and social issues. Progress in this direction is essential if Cuba is to reform its socialism and continue to create the conditions for its survival.

Notes

1. Osvaldo Dórticos Torrado, "Discurso Pronunciado en el Acto Central por el V Aniversario de la Constitución de la República," *Revista Cubana de Derecho,* No. 16 (1980), p. 6.
2. Constitución de la República de Cuba (1976), Arts. 1 and 14.
3. Ibid., Art. 16.
4. Ibid., Arts. 44–45.
5. Ibid., Art. 46.
6. Ibid., Art. 49.
7. Ibid., Art. 50.
8. Ibid., Arts. 40–41.
9. Ibid., Art. 43.
10. Ibid., Art. 42.
11. Ibid., Art. 43.
12. Ibid., Art. 52.
13. Ibid., Art. 53.
14. Ibid.
15. Ibid.
16. Ibid., Art. 54.
17. Ibid., Arts. 55–56.
18. Ibid., Art. 57.
19. Ibid., Art. 59.
20. Ibid., Art. 58.
21. Ibid., Art. 5.
22. Ibid., Arts. 68 and 73(b).
23. Ibid., Art. 88(c).
24. Ibid., Arts. 93 and 96(i).
25. The process began with public debates held in the spring and summer of 1990 pursuant to a broad call by the Party for massive discussion of the problems confronting the country in preparation for the Fourth Party Congress which was held in October 1991. While the population did not participate in discussions directed toward specific constitutional changes, opinions and concerns raised during these debates found expression in the modifications. Susana Lee, "Report on the imminent debate of the modification to the constitution," *Granma,* June 9, 1992, p. 3. At the same time, a commission created by the Central Committee of the Party, headed by Carlos Rafael Rodríguez, worked together with the commission of the National Assembly to finalize the proposed modifications. The work involved frequent meetings and discussions of drafts in the capital and in the various provinces as well. Copies of the final proposal were circulated among all the assembly delegates in early June, five to six weeks before the assembly was to meet. A number of amendments to the language of the provisions were made during the National Assembly debate.
26. Dórticos, p. 6.
27. Emilio Marill Rivero, "Acerca de la Dialéctica de la Democracia y la Legalidad Socialista," *Revista Cubana de Derecho,* No. 16 (1980), p. 105. See also, Dórticos, pp. 5–35.

28. Ibid., p. 7.

29. Marill, p. 104.

30. Julio Fernández Bulté, "Reflexiones acerca del Estado de Derecho," *Revista Cubana de Derecho,* No. 6 (1992), p. 14.

31. Marill, p. 109 (quoting Lenin).

32. Ley No. 72 (Ley Electoral), October 29, 1992, *Gaceta Oficial Ext.,* November 3, 1992.

33. Ibid., Arts. 16–41.

34. The British Broadcasting Corporation, Summary of World Broadcasts, February 10, 1993 (broadcast of speech by Fidel Castro, February 6, 1993).

35. For reports on the elections see "The Scene Behind the Elections," *Latin America Weekly Report,* March 4, 1993, p. 4; Agence France Press, "Younger Faces Grace Cuba's Assembly-Elect," February 26, 1993.

36. Fernández Bulté, p. 17.

37. The Council of State, elected by the National Assembly, exercises executive power and is empowered to enact legislation when the National Assembly is not in session. Such enactments, known as decree-laws, take effect immediately but must be submitted to the National Assembly for ratification at its next scheduled session. Unfortunately, there is virtually no information available regarding how the Council of State functions, how often it meets, or what procedures govern its deliberations. The Council of State is comprised almost exclusively of the highest level of party leadership reflected by the high correspondence between the Political Bureau of the Cuban Communist Party and the membership of the Council of State. As a result of changes in the composition of the Political Bureau, there are seventeen new members of the Council of State.

38. The election changed the make-up of the National Assembly. All but 98 of the 589 members were elected to the assembly for the first time representing an 83 percent change. The majority are younger Cubans, born after 1950. Women represent 22.75 percent. While not a requisite, Party membership continues to be an important factor; only 22 of the 589 delegates to the assembly are not members of the Party or the UJC.

39. *Este Es el Congreso Más Democrático,* report of the Party Congress, October 10–14, 1991 (Havana: Editora Polítca, 1991), pp. 6–32.

40. Ibid., p. 7.

41. Constitución de la República de Cuba (1992), Art. 9(b) (formerly Article 8(b)).

42. Constitución (1976), Art. 44.

43. Articles 56 and 57 protect the privacy of one's home and mail from illegal search.

44. James S. Rawlings and Michael R. Weir, "Race and Rank Specific Infant Morality in a U.S. Military Population," *American Journal of Disabled Children* (March 1992), pp. 313–316.

45. Steve Kerch, "Ground Broken to Help Homeless," *Chicago Tribune,* January 29, 1989 (estimates of U.S. homeless range up to more than three million).

46. Katherine Boo, "Reform School Confidential," *Public Education* (October 1992). (In many cities only half of high school students pass state examinations; in Chicago in 1988, half of the students dropped out before graduation.)

47. "U.S. Poverty Rate Highest since 1980s," *Chicago Tribune,* September 4, 1992.

48. Sarah M. Santana, "Whither Cuban Medicine? Challenges for the Next Generation," in *Transformation and Struggle: Cuba Faces the 1990s* (New York: Praeger,

1990), Sandor Halebsky and John M. Kirk, eds., p. 267. Cuba's infant mortality rate rivals that of the United States and Canada. Life expectancy in Cuba rose from 65.10 in 1965 to 73.97 in the period 1985–1990. Mortality rates from infectious and parasitic diseases, a common killer in underdeveloped nations, plummeted from 94.4 (per 100,000 population) in 1962 to 9.4 by 1987 as a result of the revolution's efforts. Ibid.

49. Ibid.

50. For a general description of Cuba's response to AIDS see Sarah Santana and Karen Wald, *Human Immunodeficiency Virus in Cuba: The Public Health Response of a Third World Country, International Journal of Health Services,* Vol. 21, No. 3 (1991), p. 511.

51. Ciro Bianchi Ross, "SIDA se condiciona el placer," *Cuba International,* No. 274 (October, 1992), pp. 13–16.

52. "Cuba Says It Slows AIDS by Quarantining Patients," *Chicago Tribune,* December 3, 1992, p. 7.

53. Gail Schmoller, "Belief About AIDS: Conflict with Reality," *Chicago Tribune,* August 16, 1992, Womanews, p 1.

54. "County Hospital Plans AIDS Ward," *Chicago Tribune,* July 22, 1987, p. 1.

55. Constitución (1992), Art. 53.

56. Fidel Castro, "Palabras a los Intelectuales," (Havana: Ediciones del Consejo Nacional de Cultura, 1961).

57. "Situation of Human Rights in Cuba," *Human Rights Questions: Human Rights Situations and Reports of Special Rapporteurs and Representatives,* United Nations, General Assembly, Doc. A/47/625, November 19, 1992 (Interim Report of the Special Rapporteur for Cuba), p. 21.

58. TV Martí, a U.S. government sponsored station which transmits from Florida directly to Cuba, is almost entirely blocked by Cuban interference. Its transmission has been criticized internationally as violating international norms governing the electronic media.

3

Development of the Legal Profession and the Practice of Law

The upheaval of 1959 had a dramatic impact on the legal profession. On the one hand, it destroyed the private practice of most Havana law firms, and by 1962, a great number of lawyers had left Cuba.[1] At the same time, the legal profession, which had previously enjoyed both prestige and influence among those with political power, fell from grace. The practice of law itself came to be considered a parasitic bourgeois profession that would be unnecessary in the "new society" in which corruption, crime and exploitation would disappear. Castro, himself a lawyer, exhorted young people to study more useful things like medicine, engineering or science, instead of law. To the observer, it could have appeared that the revolution was following, in a figurative way, the Shakespearean phrase "[t]he first thing we do, let's kill all the lawyers."[2]

The role of the established courts as centers of private dispute resolution changed as well. The centralization of authority in the state, the nationalization of the economy and the prohibition of most private economic relationships including the rental of property, eliminated many areas of private controversy over which the courts previously exercised jurisdiction. At the same time, political and social institutions emerged that would play an increasingly important role in dispute resolution. Thus, rather than seek redress for grievances in the courts, Cubans began to turn to institutions like the Communist Party, the *Fiscalia* (office of the attorney general),[3] the Committees for the Defense of the Revolution (CDRs) and the Central Organization of Cuban Workers (CTC) to resolve problems. Over time, the central role of these institutions in Cuban life, particularly that of the Communist Party and the mass organizations, further diminished the importance of the courts in civil affairs.

As the role of the courts and legal institutions in Cuban society shrank, legal

41

education as well as the legal profession began to atrophy. In 1962, as part of the process of reorganizing the newly nationalized educational institutions, the Faculty of Law lost its status as an independent faculty of the University of Havana (the only law faculty in the country at the time) and became merely a school within the Faculty of the Humanities. The numbers of university students matriculating in the study of law dwindled, and in 1964–1965 no new students enrolled in the law school.[4] Between 1965 and 1980 the median number of graduates from full-time study was fewer than fifty annually; none graduated in 1978 and 1979.[5]

Moreover, the law curriculum became very limited, partly as a result of the lack of concern for the replenishment of the profession and partly because traditional courses were no longer considered useful or relevant. For example, private enterprise law completely disappeared from the curriculum. Other courses that were regarded as having continuing but lesser value to a socialist society, such as obligations and commercial law, were reduced in scope. New courses on Marxist theory and economics were introduced. As in the past, the teaching methodology remained rigid and formalistic.[6]

Despite these adverse circumstances, the practice of law did not disappear altogether. Those who remained in private practice became occupied with dealing with a myriad of property cases, domestic relations problems and criminal defense cases. Consistent with the socialist policy of the new government, in 1965 the Ministry of Justice approved, on an experimental basis, the establishment of collective law offices (*bufetes colectivos*) in Havana that would provide legal services at modest rates or free to those who could not pay. These were small law offices that functioned as profit-making collectives, and the lawyers shared their fees and expenses. In addition, lawyers took on other responsibilities. Many lawyers who were sympathetic to the revolution began working as advisors and administrators for the institutions of the new government. Law students and young lawyers were called on to assist in the organization of the Popular Tribunals of the 1960s, which were presided over by lay judges and did not envisage a role for lawyers in the proceedings.

Recovery of the legal profession, in terms of both prestige and importance, would take several decades, but by the mid-1960s it was recognized that the legal profession not only had relevance to the development of the socialist system but was essential to the process of institutionalization. In 1965, the Party appointed a Commission on Juridical Studies to analyze the laws and institutional framework of the new Cuban socialist system and to propose legislation that would provide the system with a firm juridical base. Blas Roca Calderío, who had been a leader of the former Cuban Communist Party, presided over the commission. Although he was a shoemaker by trade, not a lawyer, he is credited with promoting the legal institutionalization of the revolution.

As a result of the commission's work, the judicial system and the legal profession gained recognition as important pillars of the socialist system. The

First Congress of the Party in 1975 specifically recognized the role of lawyers in the future development of the socialist system:

> The role of jurists must grow with the progress in perfecting our State and the new mechanisms of the System of Directing the Economy. We need more jurists better prepared and specialized in all the distinct branches of Law.[7]

In 1976 the law school was returned to its former status as an independent faculty in the University of Havana.

The *Bufetes Colectivos*

One of the first significant results of the commission's work was the Law on the Organization of the Judicial System, adopted in 1973, which established a unified court system eliminating both the Revolutionary Tribunals and the lay Popular Tribunals.[8] The statute also eliminated the private practice of law. All legal services to the population were to be provided through *bufetes colectivos* (collective law offices) organized and supervised by the Ministry of Justice.[9] Thus, in order to practice law, a lawyer had to join one of the *bufetes colectivos*.[10]

By May 1973, a month before the new law on the judicial system was adopted, the number of *bufetes colectivos* had grown to thirty-eight, distributed among the six provinces.[11] There were 227 lawyers working in these *bufetes*.[12] Building on the experience of the *bufetes* in the 1960s, the Ministry of Justice designated a national organizing commission to develop both a plan for a national structure to administer the *bufetes colectivos* and a code of conduct for the lawyers. The following year, 1974, the National Organization of *Bufetes Colectivos* (ONBC) was formally established. At the same time, the Ministry of Justice permitted eligible lawyers in private practice to join a *bufete* and issued regulations that broadened the types of judicial and administrative procedures in which lawyers were authorized to participate.[13]

The founding of the ONBC as a national institution was remarkable in several respects. It became the only vehicle through which lawyers could continue to provide legal services to individuals, thus bringing all lawyers under the code of ethics adopted by the ONBC governing bodies. It also created one of the first autonomous institutions in Cuba. Although the Ministry of Justice maintained oversight, the ONBC began to direct its own policy and administration. The importance of this independence was explained in a speech by Blas Roca at the founding of the ONBC: The lawyer could not be considered a public employee, subject to outside administrative authorities, if he were to fulfill his mission of representing the interests of his client before the courts.[14] It was not until 1984, however, that the legal basis for the autonomous, independent status of the ONBC was created by statute. Adopted at a time when substantial reforms were taking place in virtually all areas of the legal system,[15] the law is reflective of continuing concern for improvement of the legal system in general.

A primary problem in the early 1980s was the deficit in lawyers, both in quantity and quality. Great attention had been given to the drafting of new laws in the 1970s, but the replenishment of the legal profession had been completely ignored, and this neglect posed a significant impediment to progress. At the same time, the demand for legal services was increasing as new laws, such as the Housing Law of 1984,[16] gave individuals new rights and responsibilities. The meager number of law graduates was clearly insufficient. In order to address the shortage of qualified lawyers, the Political Bureau of the PCC determined that new law faculties should be created to train more lawyers. In addition, the curriculum of the law faculties was overhauled.

Increasing the numbers and quality of law graduates, however, was not sufficient to assure competent and efficient legal services. The newly appointed Minister of Justice, Juan Escalona Reguera, along with the leadership of ONBC, determined that in order to provide the legal services needed, the ONBC had to be expanded and strengthened as an institution. The result was the 1984 statute developed jointly by the ONBC and the Ministry of Justice, which set forth the structure and role of the ONBC as well as the regulation of the practice of law.

Decree-Law 81, "On the Exercise of the Practice of Law and the Organization of *Bufetes Colectivos*," which became effective on Jurist's Day, June 8, 1984, governs the practice of law and the organization of the *bufetes colectivos*.[17] The law reaffirms the autonomy of the ONBC. Article 5 provides:

> The ONBC is an autonomous national entity serving social interests and of a professional character, with its own juridical personality and property, consisting of jurists who join voluntarily, and governed by the present Decree-Law.

The law authorized the Ministry of Justice to issue more specific regulations governing the practice of law and the organization of the *bufetes colectivos*.[18] These regulations, issued in December of 1984, further defined the autonomous status of the ONBC:[19]

> Art. 6. The National Organization of *Bufetes Colectivos* develops its activities in conformity with its goals and autonomously, is subordinate only to the law and is directed solely by the organs of direction recognized in its by-laws and in the present Regulation.

> Art. 7. The National Organization of *Bufetes Colectivos* has juridical personality and its own patrimony, the capacity to acquire and dispose of its property and to enter into contracts on its own behalf; it is entitled to rights and obligations and to exercise legal actions which correspond to it. The representation of the National Organization of *Bufetes Colectivos* is exercised by its organs of direction in conformity with their respective legal authority and by the present regulation.

Although the Ministry of Justice was to maintain some oversight functions,[20] the ONBC was given authority to direct its own affairs. As an institution, the ONBC is governed by a General Assembly of delegates elected by members of the local *bufetes*. The assembly, which meets annually, elects a seven-member National Board of Directors that develops policy and administers the organization for five-year periods. The ONBC must provide the Ministry of Justice with periodic reports on its activities and any disciplinary actions taken against lawyers.

The Cuban system of *bufetes colectivos* bore some resemblance to the Soviet colleges of *advokatura*, but the Cuban institution was not patterned after the Soviet colleges and differed substantially in significant respects. Both the Soviet colleges and the Cuban *bufetes colectivos* were supervised by the respective ministries of justice and were the exclusive providers of legal services based on state-established fees. The Soviet colleges, however, never functioned with the degree of self-governance that the Cuban *bufetes* have. Until the reform movement of 1989, the Soviet colleges were largely subordinate to local party institutions.[21] Nor did they take an active role in developing policy and legal proposals as have the *bufetes colectivos*. Until fairly recently, the Soviet colleges remained passive, bureaucratic institutions of aging practitioners, a good portion of whom did not even have law degrees, and who enjoyed little prestige.[22]

As an indication of the difference in their status, salaries of Cuban lawyers have been consistently higher than their Soviet counterparts relative to average salaries among workers. Whereas the average monthly income of a Cuban lawyer in 1989 (460 pesos) was more than twice the salary of the average worker,[23] Soviet lawyers' salaries in the late 1980s were about 120 percent of average income.[24] Even in 1974, however, lawyers received a very substantial monthly salary of 231 pesos, which was almost double that of the average worker, an indication of their newly acknowledged importance and rehabilitation as a profession.[25] Legal services in Cuba also are about twice as expensive for clients relative to their monthly salaries than they were in the Soviet Union in the late 1980s.[26]

Over the years the ONBC has not only become an autonomous, self-governing institution in terms of setting policy, but it has become completely self-financing from fees charged to clients. The ONBC receives no government funding and has even occasionally contributed funds to public projects.[27] In addition, although salaries were initially set by the Ministry of Justice, today the ONBC controls these salaries which are paid out of income from client fees. As Dr. Emilio Manresa, president of the National Board of the ONBC, recently stated: "The lawyer represents the interests of a citizen, at times against decisions of an administrative nature, against a public official or another citizen. If paid by the state he would be a public official, and the independence of his function would be compromised."[28] Thus, unlike education and health care services, the costs of which are assumed by the state, legal services in Cuba are contracted for on an individual basis. Clients sign a contract with a lawyer for specific services and pay a set fee ranging from 10 pesos for drawing up a simple document to as much as 100 pesos for more complicated matters involving litigation.[29] There is no charge for the initial interview or consultation.

Although Cuba has experimented with various kinds of bonus programs as a material incentive to factory workers, the situation of lawyers is indeed unique. Today, as a result of ONBC policy changes since 1988, their income is entirely dependent on the number and complexity of the cases handled. The greater the number of cases handled, the more money a lawyer will earn. Fees are higher for more complicated legal problems, and even in simpler cases lawyers earn a higher percentage of the fee if the case turns out to be unusually time consuming. In the latter case, the fee proportion is worked out with the director of the local *bufete*. Moreover, there is no ceiling on how much a lawyer can earn; some may earn as much as 600 pesos or more—as much as the highest salary range for any professional in Cuba, including doctors, who have traditionally enjoyed both the most prestige and remuneration among Cuban workers.[30]

Decree-Law 81 also sets forth the rights of lawyers and requirements for admission to practice in the *bufetes*. First, the term *abogado,* or lawyer, refers only to those who represent and defend the rights of individuals or juridical persons before the courts, organs of arbitration or administrative agencies, both nationally and internationally.[31] The practice, however, encompasses giving consultation as well as representation.[32] Those who are carrying out functions as members of the judiciary, prosecutors, administrators or arbitrators may not practice law.[33] In order to become a lawyer, one must be graduated as qualified to practice law from a center of higher education in Cuba or in a foreign country with recognition or validation in Cuba, and be admitted to practice law by the ONBC.[34] Despite the last qualification, the Ministry of Justice may under extraordinary circumstances authorize someone to practice law during a determined period.[35] In addition, to be admitted to practice, an applicant must demonstrate good moral character and must not have been convicted of an intentional crime that would call him or her into public disrespect or be subject to criminal process for such a crime.[36] Lawyers are required to keep current with legislative developments and to continue perfecting their knowledge and skills, but there is no specific requirement of certification for continuing legal education.[37]

To join a *bufete*, a lawyer must apply to the respective provincial director who evaluates the application and sends a recommendation to the ONBC. Once admitted, a lawyer can practice anywhere in the country regardless of the *bufete* to which he belongs. Similarly, clients have the right to choose a lawyer of their preference to represent them, and they may go to any *bufete*.

The lawyer, however, is not obligated to take the case if there is a justifiable reason to reject it,[38] and in the event the lawyer does refuse, the director of the *bufete* will appoint another lawyer to represent the client.

The ONBC is governed by rules of ethics[39] and lawyers may be disciplined by the ONBC for violations. The grounds for discipline include: gross negligence, intervening in a case or substituting for another lawyer without his or her prior knowledge and consent; breach of confidential relationship; violation of regulations governing the *bufetes* or any violation of law; impeding justice; resorting to false testimony or evidence; and being disrespectful to officials and judges of the courts, prosecutors, other lawyers and persons involved in legal procedures.[40] Discipline may consist of a warning, a fine, transfer or even dismissal. In most cases the disciplinary measure is a private or public warning, but in cases of serious violation, the lawyer may be suspended or dismissed.[41] In each case the disciplinary decision may be appealed to the National Board, the decision of which is final except in cases of dismissal or denial of admission. In such cases appeal may be made to the Ministry of Justice.[42] In contrast, the Soviet *advokatura* never adopted a code of ethics.[43]

In 1982 and 1983 a number of lawyers and judges were tried for corruption. Apparently, lawyers had been taking money under the table from clients and using some of it to pay off judges in return for acquittals. Lawyers involved in this scandal, known as *toga sucia* (the dirty toga), were dismissed from legal practice and sentenced to jail.[44]

Socialist Legality and the Practice of Law

The law guarantees every lawyer the right to practice with independence[45] and with all the legal rights and guarantees to initiate proceedings and make statements related to the rights he or she defends.[46] The law also obliges lawyers to observe and contribute to the strengthening of socialist legality.[47] In a sense, this obligation is not very different from the obligations imposed on lawyers in the United States, who as officers of the court, are expected to scrupulously obey the law. It differs, however, in that Cuban lawyers are expected to support socialist ideology and to work for the perfection of socialist law, whereas U.S. lawyers have no obligation to support any particular ideology or legal philosophy. The question that might be asked with respect to Cuba, where the collective good takes precedence over the individual, is to what extent does the socialist system, particularly its political dynamic, limit a lawyer's ability to freely defend his or her client's interests against the state.

The 1977 revision of the law of judicial organization stipulated that legal representation be conducted in a manner that would "avoid abusing the legal guarantees of defense in ways that would impede the social functions of justice."[48] In addition, one of the violations listed in the Code of Ethics is conduct by an attorney that "impedes justice from fulfilling its social function."[49]

The meaning is unclear, but regardless of whether the 1977 statutory provision was interpreted to mean anything other than that lawyers are obligated to obey the law and not obstruct justice, there is little evidence to suggest that Cuban lawyers have been pressured not to vigorously represent their clients. Some jurists have noted, however, that during the 1970s lawyers in general were not very competent and frequently acted passively in encounters with state agencies.[50] According to the president of the ONBC, in the 1970s the best lawyers joined the judiciary or the *Fiscalia*. This pattern seems to have changed considerably in recent years. In fact, the new law and regulations governing the practice of law that were adopted in 1984 emphasize the independence of the attorney and the obligation to defend his or her client's interests with maximum diligence.[51] For example, the regulations specifically state:

> In the practice of law attorneys enjoy the guarantees established in law, by virtue of which no one can interfere with the decisions of a technical character made under their responsibility.[52]

This emphasis on diligence, independence and competence is consistent with the general concern and policy of strengthening the *bufetes* and the quality of legal services. It appears to be having a positive effect.

According to one researcher, Cuban lawyers in Havana's largest *bufete* obtained acquittals in criminal cases in approximately 22 to 31 percent of cases in 1991, depending on the type of crime.[53] This is much higher than the 1 percent acquittal rate for Soviet lawyers,[54] further demonstrating the dissimilarity in legal practice in the two systems. Moreover, in the area of criminal defense there is much anecdotal evidence of Cuban lawyers having worked with great dedication and diligence on their clients' behalf, even in sensitive cases. In one case related by a young criminal defense lawyer, the prosecution tried to raise the accused's homosexuality as being material to guilt. The lawyer, who admitted to being homophobic himself, nevertheless successfully blocked admission of such evidence and won a reduced sentence for his client against whom there was evidence of guilt.[55] In another case, a lawyer gained acquittal, on grounds of insufficient evidence, for a client accused of writing anti-government slogans on a wall.[56]

The national director of the ONBC has stated that "the revolutionary lawyer is the one who provides his client the best defense he can."[57] Yet despite repeated encouragement as well as examples of highly motivated and capable defense lawyers, there are still many lawyers who do not actively defend their clients, a fact that has drawn the attention of their colleagues within the *bufetes*. In a paper delivered at the National Juridical Conference of the ONBC in 1989, the proponent criticized lawyers for not actively participating in the preparatory phase of criminal prosecutions.[58]

The role of defense counsel in the trials resulting from the drug trafficking scandal of 1989 drew strong criticism from some members of the Cuban legal community. The trial of the military personnel, which included decorated General Arnaldo Ochoa, was televised nationally almost in its entirety.[59] The broadcasts inspired daily commentary among Cuban lawyers who debated the evidence and the merits of the defense counsel in informal conversations.[60] Among the lawyers with whom I spoke, none thought the defendants were innocent or that the evidence against them was insufficient for convictions, though some questioned the legal justification for the death penalty. In general, however, the consensus was that the defense counsel, with few exceptions, had been unduly passive in the face of the aggressive prosecutor.

In contrast, a second trial, that of former Minister of the Interior José Abrantes and members of his staff, which took place a month later, inspired praise for the quality of the defense counsel. The trial was video taped and shown fairly widely to groups of lawyers as well as to some Party members. Unlike the former trial, where the government had appointed military lawyers to defend the accused, the defendants in the Abrantes trial exercised their legal right to appoint their own counsel and chose from among the best criminal defense lawyers in Havana's *bufetes*. Although none of the defendants was acquitted, the defense counsel did manage to obtain reduced sentences and drew rave reviews from their peers for their performance. In fact, their energetic and intelligent defense was held up by some as a standard for all criminal lawyers.

The impact of increasing professionalization is felt in the area of civil law as well. In cases challenging administrative decisions, such as those made by the Housing Institute, lawyers have improved as advocates for their clients.[61] They have also become advocates for reform in aspects of civil law.[62]

Thus, Cuban lawyers are required to support socialist legality, but such allegiance does not require compromising the diligent representation of their clients' interests under the law. One area, however, in which lawyers are called upon specifically to contribute to the strengthening of socialist law is in the education of both their clients and other citizens with respect to their legal rights.[63]

The ONBC in the 1980s

Since 1984, the ONBC has become a dynamic organization that has created a uniquely autonomous institution providing services to the population. The number of lawyers working in the *bufetes* has increased from 634 in 1965 to approximately 2,000 in 1992.[64] The number of *bufetes* has grown to more than 250 nationwide, some of which are staffed by as many as 50 or more lawyers.[65] There are also two types of special *bufetes:* those that handle criminal cases for defendants who cannot afford to pay the fee for an attorney (*de oficio*), and those that handle appeals (*Bufete Especializado de Casación*).

The number of cases handled by the ONBC has increased by more than 50 percent, from 114,675 in 1980 to 177,015 in 1989.[66] In Havana a single *bufete* may handle 8–9,000 cases a year.[67] The most common cases are divorce, inheritance and housing matters. The number of civil cases almost doubled in the last ten years and now represents more than 70 percent of the cases handled by the ONBC.[68] During the same period, the number of criminal cases handled increased only by 13 percent.[69]

The increase in the number of cases, particularly civil, is the result of several factors. First, the new civil code and housing law provided the basis for an increased number of civil actions. Second, the ONBC itself has embarked on a promotion campaign using weekly television spots that provide citizens with legal advice and answer questions about legal problems. Newspapers also carry regular columns discussing legal issues, particularly those related to housing and workers' rights.

The campaign is part of a concerted effort to get citizens to seek the assistance of the *bufetes* to resolve legal and administrative problems, as opposed to going to local or national Party units, which, as already mentioned, had taken a major role in dispute resolution in the 1960s and 1970s. In the 1980s authorities tried to reverse this habit because it undermined efforts to strengthen the legal system. The effort appears to have met with success.

In order to meet the growing demand for legal services, the Ministry of Justice approved a program in 1982 of obligatory social service for recent law graduates: They must work at a *bufete* for three years. While at the *bufete,* the young lawyers receive additional training and are exposed to a range of practice, including civil, labor and criminal law. They receive a set salary of 198 pesos in the first and second years.[70] In their third year, they are treated as full members of the *bufete* and receive the same remuneration as other lawyers. They also receive an annual evaluation that they must pass in order to remain working at the *bufete.* Upon completion of three years' service, they may decide to continue working at the *bufete* or to seek employment in other legal areas, such as counsel to commercial enterprises or government agencies, the procurator's office, etc. As a result of this program, the number of lawyers working in the *bufetes* has increased by about 250 each year since 1988.[71] At the same time, secondary school graduates were encouraged to matriculate in law schools.

The profile of lawyers working in the *bufetes* has changed considerably in the last decade. In 1989, fewer than 21 percent of the lawyers were over 45, and almost 60 percent were under 30 years of age, reflecting the number of recent graduates who are joining the profession.[72] Although the *bufetes* are increasingly infused with young energy, the percentage of lawyers with substantial experience is dwindling. According to a 1989 report, of the young lawyers who entered between 1983 and 1986, almost 60 percent remained working in the *bufetes* after completing their three-year social service commitment.[73]

By the end of the 1990s almost all of the *bufete* lawyers will be members of the generation that graduated from law school in the 1980s. It is hoped that this will mean that they will be better prepared, if not more experienced, than their predecessors.

The organization has also become much more actively involved in the debate over legal reform, particularly in civil and criminal law, and the ONBC has sponsored a number of regional conferences on legal issues. At these conferences, lawyers not only engage in discussion of technical issues, such as resolving certain inheritance or divorce problems, but they also present papers exploring theoretical issues and proposals for reform of both law and legal practice. For example, one paper presented in 1989 called for greater diligence among criminal defense lawyers during the preparatory phase of the criminal procedure;[74] others critiqued the provision of the Criminal Code entitled "social dangerousness."[75] These exchanges have had a positive impact on professional morale among the lawyers. In a number of instances these papers have been published by the ONBC, thus adding to the growing body of legal literature in Cuba.

In addition, the ONBC has organized special commissions to study or to make legislative proposals and to draft reports that will be submitted to the appropriate commission of the National Assembly or other institutions responsible for drafting legislation. In 1988, the ONBC appointed an eighteen-member commission to make proposals for reforms to the Code of Criminal Procedure. These proposals were submitted to the national commission, in which the ONBC is a participant, designated to draw up proposed modifications.

Members of the *bufetes* also participate in the National Union of Cuban Jurists (UNJC), the national bar association. Some are active members of the various law societies organized by the UNJC, particularly the Civil and Family Law Society and the Criminal Law Society, and many attend other lectures and events sponsored by the UNJC. They have also had increasing contact with lawyers and legal service organizations in other countries resulting in important exchanges of experience and materials.

Practice in a *Bufete* Today

In many ways, Cuba's lawyers resemble their counterparts in U.S. legal service and public defender offices which have faced severe budgetary restraints in recent years. Despite the increase in the number of lawyers at Cuba's *bufetes colectivos,* lawyers carry large case loads and work under very difficult physical conditions, particularly in the last two years with the shrinkage of hard currency and imports. These problems seem to be more acute in Havana than elsewhere because of the density of Havana's population.

Inefficiencies in the Cuban economy coupled with the damaging impact of the U.S. trade embargo have made it difficult for the ONBC to obtain necessary supplies and equipment. Although there has been some effort to introduce computers, it is not unusual to find lawyers and secretaries typing legal documents on a manual typewriter with a well-worn ribbon. Cuba's telephone system dates to the 1950s and frequently the one or two telephones that a *bufete* may have are out of order. The severe gasoline shortage that has almost crippled the public transportation system poses enormous obstacles to adequate client contact and delivery of service. It is a tribute to the dedication of many of these lawyers that they persevere under such conditions to diligently represent their clients. One lawyer told me that his colleagues often pedal more than thirty kilometers from Havana to visit clients who are held in prison. It would not be surprising if lawyers became demoralized and discouraged under such conditions.

The appeals process has also reportedly been plagued by inefficiencies in telegram and mail service, which delay delivery of petitions for appeal, sometimes until after the expiration of the appeal date. The *bufete* specializing in appeals submitted a special report to the General Assembly at its meeting in June 1990.[76] In the report, it detailed the difficulties and published a series of communications to the president of the Supreme Court in which the lawyers describe the seriousness of the problem and solicit assistance in finding a solution that would preserve the rights of the appellants.[77] The report demonstrates not only the difficulties caused by inefficiencies in the postal service, but also the diligence of the lawyers in protecting the rights of their clients.

There are subjective impediments as well. As in many other countries, Cuban lawyers frequently have to contend with delay, inefficiency and ineptness in the court system, and often, it is the lawyer who is blamed by the client for the delay or unfavorable outcome. As one young lawyer complained,

> People consider us to be professionals and come to us to solve their problems. But we are not like doctors who can give a consultation and then a cure. To solve a problem, we have to depend on the efficient work of others like instructors, administrators and the courts. But we cannot solve a legal problem if others are not doing their job, and the clients sometimes think it is our fault.[78]

At the last General Assembly of the ONBC, held in June 1990, before the full impact of the impending economic crisis was felt, young lawyers in particular were highly critical of the courts and the lack of professionalism among judges in the trial courts.[79] They also had harsh words for inefficiencies in the prosecutor's office as well as for police instructors who do not produce required reports and files necessary for the defense of criminal defendants. Responses to these criticisms by representatives of the courts and the Ministry of Interior were honest and candid. There was consensus that the quality of personnel in these institutions was not acceptable and had to be improved if the legal system was to work properly.

The lawyers and the representatives of other legal institutions have expressed deep concern for these problems, but the difficulties resulting from the economic crisis is beyond their control. The introduction of computerization where possible has alleviated some of the difficulties, but shortages of paper and fuel persist in making delivery of services arduous. If material conditions get much worse, not only will the legal system be further adversely affected, but the population could lose confidence in its ability to resolve their legal problems.

Despite these problems, Cuban lawyers have reclaimed a place of importance in society and have developed considerable pride in their profession. They are very different than the lawyers practicing in the 1950s, both in attitude and training. They also have a deep understanding of the everyday problems of the Cuban population, whose interests they represent on a daily basis. For many, this experience influences their personal sense of justice. The Cuban citizen has access today to legal services that did not exist in 1959, and the role of lawyers in Cuban life will undoubtedly continue to evolve in the coming years.

Legal Advisors to State Institutions and Enterprises

For those not working at a *bufete,* one of their career options is to become a legal advisor to state agencies, ministries and commercial enterprises. As a kind of house counsel, these lawyers provide legal services and advice, particularly with respect to commercial relationships and contracts.[80] They also represent these institutions in arbitration and court proceedings, although the institution or enterprise may also choose to contract for a lawyer from one of the *bufetes* to do so. Unlike lawyers who work for *bufetes,* legal advisors receive a set salary established by the State Committee on Prices.[81]

Little has been written about these legal advisors. Their primary importance has been to assist the management of commercial enterprises in fulfilling their legal obligations under the state-controlled economic system:

> It corresponds to the legal advisor to assist in the perfection of economic contracts, in the first place, advising the chief of the enterprise and the enterprise council about the obligatory nature of contracts, its legal force and the economic and political consequences resulting from disregard for the economic legislation.[82]

The role of the economic contract is discussed more fully in Chapter nine. Since the structure of the state enterprises and centralized planning have undergone significant change in the last several years, it is inevitable that the role of the legal advisor will also change.

Yet while substantial emphasis has been placed on upgrading the quality of the *bufete* lawyers, primarily because of the strength of the ONBC, no program of similar proportion has been instituted with respect to the legal advisors, particularly in the smaller enterprises. Legal advisors have been almost universally criticized for lack of preparation and skill. The improvement of the law school curriculum has had a positive impact, but many recognize the necessity of developing post-graduate courses. Technical knowledge, however, is not sufficient to make legal advisors significant assets. Considerable effort is needed to prepare them to be advocates and not just passive technicians.

Lawyers must now adapt to the adversarial, competitive nature of market-based transactions. Under the system of a centrally planned and managed economy where even international trade was negotiated by centralized government agencies, the lawyer was relegated to a minor role in which he or she reviewed contracts solely for their technical compliance with regulatory norms. Now that the economy is increasingly decentralized and economic relationships are becoming more dynamic, the lawyer must take a more active role in protecting the interests of the enterprise. Given the critical importance of commercial law and international trade to Cuba's future, one can expect greater attention will be paid to improving the skills of this sector of the legal profession.

Some steps in this direction have been taken recently with the establishment of satellite offices (*consultorias*) of legal advisors in the provinces.[83] They are under supervision of the provincial offices of the Ministry of Justice. Each *consultoria* has two or more lawyers, and they serve clusters of enterprises that do not have their own house counsel. Services are provided on a retainer basis at 250 pesos monthly, an hourly basis or per task.[84] Generally the fee is 10 pesos per hour depending on the nature of the work; flat rates for tasks, such as the drafting of a contract, are set forth in fee schedules established by the Ministry of Justice.[85] Salaries for the lawyers are paid out of the budget of the Provincial Assembly. One day a week is devoted to education, training and discussion of new issues confronting the lawyers. Reportedly, these weekly sessions have also attracted the attendance of advisors working for specific enterprises.

In the past, a special *bufete* was established to provide legal services to foreigners on a hard currency basis. Lawyers in these *bufetes* handled marriage, divorce, inheritance and other personal matters as well as legal services related to business deals. Foreign lawyers have not been permitted to practice in Cuba, and a new law office, the *Consultoria Nacional,* was created in 1991 to represent foreign businesses that are interested in investing or that have investments in Cuba.[86]

Legal Education

The 1960 Law of the Reform of the University (Law No. 859) not only created the right to free education but it also directed the orientation of the university toward the areas of study most needed by the revolution: medicine, engineering and courses of study considered of practical importance. As already noted, the Law Faculty lost its independent status and became simply a school within the Faculty of Humanities. Moreover, the program of study in the law school became Marxist, with emphasis on philosophy and theory. Further, the curriculum incorporated the general premises of the time—that bourgeois law had to be destroyed, crime would disappear with the elimination of economic exploitation, and lawyers would not be necessary in the new society. As a result, the curriculum became very narrow and many courses disappeared altogether.

The reforms of the 1970s that established a new legal framework for the revolution naturally affected legal education, but recovery of legal education took a long time. During the 1960s and 1970s, only a handful of students graduated from full-time law school.[87] At the same time as day classes were reduced in size, a program of night school study was begun in 1969. Although fewer than 50 students matriculated in the day school during most of the 1970s, many more attended law school at night. Night classes, however, were eliminated in the early 1980s.

In 1975, the First Party Congress created the Ministry of Higher Education, and in 1976 the ministry reestablished the Faculty of Law as an independent faculty within the university. The law curriculum was reviewed and revamped to meet the needs of the evolving legal system. A new plan of study was adopted, called Plan A, which included 3,500 hours of study over a five-year period in four areas of specialty: penal, civil, international and *asesor de empresa*. Students chose a specialty area upon entering. The plan also introduced practice as a part of study, and students were given the opportunity, albeit limited, to spend time as interns at various institutions.

In 1980, this plan was criticized as insufficient to produce the quality of lawyers and legal advisors needed. The curriculum was considered still too narrow. It was thought that students should receive broader training; specialization could come after graduation. A new curriculum was introduced, but within two years it, too, came under review for modifications. So discouraged were some of the leadership with the quality of legal training, that the Minister of Justice once remarked that most lawyers who graduated before 1984 were useless.[88]

In 1982–83 a new plan was proposed to improve the quality of lawyers. This plan, which was put into effect in 1984, expanded required study to 4,500 hours, adding a semester to the program. It also broadened the subject areas from four to eight: Roman law, mercantile law, financial law, agrarian law, civil and criminal procedure, general civil, economic contract law and private property law. Practical education was expanded, and students were also expected to engage in research and analysis. In the second and third years, students were to spend four weeks as interns observing in *bufetes* and other agencies. Students in their fourth and fifth years were to engage in approximately

four weeks of practice. In addition, students were required to undertake research projects and complete two papers (*trabajos de cursos*): one in the first
two years and a more specialized investigation in the third and fourth years.

Although these were very important changes, there were still some deficiencies, and, in 1989, a committee of professors and experienced lawyers began a study of the curriculum with the goal of developing a new plan, Plan C,
which was to be instituted in 1990–91. According to then Dean Julio Fernández Bulté, the starting point of the new plan is the concept of the profession:
the definition of the legal profession and a model of the professional in socialism.[89] The plan takes into account the various activities of the different institutions and the specific challenges that lawyers face in Cuba. It therefore introduces some emphasis on basic theory and history. Substantive subjects are
organized in four areas of study: penal, civil, international (both public and
private) and commercial enterprise law (which includes economic law, labor
law, finance, etc.) Students are to take courses in all areas. Under this plan,
practical experience will increase to a total of twenty-four weeks.

Plan C had still not been implemented at the end of 1992. Apparently, the
dramatic changes in the international context, the collapse of the Soviet
model and the transformation of some of Cuba's institutions have led to re-
consideration of the curriculum. New attention is being given to corporate
and commercial law, particularly international trade law.

At the same time that the curriculum was being revised, professors at the
law faculties began to experiment with methodology, setting aside the rigid
lecture format that traditionally characterized university classes. Younger faculty, in particular, seek to engage students in discussion in class and work with
students in special research projects. Many of the older jurists who complained bitterly in the past of the poor quality of Cuba's law graduates are
more enthusiastic about the quality of recent graduates, who are viewed as
more skilled, dynamic and dedicated.

In addition to changes in the curriculum, there was general agreement
among the Party leadership that the number of law students should be increased substantially. In 1984, law faculties were created at the universities in
Camagüey, Santiago de Cuba and Villa Clara. A plan to increase enrollment
until the year 1992 was introduced, and enrollment began to increase at the
University of Havana as well. By 1988, there were 1,148 students at the University of Havana and approximately 3,500 in the entire country in all five
years of school.[90]

At first, the study of law did not attract the most qualified students, who
continued to pursue more prestigious careers in science and medicine. As the
legal profession became more respected and independent—as well as better
paid—admission to law school became increasingly competitive. More and
more women also entered the profession and now make up between 60 and

70 percent of all law students as well as more than half of the lawyers in the *bufetes*.[91]

Entrance requirements have now become more rigorous as the number of students wishing to attend law school has increased. In general, universities are under pressure because parents want their children to be professionals and greater numbers of young people are completing pre-university with the hope of entering university. In 1987, 35,000 applicants were refused entrance into the university.[92] Those denied entry as full-time students may, however, still pursue a degree in almost all areas of study through a system known as *enseñanza libre*, a kind of correspondence course. Students in this program buy books and follow a program of study worked out with the faculty. They do not attend classes, but may view classes on video tapes. They take three exams a year. More than two hundred students received a law degree in this way in 1988.[93]

Until 1987, students were admitted to law school based solely on grades and entrance examination scores. Now, there are two ways in which students are selected: 40 percent are chosen solely on the basis of pre-university scores; and 60 percent are chosen by special exam. The exam consists of mathematics, Spanish language (writing and grammar) and history. Many of those applying by way of special exam are students seeking admission after doing their military service or who wish to change careers. Applicants must also submit to an interview by the National Union of Cuban Jurists to assure their moral aptitude.

Although professionalization can also breed elitism, several factors are likely to slow, if not prevent, its happening in the legal profession in Cuba. First, education from grade school through post-graduate degrees is free in Cuba. Thus, tuition to law school is free for Cuban residents, as is room and board. Students must pay for books, but the price of books in Cuba is very modest as production is subsidized by the government. As a result, university students come from a broad range of backgrounds, and it is not unusual to find that the daughter of a small farmer or a hotel floor sweeper is a law student.

Further, as already mentioned, upon graduation, all students are required to do social service as a way of repaying society for its investment in their education.[94] For most law graduates this means three years' service in a *bufete colectivo* after which time they may choose to apply to stay or seek other employment. While at the *bufetes*, these young lawyers come into daily contact with average working people and develop a good understanding of the problems they confront.

The National Union of Cuban Jurists

The taking over of the Havana Bar Association in 1960 by revolutionary militants did not signal the establishment of a new professional association of any permanence. There is no mention in the literature of the association's activities after the early 1960s. Its dissipation is not surprising given the general demise of the profession. The restructuring of the judicial system and the renewed attention given to the legal profession in the mid-1970s, however, gave impetus to the establishment of the National Union of Cuban Jurists (UNJC), in 1977.

Approximately 85 percent of jurists in Cuba belong to this association, although membership is not obligatory. Membership includes lawyers, legal advisors, judges, prosecutors, law professors and notaries. It is headquartered in an elegant house formerly occupied by one of Havana's elite. Small offices and meeting rooms open onto a central courtyard. The upstairs is occupied by a modest law library. Like other non-governmental associations, the UNJC is now self-financed from membership dues, sale of publications and conference fees.

During a short period after the death of its first president, Francisco Varona Duque Estrada, in 1986, the UNJC's professional activities declined, and it was criticized as being little more than a social club. More recently, however, it has become extremely important as a professional association which brings together jurists working in the many areas of law. The UNJC plays a major role in organizing national and international legal conferences and programs for continuing legal education. It also has established relations with bar organizations in other countries and contributes to the exchange of information between Cuban lawyers and those in other countries.

Law societies organized by the UNJC meet regularly to debate legal issues. The societies bring together specialists in the areas of family law, criminal law, civil and administrative law, commercial and economic law, labor law, constitutional law and international law. Members of the societies come from the *bufetes,* the *consultorias* and the state enterprises, the ministries, the judiciary, the attorney general's office, the notariate, and the law faculty. Because of the breadth of participation and experience, they often provide consultation to the legislature on matters in their area of expertise.

The UNJC also publishes a quarterly law review, *Revista Cubana de Derecho,* and a bi-monthly bulletin. In addition, it produces video tapes on various aspects of the law that are sent to branches of the UNJC around the country. Lawyers frequently visit the UNJC to use its library or to purchase legal books and literature at the small bookstand on the front porch.

As a measure of its importance, jurists increasingly look to the UNJC as a center for holding activities and discussions. A series of forums sponsored in 1992 on the law of joint ventures drew a large audience that overflowed the main hall, which seats about one hundred. Similarly, registration for an interdisciplinary forum on abortion law had to be closed several days in advance because of lack of space.

The UNJC has also been instrumental in organizing several important national and international legal conferences in Cuba. In 1984, it sponsored the first national legal symposium on socialist law. The symposium, which was primarily for Cuban jurists, included papers on all major areas of Cuban law. In 1987, the UNJC hosted a major international conference on labor law co-sponsored by the American Association of Jurists. Together with the Ministry of Justice and the *Fiscalia,* the UNJC hosted the United Nations Conference on Criminal Law in August of 1990. Even in the midst of economic difficulties, Cuba continues to be the forum for important legal conferences. For example, in the fall of 1992, Cuba hosted an international conference on environmental protection. It has also sponsored other smaller conferences on such subjects as forensic medicine, the use of computers in legal practice and criminology.

Conclusion

Once denigrated, the legal profession has been rehabilitated and is today an important sector in Cuban socialist society. Along with the elevation of status, lawyers are playing an increasingly important role in the shaping and drafting of legislation and have already had a positive effect on the expansion and protection of legal rights as is evident in recent advances in the criminal justice system. It is likely that the impact will be felt in other areas as well.

At the same time, the population has come to expect relatively easy access to legal services in a system that has substantially diminished, if not eliminated altogether, inequality in its law and legal process. Legal representation is no longer a privilege of class. The expansion and improvement of services provided by the *bufetes colectivos* has strengthened the functioning of the legal system and the rights of Cuban citizens. Access to justice is an important right, and Cuba is closer to guaranteeing this right to all its people than most countries in the world.

With respect to commercial and business law, the current situation poses particular challenges to the legal profession. Lawyers must not only cope with material shortages, but they must prepare to deal with legal issues raised by the collapse of the socialist community and the new demands of the economic transformation of Cuba. Whether that transformation brings a reshaping of socialism, a return to raw capitalism, or something in between, Cuban lawyers will have to sharpen their ability to represent Cuban interests in international competition. Despite the progress of the past decade, the Cuban legal profession is not yet adequately prepared to take on this challenge.

Notes

1. For a description of the disintegration of one of Havana's leading law firms in 1959, see, Augustín Cruz, "It Took Only Three Years: The Destruction of a Law Firm," *American Bar Association Journal,* vol. 50 (January 1964), p. 63.

2. *Henry VI,* Part 2, Act IV, scene ii.

3. The *Fiscalia* is an independent institution answerable only to the National Assembly. Its primary functions are to prosecute crime and to assure enforcement of the laws. The Ministry of Justice is responsible for the administration of the court system and the regulation of legal practice. It also participates in the drafting of legislation both in its initial stages as well as in the final stages of codification.

4. Interview with Julio Fernández Bulté, Dean of the Faculty of Law at the University of Havana, December 21, 1988. Enrollment in the Faculty of Law, the nation's only law school, dropped precipitously from 2,853 in 1958–59 to 159 in 1971–72. Luís Salas, "Emergence and Decline of Cuban Popular Tribunals," *Law & Society Review,* vol. 17 (1983), p. 598.

5. *Tesis Sobre la Vida Jurídica del País* (Havana: Unión Nacional de Juristas de Cuba, 1987), pp. 19–21.

6. Interview with Manuel Hevia, January 6, 1992, Havana, Cuba.

7. "Informe Central," *Primer Congreso del Partido Comunista de Cuba* (Havana, 1975), pp. 151–52.

8. Ley No. 1250 (Ley de la Organización del Sistema Judicial), *Gaceta Oficial,* June 23, 1973.

9. Ibid., Arts. 171, 173.

10. Ibid., Art. 171.

11. The distribution was as follows: Pinar del Rio, 1; Havana, 16; Matanzas, 3; Las Villas, 8; Camagüey, 2; and Oriente, 8. Report of Dra. María Luisa Arteaga Abréu, president of the provisional National Board of Directors of the *Bufetes Colectivos,* published in *Discursos en el Congreso de Constitución de los Bufetes Colectivos* (Havana, 1974), p. 20. In 1973, Cuba was still divided into six provinces; the 1976 Constitution increased the number to fourteen.

12. Ibid.

13. Acuerdo No. 34 (Reglamento de los Bufetes Colectivos y Código de Ética Profesional [Abogados]), *Gaceta Oficial,* March 7, 1974.

14. Speech of Blas Roca at the closing of the National Constitutive Congress of the *Bufetes Colectivos,* January 13, 1974, in *Discursos en el Congreso de Constitución de los Bufetes Colectivos* (Havana, 1974), p. 34.

15. A series of important reforms was instituted starting in 1983, the year in which Juan Escalona Reguera became Minister of Justice. Within a year, the Criminal Code, including the sentencing structure, was reviewed for modification. Other important developments concerned the arbitration system, the labor code, and revision of the Civil Code.

16. Ley No. 48 (Ley General de la Vivienda), *Gaceta Oficial Ext.,* December 27, 1984.

17. Decreto-Ley No. 81 (Ley Sobre el Ejercicio de la Abogacía y la Organización Nacional de Bufetes Colectivos), *Gaceta Oficial,* June 8, 1984.

18. Ibid., Disposiciones Especiales, Primera.

19. Resolución 142 (Reglamento sobre el Ejercicio de la Abogacía y la Organización de Bufetes Colectivos) (Ministry of Justice), *Gaceta Oficial,* December 18, 1984.

20. Ibid., Art. 42. The primary areas of oversight concern programs of continuing legal education, evaluating performance of lawyers before the courts and other tribunals. The Ministry of Justice also has the right to review and approve changes in the fees

charged, number of *bufetes* and number of lawyers assigned to each. By law, and in practice, these functions are carried out in coordination with the ONBC and the Ministry rarely, if ever, sets aside an ONBC decision. It also conducts an audit of the financial activities of the ONBC.

21. Eugene Huskey, "The Limits to Institutional Autonomy in the Soviet Union: The Case of the *Advokatura,*" *Soviet Studies,* vol. 34, no. 2 (April 1982), pp. 200–227.

22. Ibid., pp. 202, 217. See also, Peter Solomon, "The Role of Defence Counsel in the USSR: The Politics of Judicial Reform Under Gorbachev," *Criminal Law Quarterly,* vol. 31 (December 1988), p. 84.

23. Interview with Emilio Manresa Porto, December 29, 1989, Havana, Cuba.

24. Robert Rand, *Comrade Lawyer* (Boulder, Colo.: Westview Press, 1991), p. 12. Solomon suggests that the low salaries and prestige of lawyers in the Soviet Union posed a barrier to reform even in the late 1980s. According to Solomon Soviet lawyers themselves opposed reforms which would give defense counsel greater participation in the criminal process because it meant more work for no extra pay. Solomon, p. 88.

25. Arteaga Abréu, p. 24.

26. Raymond Michalowski, "Socialist Legality and the Practice of Law in Cuba," (unpublished manuscript, 1992), pp. 29–30.

27. Interview with Emilio Manresa.

28. Esther Mosak, "En la Balanza," *Cuba Internacional,* no. 267 (March, 1992), pp. 37–42.

29. Michalowski, pp. 29–30.

30. Interview with Emilio Manresa. Dr. Manresa reported in 1989 that one lawyer had earned upwards of 1,000 pesos in one month, although that was unusual.

31. Decreto-Ley 81, Art. 1.

32. Ibid.

33. Ibid., Art. 16(c).

34. Ibid., Art. 3. Lawyers wishing to join the ONBC make application to the corresponding Provincial Director where they want to practice. The application is sent by the Provincial Director, along with his recommendation, to the National Board of Directors (JDN). Ibid., Art. 17.

35. The Ministry of Justice gave special permission to a retired lawyer whom Elizardo Sánchez, leader of the Comité Cubano Pro Derechos Humanos, had requested to defend him at his trial in the fall of 1989.

36. Ibid., Art. 16.

37. Both the ONBC and the UNJC organize courses and seminars for lawyers on legal developments.

38. The regulations governing the practice of law specify justifications for refusing to take a case. These generally include situations where there is a conflict of interest by virtue of blood relationship, friendship or other compromising relationship with the opposing party. Resolución 142 (Ministry of Justice, 1984), Art. 50. Although the regulation does not address situations where the lawyer simply has too many cases already to be able to attend to another, this often happens, and he or she is excused from taking the case.

39. A Code of Ethics was adopted in December 1978 which set forth the kinds of infractions for which a lawyer could be disciplined. This code seems to have been sub-

sumed by Resolución 142 of December 1984 which sets forth not only the infractions for which a lawyer may be disciplined but also the procedure for such discipline and the appeal process. Resolución 142 (Ministry of Justice, 1984), Arts. 59–70.

40. Ibid., Art. 59.

41. Decreto-Ley 81 (1984), Art. 27.

42. Ibid., Art. 29.

43. Michael Burrage, "Advokatura: In Search of Professionalism and Pluralism in Moscow and Leningrad," *Law and Social Inquiry* (Summer 1990), p. 462.

44. Interview with Emilio Manresa Porto, December 20, 1988, Havana, Cuba. According to Manresa, some of these lawyers have been released after serving their sentences.

45. Decreto-Ley No. 81, Art. 2(a).

46. Ibid., Art. 2(b).

47. Ibid., Art. 2(c).

48. Ley No. 4 (Ley de Organización del Sistema Judicial), Art. 143, *Gaceta Oficial,* August 25, 1977.

49. Código de Ética, Art. 2 (10), *Gaceta Oficial,* December 27, 1978.

50. Interview with Emilio Manresa Porto, December 20, 1988.

51. Resolución 142 (Ministry of Justice, 1984), Art. 34 (b).

52. Ibid., Art. 2.

53. Michalowski, p. 45.

54. Peter Solomon, "The Case of the Vanishing Acquittal: Informal Norms and the Practice of Soviet Criminal Justice," *Soviet Studies,* vol. 39, no. 4 (1987), p. 547. See also, Solomon, "The Role of Defence Counsel in the USSR," p. 84.

55. Interview with Prof. Jorge Arránz, June 11, 1990, Havana, Cuba.

56. Interview with Menelao Mora, January 7, 1992, Havana, Cuba.

57. Interview with Emilio Manresa, December 29, 1989, Havana, Cuba.

58. Mariano Mieres Martí, "Los Abogados en el Fase Preparatorio," published in a collection of papers entitled *Ponencias Derecho Penal* (Havana: Organización Nacional de Bufetes Colectivos, 1989), pp. 55–77.

59. Although it is impossible to know exactly what portions were omitted from broadcast, several persons who were present at the trials commented to me that they were quite surprised at the extensiveness of the television broadcasts.

60. I was in Cuba during the trials. This information is based on conversations with Cuban lawyers during that period.

61. Interview with Rodolfo Dávalos Fernández, Legal Director of the National Housing Institute of Cuba, Havana, March 24, 1989.

62. See papers collected in *Ponencias Derecho Civil* and *Ponencias Derecho Penal,* both published by the ONBC in 1989.

63. Decreto-Ley 81 (1984), Art. 2(ch).

64. Mosak, p. 38.

65. Ibid.

66. "Principales Indicadores de la Prestación de Servicios Jurídicos," mimeograph (ONBC 1989).

67. Mosak, p. 39.

68. "Principales Indicadores de la Prestacion de Servicios Juridicos," mimeograph (ONBC, 1989). More than half of the civil cases handled are divorce petitions. Mayra Contreras Contreras, Marisela Casanova Alvarez, Arelys Morlans Barrios y Mario Perdomo González, "El Proceso Especial de Divorcio for Mutuo Acuerdo y Justa Causa," *Revista Cubana de Derecho,* No. 35 (1988), p. 141.

69. "Principales Indicadores de la Prestación de Servicios Jurídicos," mimeograph (ONBC, 1989). In 1980 the *bufetes* handled 43,640 criminal cases; in 1989 the number had risen to 49,480 as compared to 127,535 civil matters.

70. Interview with Emilio Manresa, December 20, 1988.

71. Ibid.

72. "Composición por Grupos de Edades de los Abogados Miembros y Jóvenes Juristas que Cumplen el Servicio Social en la ONBC," mimeograph (ONBC, 1989).

73. "Promoción de Jóvenes Juristas Que Han Cumplido el Servicio Social en la ONBC," mimeograph (ONBC, 1989).

74. Mieres Martí, pp. 55–77.

75. For example, see Mario Alberto Taglo y Babé, "Contribución para el Perfeccionamiento del Vigente Código Penal Cubano," in *Enfoques Jurídicos de Abogados Cubanos,* (Havana: ONBC, 1989), pp. 202–264; Carmen López González, et al., "Algunas Consideraciones Sobre el Estado Peligroso en Cuba," published in a collection of papers entitled *Ponencias Derecho Penal* (Havana: Organización Nacional de Bufetes Colectivos, 1989), pp. 153–178.

76. Bufete Especializado de Casación, *Información,* mimeographed report distributed at the General Assembly of the *Bufetes Colectivos,* Havana, June 8, 1990. According to the report, the *bufete* handled 2,564 appeals in the first five months of 1990. Ibid., p. 29.

77. Ibid.

78. Interview with Avelino González González, June 10, 1990, Havana, Cuba.

79. I attended this General Assembly meeting, June 8–9, 1990, and this information is based on my observations and notes.

80. The functions of legal advisors are governed by Decreto No. 138 (Council of Ministers, March 20, 1987).

81. Ibid., Art. 9.

82. Pablo Prendes Lima, "Algunos Apuntes Acerca del Contenido Político-Ideológico en la Actividad de la Asesoría Jurídica de las Empresas Estatales," in *Política Ideología y Derecho* (Havana: Editorial de Ciencías Sociales, 1985), p. 212.

83. These offices were established by Resolución No. 20 (Ministry of Justice, February 5, 1988).

84. Resolución No. 31 (Ministry of Justice, March 19, 1988), *Gaceta Oficial,* March 21, 1988.

85. Ibid.

86. Since 1982, foreign firms have been permitted to make investments in Cuba in joint venture with the Cuban government. The subject is treated more fully in Chapter nine.

87. Interview with Julio Fernández Bulté, former Dean of the Faculty of Law at the University of Havana, December 21, 1988.

88. Interview with Juan Escalona Reguera, former Minister of Justice, December 19, 1988, Havana, Cuba.

89. Interview with Julio Fernández Bulté.

90. Ibid.

91. Ibid. Women are also well represented in other areas of legal work. One-third of the judges of the Supreme Court were female in 1990.

92. Ibid.

93. Ibid.

94. This requirement was established for law graduates and other graduates of technical schools by law in 1973. Ley No. 1254 (Servicio Social de Egresados) *Gaceta Oficial,* August 2, 1973.

4

The Judicial System

The three institutions primarily responsible for promoting and guarding socialist legality in Cuba are the court system, the Procurator General (*Fiscalía*) and the Ministry of Justice. Although each was fairly weak and riddled with corruption under the prior regime, they did not fare very well in the early years of the revolution either. The change in personnel effected by the new government eliminated officials known to be corrupt, but it did not bring vitality to the role of these institutions in the legal system. Unfortunately, the deliberate neglect in the 1960s of these institutions and of the legal profession in general impeded the development of legal culture and left Cuba with an inefficient court system and a poorly trained judiciary. It is only in the last decade or so that significant attention has been given to these institutions, clarifying their roles and strengthening their leadership and personnel.

The Evolution of the Current Court System

The courts and the judiciary have gone through substantial transformation and modernization since the revolution. As noted in Chapter three, in the first two decades, other institutions, particularly local party organs and work place councils, became the primary forums for dispute resolution, thereby reducing the role of the courts in civilian affairs. Moreover, the number of private property and commercial disputes declined dramatically as most commercial activity was nationalized. Since the mid-1970s, however, the courts have steadily gained greater prominence in the legal system as their jurisdiction has expanded in response to the evolution of substantive socialist law. At the same time, Cuba continues to experiment with and develop non-judicial forums for the resolution of claims in the areas of labor rights and domestic relations.

The Pre-Revolutionary Judiciary

One of the early acts of the revolutionary government was to bring the judiciary under its control and influence. The Constitution was amended in early January to permit removal of judges who had been tainted by association with the Batista regime.[1] In addition, Revolutionary Courts were established outside the jurisdiction of the ordinary courts, initially to try war criminals and later to try those accused of counter-revolutionary acts. These and other actions converted the judicial system into an instrument of the revolution. It cannot be said, however, that by doing so the revolution destroyed a judicial system that had legitimacy or a deep-rooted tradition of independence. To the contrary, Cuba's judiciary was historically allied to the ruling political interests, and in the decade before the revolution it was notoriously corrupt.

Influenced by the U.S. occupation at the turn of the century, Cuba granted the Supreme Court the power to determine the constitutionality of laws, decrees and regulations at the very beginning of the Republic in 1902. The court, however, rarely challenged government action except when legislation affected its own authority or jurisdiction. Despite its power of judicial review, the court was not only powerless to stop Batista from suspending the Constitution and violating the rights of Cuban citizens, but it expressly declined to hear a challenge to Batista's coup of March 10, 1952, and made no pronouncements in opposition to the dictatorship.[2] One of the few judges who questioned the legality of Batista's tyranny was forced into exile.[3]

The alliance of the judiciary with the dominant political forces, however, was not the court's only defect. The system's structure was woefully inefficient and antiquated as well. The nineteenth-century judicial system bequeathed by colonialism had progressed little since the beginning of the Republic. Despite appreciable population growth, the number of courts was exactly the same in 1959 as it was in 1911.[4] Even the provisions of the liberal Constitution of 1940 that were intended to strengthen judicial power did not breathe life into the court system; the Supreme Court, which supervised the functioning of lower courts, made no proposals for improvement during the entire period from 1940 to 1959.[5]

Perhaps one explanation for the judiciary's reluctance to exert its independence is that the 1940 Constitution, while declaring the independence of the judiciary, also provided for a system of political appointment to the Supreme Court. Prior to 1959, judges of the Supreme Court were chosen by the President from a list of three names proposed by a nine-member electoral college. Members of the electoral college were appointed by the full bench of the Supreme Court (four members), the President (three members) and the University of Havana (two members).[6] Judicial appointments were then submitted to the Senate for approval.[7] The general lack of legitimacy of Cuba's political institutions historically, however, precluded the development of a strong, independent judiciary. As would be expected, the result was a Supreme Court representative of and subservient to the dominant class interests as reflected in the government.

Typical of the continental civil law systems, the lower-level judiciary were civil servants who rose through the ranks on the basis of seniority. While judges were criticized for being passive and politically dependent, the greatest concern with respect to the lower courts was widespread corruption.[8] Decisions were routinely purchased through bribery. In a few instances, judges who went against the prevailing political power were forced from the bench.[9] Prosecutors were also notorious for corruption and extortion, demanding payment or favors in exchange for relief from prosecution or fines.[10]

Conflict with the Judiciary

Not surprisingly, in early 1959, there was broad consensus among Cuban jurists that the halls of justice were rotten to the core and substantial reform was needed. Even moderates, who eventually condemned the more radical policies of the revolution, believed that creating a judicial system supportive of democratic change would require an extensive purge of judges and court officials loyal to Batista as well as those "who because of their aristocratic mentality" obstructed reform.[11] In the view of Francisco Alabau Trelles, a magistrate of the Supreme Court who was himself removed in the judicial purge of December 1960,[12] the pre-1959 judicial system required "complete reorganization" if it were to become independent, honest and effective in the administration of justice.[13] Thus, there was little opposition to the January 13, 1959, decree that suspended the non-removability of the judiciary. The authority to remove judges was granted for limited periods of thirty to forty-five days at a time,[14] and this authority was renewed when necessary.[15] New judges were named by the Council of Ministers.

Thus, the rationale behind the principle of the non-removability of the judiciary notwithstanding, its suspension was acceptable under the prevailing political context. Demand for establishment of a judiciary independent of the legislative power began to emerge in late 1959. The National Association of Judicial Officials convened a forum on judicial reform in November. At the forum, representatives of the National College of Lawyers argued that judges should be named by the Supreme Court, the Law Faculty and officials of the bar association. Opposition to the removal of judges increased when the socialist goals of the revolution began to emerge at the end of 1960. Thus, the liberals, who supported the revolution at the beginning and condoned the removal of judges sympathetic to the Batista regime, later insisted on the guarantee of irremovability and protested removal of newly appointed judges who resisted the revolutionary agenda of the new government.

Emilio Menéndez y Menéndez, a close associate of Urrutia, was appointed president of the Supreme Court in January 1959. By all accounts he was a decent man, untainted by collaboration with the Batista regime, although undistinguished as a jurist. He was a moderate who, in his address to the opening of the 1959 court session in September, exalted the liberal philosophy of Descartes.[16] Menéndez believed that justice lay in the inherent value of individual freedom and exercise of will, principles that did not vary with changing social context.

In contrast to Menéndez y Menéndez and liberal reformers, José Santiago Cuba Fernández, who had fought in the revolution and had been appointed public prosecutor of the Supreme Court, projected a much more radical vision of the role of the judiciary. At the same 1959 inauguration of the court session, Santiago Cuba declared that the laws of the revolution had to be applied and interpreted "according to revolutionary criteria."[17] Judges could not be blind instruments:

> Society demands less blindness and more vision of the people, a vision which makes possible that the Revolutionary Law is applied not as a cold norm but as living law dictated by the Revolutionary Power to serve the people.[18]

The conflicting legal philosophies of Santiago Cuba and Menéndez manifest the fundamental incompatibility of the bourgeois concept of the judiciary and the radical nature of revolutionary justice. The moderates who came from middle- and upper-class backgrounds saw themselves in the lofty role of "impartial" interpreters of the revolutionary laws applying "neutral" principles rooted in the precepts of individual and property rights of bourgeois democracy. The revolutionaries, on the other hand, argued that the judiciary must be an instrument of the revolution obligated to apply the law in a manner consistent with revolutionary goals and principles to which other interests were subordinated.

Within a short time, concern mounted that the judiciary presented an impediment to the social and economic policies of the revolution. In early 1960, the Supreme Court opposed some of the government's laws and frequently ruled in favor of landowners in disputes arising under the agrarian reform law.[19] Antagonisms within the legal profession increased as the Havana Bar Association tacitly aligned itself with the propertied interests as well. In reaction to these developments, lawyers loyal to the revolution took over the association in July 1960, unseating its former leadership and issuing harsh verbal attacks against the judiciary for undermining government policy. Increasing polarization led to a final purge of the judiciary in late 1960. By late fall most of the judges who had not joined cause with the revolutionary government had left the country. They wrote a stinging condemnation of the revolution from exile in Miami.[20]

New judges loyal to the revolution were appointed, including Enrique Hart Ramírez, a practicing Roman Catholic, who remained president of the Supreme Court for almost twenty years from 1961 to 1980.[21] Hart opened the

1961 court session with a statement embracing the task of helping in the construction of the socialist state. In his address, he declared his loyalty to the revolutionary government and warned that the judicial system was in a transitional period that necessitated cautious attention to the strict application of the law.[22] Further, he expressed his support for the removal of the justices who were opposed to the social and economic reforms of the government.

Not surprisingly, the newly appointed judiciary was uncritical in its support of the socialist regime. This loyalty did not necessarily mean, however, that all prosecutions resulted in conviction. The Supreme Court insisted that lower courts apply the law and follow procedure faithfully, reversing their decisions when they did not. A substantial number of trials ended in acquittal, and many convictions were overturned.[23]

However, like their predecessors, the new judiciary passively maintained the structure of the colonial system and undertook no initiative to reform the judicial system in the 1960s. Aside from the creation of the Revolutionary Courts and the People's Popular Tribunals, the ordinary courts remained virtually unchanged in structure and jurisdiction until 1973. In fact, the modifications to the Organic Law of Judicial Power that were enacted in December 1960 maintained the pre-revolution structure of the ordinary courts virtually intact, although the power of judicial review had been eliminated.[24]

The People's Popular Courts

The People's Popular Courts, on the other hand, reflected the idealistic desire to democratize justice, at least at its most popular level. They were neither developed in consultation with the existing judiciary nor were they supervised by them. Rather, they were established by a commission organized by the law faculty in October 1962 at the urging of Fidel Castro.[25] These courts represented an innovative experiment designed both to develop mass participation in the justice system and to educate the population to the new socialist ethic. As stated by Castro, the goal of the popular courts was to correct antisocial behavior "not with sanctions, as in the traditional style, but rather with measures that would have a profound educational spirit."[26]

The first such courts were established in 1962 in rural areas that had not been served previously by the judicial system. Staffed by part-time judges who were elected from the neighborhood or workplace, these courts handled private disputes and charges of petty crimes.[27] The use of judges selected from the community introduced a lay participation in the judicial system in Cuba for the first time. Candidates for positions as judges were screened for moral fitness and revolutionary commitment, and those selected received training of up to forty-five days. The establishment of these courts was frequently overseen by young lawyers and law students. By the end of the decade, there were more than 2,200 such courts functioning in all parts of the country, including the cities.

There are numerous accounts of the positive impact of these courts in the communities they served and on the development of concepts of popular justice.[28] The tools to resolve disputes were not found in codes of law, but emerged from common experience and community values. Trials were public and attendance was encouraged to maximize their educative function.

The duality of judicial systems, however, caused much confusion, overlapping jurisdiction and inconsistency in the application of law. In the late 1960s criticisms of the system began to surface,[29] and a number of jurists perceived the need to rationalize the system in order to create greater predictability and fairness in the resolution of disputes. Analysis of the problems and the development of a proposal for a unified court system were entrusted to the Commission on Legal Issues appointed by the Party in 1965.

Revolutionary Courts

Another system of courts outside the jurisdiction of the ordinary courts was that of the Revolutionary Courts, established in January 1959 to try Batista's henchmen and collaborators, who were accused of atrocities and criminal acts during the struggle against the dictatorship. A continuation of similar courts created by the rebel forces in the Sierra Maestra to prosecute war crimes during the armed rebellion, the Revolutionary Courts were placed under the control of the military rather than the ordinary criminal courts. The jurisdiction of the Revolutionary Courts was suspended in early July 1959 when most of Batista's supporters had either been convicted or had fled. In November, however, in response to growing violence and armed resistance to the revolution they were re-opened and given jurisdiction over crimes designated as counter-revolutionary.[30]

The Revolutionary Courts used a summary procedure that substantially limited the opportunity for trial preparation. Defendants frequently did not communicate with defense attorneys until shortly before trial. Yet there was by some accounts a genuine effort to establish the guilt or innocence of the accused, and not all of those arrested were convicted.[31] Because of public outrage over the atrocities of the Batista regime, even moderates deemed the Revolutionary Court proceedings justified under the circumstances.[32] More than one observer has noted that the Revolutionary Courts, despite having meted out death sentences to hundreds, spared Cuba a repeat of the bloodbath that followed the fall of the Machado dictatorship in 1933[33] or that erupted in Venezuela following the fall of Pérez Jiminez in 1958. Nor has Cuba experienced institutionalized mass killings, as took place in Chile in 1973, or extra-judicial executions, reported in Argentina, Colombia, El Salvador, Guatemala and other Latin American countries.

Although the Revolutionary Tribunals and the ensuing executions grabbed headlines in the United States, fueling anti-Castro sentiments in Congress, it was the loss of power and property, not the Revolutionary Tribunals, which inspired the counter-revolution.

Reform of the Judicial System

By 1967, the turmoil that ensued from revolutionary transformation had subsided and most counter-revolutionary violence had ended. The revolution entered a new phase, and as institutionalization of the revolutionary regime continued, the Party began to pay attention to the long-neglected legal system. The Commission on Legal Issues began its work on the reform and modernization of the judicial system. As a result of the commission's work, a new law on the organization of the judicial system was adopted by the Council of Ministers in 1973.[34]

This law re-established a unified court system that provided for four levels of jurisdiction: base, district, provincial and national (the Supreme Court).[35] The People's Courts were abolished, as were the Revolutionary Courts. Although the 1973 statute maintained the principle of judicial independence by which judges owe obedience only to the law, judges were no longer appointed by the Council of Ministers for life but rather for a renewable term of years.[36] Further, the statute separated the Procuracy General administratively from the Court System and set out a new structure for its functions.[37] The Procurator General, however, maintained a seat on the governing body of the Supreme Court.

The Supreme Court was given appellate review over all judicial proceedings, even those of the military courts. Thus, while military trials remained under the supervision of the armed forces, a military chamber of the Supreme Court was established to review military court decisions. Although the Revolutionary Courts were eliminated, crimes against state security continued to be treated differently than ordinary crimes, and special chambers in the provincial courts and in the Supreme Court were created with jurisdiction to hear and review such cases. The Supreme Court structure was modified in other ways. The Chamber for Constitutional and Social Guarantees was eliminated, and violations of such rights were reviewed by other chambers when cases arose relevant to their jurisdiction. Thus, there were four chambers of the Supreme Court: civil and administrative, criminal, state security and military.[38]

In addition, the statute outlawed the private practice of law.[39] Henceforth, all lawyers wishing to provide legal services to individuals and to represent individuals before the courts were required to join the *bufetes colectivos.* The Ministry of Justice, which also maintained the registry of lawyers, supervised the organization of the *bufetes,* and most of the remaining lawyers joined them.

The 1973 law on the judicial system retained an important innovation to the Cuban court system first introduced in the People's Courts—the lay judge. The inclusion of lay judges, who were to serve on the bench along with professional judges, thus preserved the popular participation in the judicial process. This unique feature has been considered by Cuban officials to be one of the democratic attributes of the system. The selection and role of the lay judge is discussed below.

The 1973 law was the first renovation of the Cuban judicial system since the revolution. Although it represented an attempt to strengthen the system, insufficient attention had been given to the internal administration of the courts and the training of judges. Incompetence, particularly at the trial level, was widespread and impeded improvement of the judicial system.

A second, more thorough, overhaul took place in 1977, when a new statute on judicial organization adjusted jurisdictional lines to the new political administrative districts established in the 1976 Constitution. Moreover, the 1977 statute more clearly defined administrative accountability. Whereas the Supreme Court had previously been appointed by the Council of Ministers, under the 1976 Constitution, judges of the Supreme Court were to be elected by the National Assembly,[40] and judges of the provincial and municipal courts were to be elected by the corresponding legislative body.[41] The new law also contained sections strengthening the structure of the *Fiscalía*[42] (even though it was no longer affiliated institutionally with the courts), provisions governing the *bufetes colectivos*[43] and a provision establishing the National Union of Cuban Jurists.[44] Thus, all three institutions were considered to be functionally part of the judicial system even if administratively independent. In the case of the *bufetes,* they were evolving into an increasingly autonomous institution.

Although the Ministry of Justice is not mentioned in either statute, it continued to exercise supervisory responsibility over the organization and general administration of the provincial and municipal courts as well as over the *bufetes.* In addition, among the ministry's responsibilities related to the courts is the training and screening of judicial candidates to be proposed to the respective legislatures.

The 1980s brought further reforms. The retirement of Enrique Hart in 1980, after nineteen years as president of the Supreme Court, opened the way for younger judges to assume leadership in judicial administration. The governing council of the Supreme Court began to work closely with the Ministry of Justice in analyzing the deficiencies in the judicial system, which were numerous: poorly trained judges, inefficient organization and procedures and lack of mechanisms for analysis and evaluation of the court system. Reform of the judicial system over the last ten years has paralleled important developments, not only in criminal law and procedure and in civil law, but also in legal education.

In 1990 the National Assembly adopted another comprehensive law on the structure and administration of the judicial system, entitled simply "Law on the Popular Courts," to replace the 1977 law.[45] Its express goal is to improve further the court system. In particular, it declares the necessity to "institute a judicial organization which favors, by its structural flexibility, solutions to new situations," and to develop mechanisms for the continuous evaluation of the effectiveness of the system and to "strengthen ... the quality of judicial work, with a view towards its constant perfection."[46]

The Courts in the 1990s

Starting in the mid-1980s, Cuba undertook a number of steps to improve the quality of the legal system. In particular, attention was given to increase access to and respect for the courts and the legal process. Law No. 70 and subsequent modifications to the municipal and provincial courts have revised jurisdictional lines, clarified and strengthened administrative functions, and increased access to judicial process. These measures coincided with efforts to improve legal education and to increase the number and quality of lawyers as well as the efficiency of legal services.[47]

Cuba has not been immune to the problem of an overcrowded court calendar, which negatively affects the quality of justice both because of delays and because of insufficient time for analysis of individual cases. Some of the backlog has been the result of increasing criminal activity in the last few years due to the economic crisis; some of it is attributable to the expanding role of the courts in resolving civil matters. On the practical side, an additional, and equally serious, problem is created by the lack of fuel and spare parts that has paralyzed both public and private transportation, making it extremely difficult for litigants, witnesses and attorneys physically to get to the courtroom.

In response to the situation, the procedure for handling misdemeanors has been streamlined in the municipal courts,[48] and there are proposals to widen the jurisdiction of the municipal courts as courts of first instance to relieve crowded court dockets in the provincial courts. Moreover, some cases have been removed from court jurisdiction altogether. For example, labor disciplinary matters are now resolved by workplace hearing boards with right of appeal to the courts when the disciplinary measure imposed affects continued employment or promotion.[49] It has also been proposed that non-adversarial cases, such as uncontested divorces, be handled administratively.[50] On the other hand, the system of state arbitration boards, which ruled on contract and economic disputes between state enterprises, was eliminated in August of 1991.[51] Jurisdiction over such disputes has been entrusted to new Economic Law Chambers of the provincial courts and the Supreme Court.

At the same time, Law No. 70 permits provincial and municipal courts to hold trial in locations outside the official court building when it is necessary to serve justice.[52] Whereas changes in jurisdiction require legislative action, the Governing Council of the Supreme Court is empowered to propose to the

Ministry of Justice the creation of new chambers of the provincial courts and new municipal courts or sections of these courts.[53] In mid-1992, trial courts were opened in each of the Popular Councils, special councils established in zones of the larger municipalities, to address local administrative issues.[54] These courts are considered sections of the respective municipal courts and hold sessions three days a week. The other two days are devoted to continued training and preparation of the judges.

Thus, increasingly trials are held closer to the domicile of the litigants to reduce the burden of travel and to better assure the presence of the parties and necessary witnesses. To some extent, these new neighborhood courts, opened to enhance access and efficiency, recall the popular courts of the 1960s. But there are some important differences. The contemporary courts lack the informality of the popular courts. First, trials are presided over by professional judges as well as lay judges. Second, procedure and applicable substantive law are strictly governed by legislation.

Although the Ministry of Justice does not monitor or evaluate the judgments of the courts in particular cases, it does have an important role in overseeing the selection of the judiciary and in the financing and general administration of the courts. The Ministry of Justice (as well as the Governing Council of the Supreme Court) has increased its supervision of the administrative aspects of the courts and has developed and regularized procedures for evaluating the performance of the courts. To this end, staff at the Ministry of Justice have designed computer systems for data processing and record keeping with respect to the courts. The Ministry of Justice has also devoted considerable attention to the evaluation and training of judicial candidates.

The efforts of the Ministry of Justice are supported by parallel developments in the courts themselves. Regulations adopted in 1991 as a result of the joint work of the Governing Council of the Supreme Court and the Ministry of Justice set out the framework for the internal administration of the courts.[55] The regulations outline and strengthen administrative responsibilities of court officials and establish a system of reporting, analysis and evaluation at all levels.

All of these measures have been designed and undertaken with a view to improve the efficiency and the quality of the judicial system. The efforts of the Supreme Court and the Ministry of Justice in this regard have been impressive, and officials have devoted substantial time and resources to the project of modernizing the court system. The reform process involved frequent exchange and dialogue with judges and court officials at all levels. Moreover, many judges and officials traveled abroad to study the judicial systems of other countries, and Cuba invited foreign judges to visit its institutions and engage in discussions on judicial administration. There is considerable enthusiasm among officials that Cuba will be in the forefront of developing countries in achieving a professional, modern judicial system.

The Judiciary

Clearly, a well-trained, competent judiciary is a necessary ingredient for a strong judicial system. Incompetency among judges, particularly trial judges, is not unique to Cuba, but in Cuba's case the deliberate neglect of legal education resulted in the loss of more than a generation of skilled jurists, including lawyers, judges and prosecutors. This was particularly true in the trial courts, resulting in a heavy burden on the appellate courts, which reviewed and frequently reversed the lower courts.[56] Only in the last five to ten years has renovation of legal education begun to recoup the loss.

Selection and Training of Professional Judges

As in most systems based on the civil law tradition, the vast majority of professional judges in Cuba are career civil servants who enter the judiciary after receiving special training during or immediately following law school. In 1991, entry to the judiciary was opened to the legal profession to help ease the shortage of judges. Somewhat more than 150 lawyers sought positions on the bench in 1992.[57] At the same time, the Ministry of Justice initiated a competitive examination for all those applying to enter the judiciary. Those who pass and who have the other requisites for judicial positions are further screened by the Ministry of Justice, which presents slates of candidates to the respective legislatures for election.

The requirements for the judiciary are set out in Law No. 70. In addition to age and citizenship requirements, candidates must demonstrate good moral character and have the requisite years of legal experience either as a judge or lawyer: The requirement is eight years for the Supreme Court, five for the provincial courts and two years for the municipal courts. Party membership is not a requisite for the judiciary, and according to one study, a substantial proportion of the professional judges are not members of the Party.[58]

Those who are elected from the list of proposed candidates undergo further training at an institute established by the Ministry of Justice. Special continuing courses are also offered to judges at the University of Havana and at the National Union of Cuban Jurists to assure that judges stay current on legal developments. In addition to increasing time for study of case files, the reductions of the workload for judges is also intended to provide time for continuing education.

Lay Judges

One of the innovations of the Cuban revolution was the introduction of lay judges, who serve along side professional judges in all cases. The use of lay judges was generally practiced in all former European socialist countries, but as in other spheres, the Cuban model developed its own character. The practice is comparable to the mixed courts of Germany and France but with important differences. In Cuba, lay judges serve at all levels of the judicial system and in almost all cases. They are an integral part of the system, participating both in trial and appellate proceedings. In contrast, German lay judges primarily serve the function of juries and participate only in trials of serious crimes;[59] in France lay judges serve only in trials involving misdemeanors and in special tribunals such as those dealing with labor and commercial disputes.[60]

With some exceptions, sessions of the courts are presided over by three judges: In the Supreme Court there are two professional judges and one lay judge;[61] in the provincial and municipal courts there are one professional and two lay judges.[62] In the provincial courts an additional professional judge presides in criminal cases where the maximum penalty is eight years or more, when the amount in dispute in civil matters is considerable and in other similar instances. On the other hand, in the case of a misdemeanor, the accused will be tried by a single professional judge.[63]

Like professional judges, lay judges are elected by the corresponding legislature for a period of five years, but each lay judge only serves a maximum of thirty days a year.[64] Thus, they keep their regular jobs elsewhere. At the municipal and provincial levels, lay judges are selected from within their local communities. Nominations of candidates for lay judges are made by the mass organizations, the most important of which is the Confederation of Cuban Workers, which draws candidates from nominations made at workplace assemblies. Nominations are screened by the Ministry of Justice to assure that the candidates meet the formal requirements. Those who are elected as lay judges receive special training before participating on the bench.

By law, lay judges have the same rights and duties as professional judges, except that only a professional judge may be designated as president of the session.[65] They have the same right to participate in the trial and to ask questions as professional judges. There is a natural tendency for lay judges to be persuaded by the superior knowledge of the professional judge on issues of law, but according to one study, it is not extraordinary for the lay judges to prevail over the professional judge, particularly in the simpler cases tried in the municipal court.[66] As representatives of the community, lay input seems to be most significant in the area of sentencing. In contrast to Soviet lay judges, who seemed to simply rubber-stamp the decisions of professional judges, the Cuban lay judges appear to play a more dynamic role and are respected by their professional colleagues.[67] Attitudes of other members of the legal profession, as well as the general population, towards the lay judiciary is an area ripe for analysis.

Party membership has never been a requirement for the judiciary, but prior to 1976 the Party did review the nominees. Today, the members of the judiciary are increasingly less likely to be members of the Party. A recent study found that 43 percent of lay judges were not members of the Party in 1988.[68] In contrast, all judges in the former Soviet Union were Party members,[69] and in other former Marxist systems the percentage was substantially higher as well.[70] Moreover, the 1990 law also deleted previous provisions requiring that all judges, either lay or professional, demonstrate "active revolutionary involvement." Elimination of this requirement may reflect either the difficulty in assessing "revolutionary involvement" or the general move away from dogmatism since the late 1980s.

Thus, although lay judges, as well as professional judges, are likely to share the values of the system, there is no overtly political measure of their qualifications. In addition, they fairly reflect the population at large and are diverse both with respect to race and gender.[71] Almost all attained a ninth-grade education or higher, and most occupation categories are well represented.[72]

The expansion of the courts has required expansion in the numbers of judges, both professional and lay. However, the reduction of the number of judges required in less serious cases may relieve some of the shortage.

Judicial Autonomy

Cuban law provides that judges are independent in their judicial function. The 1990 law incorporates language that has been part of the law governing judicial power from well before the revolution: "Judges exercising their function of imparting justice are independent and owe obedience only to the law."[73] Not only are judges free of required membership in the Party, but they have shown themselves to be independent from other organs of government in their deliberations.

As noted earlier, judges at all levels are elected by the corresponding legislative body: The National Assembly elects judges to the Supreme Court and the provincial and municipal assemblies elect judges to the provincial and municipal courts. The term of office for judges is five years, and judges may be reelected.[74] Although there is no longer a sweeping guarantee of irremovability, the new law sets forth defined reasons for the revocation of a judge's mandate. None of these reasons involves lack of political orthodoxy. The statutory reasons include physical or mental incapacity to continue his or her judicial function; loss of any of the requisites for election (citizenship, good moral character); demonstrated negligence or incompetence; and becoming the subject of criminal prosecution. Only the legislative body that elected the judge may revoke the mandate, and the revocation process is a legislative, not an administrative one. There is, therefore, no appeal.

Disciplinary measures taken against sitting judges are appealable. One of the contributions of the 1990 law was to establish guidelines and procedures for disciplinary proceedings. Thus, the statute sets forth an administrative process in which the judge is to be informed of the charges and given an opportunity to rebut them.[75]

Observers of the former socialist countries in Europe have noted the lack of judicial independence illustrated by what has been termed "telephone justice."[76] That is, the direct interference with the judicial process by officials who order a specific outcome by making a timely telephone call to the presiding judge. Studies of judicial behavior in Cuba demonstrate substantial autonomy in ordinary criminal cases. According to Salas, in 1977, the courts dismissed 43 percent of all criminal cases filed by the Procuracy for lack of sufficient evidence.[77] Further, defendants were acquitted in 39 percent of the cases tried in the base courts, 37 percent in the regional courts and 28 percent in the provincial courts.[78] Similar statistics for dismissals and acquittals (31.5 percent) have been reported in a more recent study of sample cases handled by a large *bufete* in Havana in 1991.[79]

Clearly judges in all societies, socialist or otherwise, are influenced by the social and political environment in which they live and work. Thus, even though they do not receive direct interference, sentences can and do reflect the prevailing social ambiance. For example, in Cuba, when political leaders make a point of denouncing theft of state property, especially organized black market activity, courts are likely to respond by meting out stiff penalties for those found guilty of such crimes. On the other hand, there are cases in recent years, where those tried and found guilty of the crime of "enemy propaganda" or other crimes against state security, received sentences lighter than what had been requested by the prosecutor.[80]

Judicial Review

Cuba, like most Marxist systems, as well as some capitalist systems,[81] has rejected the notion of judicial review. Like the 1976 Constitution, the 1992 constitutional modifications do, however, maintain the principle of judicial independence and absolute judicial authority over state organs within the limits of their competency.[82] Although the Constitution speaks of the judiciary as "independent," it does not constitute the judiciary as an autonomous, independent power with authority to review the constitutionality of legislation or regulations.

As explained in 1987 by Raul Amaro Salup, president of the Supreme Court: "Here there is only one power—the revolutionary power—and all the organs of the state are precisely integral elements of this power."[83] Although any institution, including the Supreme Court, may advise on the constitutionality of any provision, only the National Assembly, as the elected representatives of the people, has the formal power to decide the constitutionality of any particular law or provision. However, according to Amaro Salup, it is not uncommon for the Supreme Court to be requested to submit an advisory opinion on the constitutionality of proposed legislation.

As part of the legislative process, all draft legislation must be sent to the Commission on Constitutional and Legal Issues, a permanent commission of the National Assembly. The commission then submits a written opinion to the National Assembly detailing any perceived violations of or conflicts with the Constitution. Proposed reforms of the National Assembly could strengthen the work of this commission. Previously, the elected representatives who served on this commission continued to work at their regular jobs. New regulations governing the National Assembly purportedly will establish a number of elected representatives who will serve as full-time, professional members of this commission. In addition, it has been the practice for prominent academics and lawyers to serve as technical advisors to the commission.

Cuba's rejection of judicial authority to review constitutionality goes against the general trend in Latin America and other parts of the world where the empowerment of the judiciary is seen as an important guarantee of constitutional and human rights. In fact, judicial review was introduced in Cuba in the first constitution of the republic, drafted during the U.S. military occupation and effective May 20, 1902. However, as noted previously, the judicial power was rarely, if ever, an important countervailing force to the executive or legislature. Similar experience with judicial review is reported in other Latin American countries.[84] Judicial review in Cuba was eliminated after 1959.[85]

Although the courts have become increasingly viewed as an important pillar in the Cuban legal system, there has been little evidence to suggest consideration of granting the courts independent powers of constitutional review. One perspective on judicial review is reflected in a recent article entitled "Reflections on the 'Rule of Law,'" by Julio Fernández Bulté, former dean of the University of Havana Law School, in which he argues that the errors of the Soviet socialist model should not lead to the abandonment of basic theories of Marx and Lenin in favor of the formalities of bourgeois representative democracy, which, he states, "each day is less representative and never was democratic."[86] Bulté derides what he considers "false formal measures of democracy," which are defined by regimes that themselves have not achieved democratic results. Although he does not specifically refer to judicial review as one of these formal measures, Bulté does suggest that Cuba must improve its democratic system.

Bulté contends that Cuba must rescue from history the true basis of democracy derived from "the direct and nondelegable power of the people."[87] At the same time, however, he acknowledges that the "Rule of Law" requires mechanisms to assure absolute guarantees against arbitrariness and the "abuse of the power or ignorance of the will of the governed."[88] This is to be achieved not simply by establishing the appropriate balance of authority within the machinery of government, but by the constitution of state power which presupposes the active and direct participation of the people, the Rousseauian "permanent plebiscite."[89]

Consistent with this view, recent modifications of the Cuban Constitution did not expand judicial power but rather took steps to broaden popular participation in the election of national and provincial representatives by instituting direct vote. Yet such measures fall substantially short of the Rousseauian ideal because of the complex nature of the nominating process, the lack of choice of candidates and the limited information upon which the electorate makes its decisions.[90] Of course, similar criticisms can also be made of the U.S. electoral system as well. Perhaps foreseeing that the electoral reforms would only represent a first step, Bulté concludes that Cuba now faces the unique challenge of developing new democratic models for socialism, and he regrets that rigorous, thoughtful analysis of these problems did not take place before.[91]

Judicial review is a fundamentally conservative force, preventing government from stepping outside accepted principles. In addition to the ideological rationale given by Bulté for rejecting judicial review, there are other factors that disfavor its adoption in Cuba now or in the near future. Socialist law in Cuba has been anything but stable. It continues to evolve and change. Fairly radical changes have taken place since 1990 in response to the economic crisis. Even the fundamental principle of exclusive state ownership of the means of production was modified in the 1992 constitutional revisions. In a context of continuous evolution and experimentation, there are few cornerstones on which to base judicial review of legislative action. Nor is there any persuasive argument for imposing the conservatism of a particular institution in a situation that demands simultaneously bold experimentation and pragmatism.

What is important to the future of the Cuban judicial system is its continued administrative development and professionalization. The seriousness with which officials now approach the role of the judicial system augurs well for its self-governance and independence. Progress will undoubtedly be seriously impeded, however, by the deepening economic crisis, which deprives the judicial system of needed material resources.

The *Fiscalía* (Procuracy)

Over the past twenty years, the *Fiscalía* has developed into an independent institution with an increasingly important function in the Cuban legal system. Prior to 1973, the government maintained the pre-revolution structure in which the *Fiscalía* was administered by the courts and was dependent on them for its budget. Although the law said that the *Fiscalía* was independent, its fundamental role as prosecutor in criminal cases and the fact that its offices were located in the court buildings necessitated its close ties to the court system.[92] In 1975, the *Fiscalía* came under the administration of the Ministry of Justice. Since 1977, however, it has become completely independent, both legally and administratively.[93]

Whereas the 1977 law contained provisions establishing the functions and structure of the *Fiscalía*, the 1990 law on the courts does not contain any provisions dealing with the operation of the *Fiscalía* at all.[94] Pursuant to the 1977 provisions, which continue to govern its structure,[95] the *Fiscalía* has been separated legislatively from the court system,[96] with the exception that the *Fiscal General* participates as a member of the Governing Council of the Supreme Court.[97] The participation of the *Fiscal General* assures interchange on questions pertaining to procedure and criminal justice, but it does not indicate institutional influence in either direction.

The *Fiscal General* and the vice-fiscals are elected by the National Assembly, and the *Fiscalía* receives a separate budget from the national government. Like other national institutions, the *Fiscalía* has a vertical structure with national, provincial and municipal offices. Its primary function is not only to prosecute criminal activity in the name of the society but to guarantee socialist legality by insuring strict compliance with the law by government and economic institutions and agencies, officials and individuals. The *Fiscalía* thus has authority to carry out investigations and to request information from officials and institutions. When it finds infractions it reports them to the body that is administratively superior to the one found in non-compliance. It also has authority to bring legal action against those who are in violation of the law and to enforce compliance with regulations.

With respect to its function of promoting and protecting socialist legality, the *Fiscalía* established in 1978 a Department of Public Attention that receives and investigates complaints by citizens who feel their rights have been violated. These complaints are studied for their validity and may be resolved in a number of ways. First, the official may explain to the citizen that there has been no violation. Second, if there is some question, the official will communicate with the agency against whom the complaint has been lodged to get clarification. If there has been a violation, the official will seek compliance. In other cases, the official will suggest to the citizen that he or she take legal action or pursue administrative remedies. Over the years, this department has become quite active, primarily assisting citizens in understanding their rights and procedures for vindicating them within the law.

Like the legal profession and the judiciary, the *Fiscalía* has suffered from the neglect of rigorous training of its personnel, particularly prosecutors functioning in the municipal and provincial offices and courts. Parallel to improvements in the law curriculum, the *Fiscalía* has developed special advanced training programs to increase the level of expertise and professionalism.

Notes

1. *Gaceta Oficial, Edición Especial,* January 13, 1959.

2. Jorge Domínguez, *Cuba: Order and Revolution* (Cambridge, Mass.: The Belknap Press, 1978), p. 111.

3. Hugh Thomas, *Cuba: The Pursuit of Freedom* (New York: Harper & Row, 1971), p. 1347.

4. Francisco Alabau Trelles, *La Revolución y el Poder Judicial, Proyecto de Ley Orgánico del Poder Judicial* (Havana: Editorial Luz-Hilo Luz, 1959).

5. Ibid.

6. Constitución (1940), Art. 173.

7. Ibid., Art. 180.

8. Stories of corruption are recounted by many lawyers who practiced before the revolution. See also, Domínguez, p. 116; Thomas, p. 1348.

9. Interview with Emilio Marill, October 13, 1992, Havana, Cuba.

10. Interview with Manuel Herryman, former police official under the Batista government, June 10, 1988, Jaimanitzas, Cuba.

11. Alabau Trelles, p. 5.

12. Decreto No. 2896 (Ministry of Justice), December 21, 1960.

13. Alabau Trelles, p. 5.

14. Ley Fundamental (February 7, 1959), Provisiones Adicionales Transitorias, Quinta.

15. The irremovability provision was suspended again in November 1960 in order to purge opposing justices from the courts. International Commission of Jurists, *Cuba and the Rule of Law* (Geneva: ICJ, 1962), p. 110.

16. Dr. Emilio Menéndez y Menéndez, *Discurso en la Solemne Apertura de los Tribunales Celebrada el 1 de Septiembre de 1959* (pamphlet, undated).

17. *Memoria leído por el Fiscal del Tribunal Supremo, José Santiago Cuba Fernández en el acto de la Solemne Apertura de los Tribunales Celebrada el 1 de septiembre de 1959* (pamphlet, undated).

18. Ibid.

19. Luís Salas, "The Judicial System of Postrevolutionary Cuba," *Nova Law Journal,* Vol. 8 (1983), pp. 43–70.

20. The International Commission of Jurists report, *Cuba and the Rule of Law,* contains numerous statements of former members of the Cuban judiciary exiled in Miami that condemn the revolutionary government for violations of human rights and the rule of law.

21. Enrique Hart Ramírez was the father of Armando Hart, one of the early student leaders jailed with Fidel Castro after the Moncada attack. Armando Hart first served as Minister of Education and was later named Minister of Culture, a position he continues to hold.

22. *Discurso leído por el Dr. Enrique Hart Ramírez, Presidente del Tribunal Supremo, 1 de septiembre de 1961, La Habana, Cuba* (pamphlet, undated).

23. Salas, p. 46.

24. In the Supreme Court, the civil law chamber was joined with the chamber on administrative law, but the chambers on criminal law and on constitutional and social guar-

antees remained. Law No. 898, December 21, 1960, Art. 2. The latter chamber, however, no longer was empowered to review acts of the Council of Ministers.

25. *Tribunales Populares,* pamphlet published by the School of Juridical Sciences, Faculty of Humanities, University of Havana (1963). This pamphlet contains documentation pertaining to the formation and functions of the organizing commission.

26. José Santiago Cuba, "Los Tribunales Populares," *Verde Olivo,* October 16, 1966, p. 24.

27. For a discussion of the development of the Popular Tribunals, see Adele Van Der Plas, *Revolution and Justice: The Cuban Experiment* (Amsterdam: Forris Publications, 1987); Luís Salas, "Emergence and Decline of Cuban Popular Tribunals," *Law and Society Review,* Vol. 17, No. 4 (1983), pp. 588–612.

28. See, generally, Van Der Plas; Salas, "Emergence and Decline;" Harold J. Berman, "The Cuban Popular Tribunals," *Columbia Law Review,* Vol. 69 (1969), p. 1317.

29. Salas, "The Judicial System," p. 51.

30. Ley No. 634, November 20, 1959 (Normas para el pase de los juicios y causas por delitos contrarevolucionarios de la jurisdicción ordinaria a los Tribunales Revolucionarios).

31. Thomas, p. 1074.

32. In his biography of Fidel Castro, Tad Szulc quotes several people connected with these tribunals who had since left Cuba and who felt the tribunals were justified since they prevented mobs from taking justice into their own hands. Tad Szulc, *Fidel: A Critical Portrait* (New York: William Morrow, 1986), pp. 482–485.

33. Ibid.

34. Ley No. 1250 (Ley de Organización del Sistema Judicial), *Gaceta Oficial,* June 23, 1973.

35. Ibid., Art. 2.

36. The term for the presidents of the courts was seven years, for professional judges five years, and for lay judges it was three years. Ibid., Art. 85.

37. Ibid., Art. 3.

38. Ibid., Art. 19.

39. Ibid., Art. 171.

40. Constitución (1976), Art 75(m).

41. Ibid., Art. 105(h).

42. Ley No. 4 (Ley de Organización del Sistema Judicial), Arts. 119–142, *Gaceta Oficial,* August 25, 1977.

43. Ibid., Arts. 145–153.

44. Ibid., Art. 154.

45. Ley No. 70 (Ley Sobre Los Tribunales Populares), *Gaceta Oficial, Edición Especial,* July 24, 1990.

46. Ibid., third *Por Cuanto*.

47. See Chapter three.

48. Decreto-Ley No. 128, *Gaceta Oficial,* June 18, 1991.

49. Decreto-Ley No. 132, *Gaceta Oficial,* April 9, 1992.

50. Interview with Dr. Carlos Amat Fores, Minister of Justice, Havana, Cuba, October 12, 1992; interview with Drs. Emiliano Manresa and José Mendoza, National Directorate of the *Bufetes Colectivos,* Havana, Cuba, October 12, 1992.

51. Decreto-Ley No. 129, *Gaceta Oficial,* August 19, 1991.

52. Ley Sobre los Tribunales Populares (1990), Art. 12.

53. Ibid., Art. 20.1(m).

54. Interview with Carlos Amat Fores, Minister of Justice, Havana, Cuba, October 13, 1992.

55. Reglamento de los Tribunales Populares, *Gaceta Oficial Ext.,* February 22, 1991.

56. There are no statistics on reversals. The statement is made based on a review of Supreme Court decisions and anecdotal evidence provided by lawyers.

57. Interview with Dr. Carlos Amat Fores.

58. Marjorie Zatz, *The Production of Socialist Legality in Cuba,* unpublished manuscript. This manuscript is scheduled to be published by Rutledge Press in 1994.

59. John Langbein, "Mixed Court and Jury Court: Could the Continental Alternative Fill the American Need?" *American Bar Foundation Research Journal,* No. 1 (1981), p. 198.

60. John Henry Merryman, *The Civil Law Tradition* (Stanford, Calif.: Stanford University Press, 1985), pp. 40–41.

61. Ley Sobre los Tribunales Populares (1990), Art. 21.3.

62. Ibid., Art. 35.1.

63. Decreto-Ley No. 128 (1991), Gaceta Oficial, June 18, 1991.

64. Ley Sobre los Tribunales Populares (1990), Art. 48.3.

65. Ibid., Arts. 8.2 and 23.3; Constitución (1992), Art. 124.

66. Zatz, p. 270.

67. Ibid.

68. Ibid., p. 275.

69. George Ginsburgs, "The Soviet Judicial Elite: Is It?" *Review of Socialist Law,* Vol. 11 (1985), p. 300.

70. Inga Markovits, "Law and *Glasnost:* Some Thoughts About the Future of Judicial Review Under Socialism," *Law & Society Review,* Vol. 23, No. 3 (1989), p. 424, n. 32.

71. Zatz, p. 275.

72. Ibid.

73. Ley Sobre los Tribunales Populares (1990), Art. 2.

74. Ibid., Art. 47.

75. Ibid., Arts. 60 and 61.

76. See, for example, Markovits, p. 424.

77. Salas, "The Judicial System," pp. 59–60.

78. Ibid.

79. Raymond Michalowski, "Socialist Legality and the Practice of Law in Cuba" (unpublished manuscript, 1992), p. 45.

80. For example, Elizardo Sánchez and two others, who were tried in November 1990 for spreading false information, received sentences of two years and eighteen months. The maximum sentence provided in the Criminal Code, Art. 115, is four years. Maria Elena Cruz Varela, was sentenced in November 1991 to two years in prison on similar charges. In both cases, the accused were released before the termination of their prison sentences.

81. France, for example, does not have a court of constitutional review. In 1958, France created a new governmental organ, the Constitutional Council, which is autho-

rized to review laws for conformity with the Constitution. It is not, however, a court of recourse for citizens who challenge the constitutionality of legislation.

82. Constitución (1992), Arts. 120–124.

83. Interview with Raul Amaro Salup, June 9, 1987, Havana, Cuba.

84. Merryman, p. 156.

85. Abolition of judicial autonomy and the notion of separation of powers did not come without controversy. Luís Salas, "Emergence and Decline," p. 594.

86. Julio Fernández Bulté, "Reflexiones acerca del Estado de Derecho," *Revista Cubana de Derecho,* No. 6 (1992), pp. 9, 14.

87. Ibid., p. 17.

88. Ibid.

89. Ibid.

90. For an explanation of the electoral system see Chapter two.

91. Bulté, p. 18.

92. Interview with Miguel Angel Garcia Alzugaray, Director, Department of International Relations of the Procuracy, December 16, 1992, Havana, Cuba.

93. Ley de Organización del Sistema Judicial (1977), Art. 108.

94. Ley Sobre los Tribunales Populares (1990).

95. Ley de Organización del Sistema Judicial (1977), Arts. 106–142.

96. Ibid., Art. 108.

97. Ley Sobre los Tribunales Populares (1990), Art. 19.

5

Law and Equality

Egalitarianism is one of the principle goals of Cuba's socialist system and was thought to be achievable by abolishing private ownership of the means of production, thus eliminating the economic inequality produced by the exploitation of workers. In large measure, the Cuban revolution did achieve a more egalitarian distribution of goods and services. Everyone in Cuba has food, shelter, access to education, health care and employment. Moreover, opportunities have been opened to large numbers of people who were excluded previously from everything but the most menial work. Visitors to Cuba who have occasion to ask a factory worker or a chamber maid what the revolution has meant generally receive some version of this answer: "My child is studying to be an engineer (or a doctor), which could never have happened before the revolution."

In addition to correcting social and economic inequities, the revolution took specific initiatives to remedy gender and racial discrimination. Women, who constituted the largest class of persons suffering from inequality before the revolution, were the recipients of concerted efforts to make them full participants in the new political and economic order. Cubans of African descent also benefitted from the revolution's express policy of eradicating racial discrimination and providing access to services as well as economic and educational opportunities previously closed to them. Despite impressive advances, however, neither women nor blacks have achieved full equality in Cuba.

Moreover, until recently, the government encouraged and enacted some forms of religious discrimination and discrimination against homosexuals, which it has now begun to redress. Religious groups in general have not suffered persecution or denial of their right to exercise their religious beliefs,[1] but until 1991 the established atheist character of the Marxist regime excluded individuals who professed a religious belief from full participation.[2] Repression of homosexuals, which was at its worst in the 1960s and 1970s, is no longer official policy, and a new tolerance is filtering into both societal and governmental attitudes.

This chapter describes and analyzes the issues of gender and racial equality in Cuba and the progress made since the revolution. The rights of religious believers and homosexuals are discussed in other chapters. Fuller treatment is given to gender rather than racial equality, not because of its greater importance, but because it has received considerably more attention in Cuba and, therefore, more information is available. The question addressed is not simply why women and Cubans of African descent have yet to achieve full equality; rather, it is whether or not the legal conditions and institutional framework are supportive of and conducive to its achievement. There is evidence that they are.

Women and the Law

The day must come when we have a Party of men and women, and a leadership of men and women, and a State of men and women, and a Government of men and women.

—Fidel Castro[3]

The advancement toward women's equality in Cuba has often been referred to as the "revolution within a revolution."[4] In fact, women's incorporation into the economic, political and social life of the country has been impressive and far surpasses the progress of women in other Latin American countries. Further, the revolution has provided significant advances for women in health care and education. Reproductive choice is secure as a right.

In the revolutionary context, law is far from "neutral." As discussed earlier, it is an instrument of social change, providing both a vehicle for shaping new values and attitudes and a mechanism for enforcing societal norms. Law has had an immediate impact on women's equality in Cuba. For the most part, legislation in Cuba has been supportive of progress for women, though some legislation indirectly or inadvertently still perpetuates inequality. Recent modification of the Constitution has strengthened the concept of equality.

Advances in equality for women in Cuba (or anywhere), however, cannot be simply brought about by writing formal equality into the law. Although the revolution's project has included affirmative efforts that go far beyond insuring numerical parity in work and pay, social norms and attitudes have changed more slowly and remain a barrier to women. Thus, women still bear most of the burden of household and childcare duties, and, despite Party and government support for and a steady rise in the number of women in decision-making positions, Cuban women have yet to share authority equally with men. The reasons Cuban women have still not reached this goal can be partly understood from the historical and social context of women in Cuba before and since the Cuban Revolution. Thirty-three years—the span of one generation—is not a very long time for completion of such a radical social transformation. In addition, the demands and dynamic of the revolution itself have impeded the development of an analysis of gender inequality which goes beyond legal formalism.

Without doubt, the economic crisis that began in 1989 has had a particularly negative impact on women. Scarcities make domestic life ever more difficult by increasing the amount of time women, still the primary caretakers, must spend on household chores. Moreover, the stagnation of the economy and shrinkage in many sectors halts advancement for women as well as men. Yet despite these setbacks, and, although machismo continues to dominate sexual politics, there is already a national consciousness of gender equality in Cuban public life that is firmly established and that provides a good basis for progress.

Beginning the Revolution: The First Decade

Prior to 1959, women constituted only about 15 percent of the work force.[5] For most of those women, work was an absolute necessity that provided no opportunity for development or self-fulfillment: Well over half were maids or domestic servants,[6] and a substantial number were exploited by the hundreds of notorious brothels of prerevolutionary Cuba.[7] The remainder were primarily teachers, clerks, and factory workers. Economic and educational opportunities were available only to women of the middle and upper classes. Even among these classes, the few women who did enter professions were relegated to subordinate roles; the vast majority of women did not depart from their socially assigned function of housewife and caretaker. Even absent the mores of a strong patriarchal culture that prevented women from participating in political and economic activity, high unemployment and underemployment among men limited possibilities for women.[8]

A number of women, however, did play an active role in the revolution. Women helped organize demonstrations to protest the repression of the Batista regime and the jailing of opposition leaders. During the armed struggle, women acted as couriers, raised funds, and transported guns and supplies to the guerrillas fighting in the mountains. A small number of women also participated in combat. One platoon, the Mariana Grajales Platoon, consisted entirely of women.

Although women in general constituted an oppressed class in prerevolutionary Cuba, and women actively participated in the liberation movement, women's rights per se were not on the agenda of the armed revolutionaries. Equality for women was not mentioned once in Fidel Castro's famous defense speech, known as "History Will Absolve Me," which put forth the vision of the just society for which the revolutionaries fought; nor was women's equality included in the Manifesto of the Sierra Maestra. Although suffrage had been won throughout the hemisphere, and middle- and upper-class Cuban feminists had left a mark prior to 1959,[9] there was little to suggest in 1959 that the revolution would radically change the position of women in Cuban society. Even in the United States a broad movement against sex discrimination did not emerge until after the civil rights struggle of the mid-1960s.

The decade following the triumph of the revolution transformed women's lives. Concerted efforts were made to integrate the masses of women into the economic and political life of the country. To do so required an abrupt departure from the patriarchal tradition, which dictated for the vast majority of Cuban women that identity and life revolved completely around home, marriage, and family. The process awakened women's consciousness to new possibilities offered by education, volunteer service, work outside the home, and control over reproductive choices. From this awakening would emerge more clearly defined goals of self-realization and full equality for women in Cuba.

Within one year of the fall of the Batista regime and the takeover of political control by the revolutionary movements, a national organization of Cuban women was founded—the Federation of Cuban Women (Federación de Mujeres Cubanas, or FMC). However, the FMC was created not by women to secure equal rights, but by the revolutionary government seeking to mobilize women to take on emergency tasks at a time of great urgency. Vilma Espín, a founding member and FMC president since 1960,[10] recounts that, although she and other Cuban women fought in the revolution, they never once considered the idea of creating a distinctly women's organization.[11] According to Espín, who was a leader of the Santiago de Cuba underground, it was Fidel Castro who convinced her and other women active in the revolutionary movement that a women's organization was necessary to incorporate women into the revolution.[12]

At the founding meeting of the FMC on August 23, 1960, Fidel Castro, while paying homage to the women who fought in the revolution, spoke primarily of the grave economic and military situation confronting the nation.[13] Growing hostility in the middle and upper classes, pockets of armed opposition and incidents of sabotage threatened consolidation of the revolution. In addition, the new leadership was faced with the staggering implications of the emerging U.S. trade embargo. Strong support for the revolution among the population was essential in order to develop an independent economy and to diffuse counter-revolutionary activity.

Thus, the sole agenda of the FMC at its founding was to strengthen support for the revolution by organizing women into the social organization and productive forces of the new society. The governing statutes adopted by the FMC at its first congress in 1962 do not even mention women's equality as one of its goals:

The Federation of Cuban Women, founded in 1960 with the objective of uniting all women and incorporating them in the process of transformation begun with the triumph of the revolution, ... confronts a new and great objective: the effective and full incorporation of the Cuban woman from all sectors of the population in the construction of the socialist state.[14]

A great many tasks needed to be done, and women were an enormous untapped resource that could serve the revolution.

The FMC, headed by Vilma Espín, was up to the task. It quickly launched a major campaign to get women out of the house and into productive work. The first activities into which women were recruited related to health and education. FMC members went from house to house to persuade women to undertake these tasks. Women were given first-aid training and organized into health brigades, which carried out the first nationwide vaccination programs against tetanus and polio.[15] They were also mobilized to help repel the Bay of Pigs invasion in 1961.[16] As a result of FMC organizing, young women, including adolescents, venturing away from their homes for the first time, joined the tens of thousands of youth who carried out the famous literacy campaign of 1961.[17] In addition, the FMC was instrumental in providing training programs and social services that enabled thousands of former prostitutes to find new jobs.[18]

Another strategy to expand women's participation in the revolution, particularly in rural areas, was the organization of educational programs that had both an ideological and skill-oriented content. Rural women were encouraged to attend special sewing classes. Traditionally a female-identified skill, sewing appealed to women who had never worked and was an acceptable activity to reluctant parents and spouses.[19] Among the first such schools were the Ana Betancourt Escuelas Campesinas for rural women. Thousands of *campesinas* were brought from rural areas into the city of Havana to attend these schools.[20] In addition, approximately 20,000 former domestic servants attended special schools for the Advancement of Domestic Servants established in Havana in 1960. Many of these women were trained to staff the child-care centers established the following year.[21] Once in classes, however, the young women were not only taught new skills but were given an elementary education, including basic hygiene, and were exposed to the social and political ideas and goals of the revolution.[22]

At the same time, the government provided material support for women to enter the work force: The first day-care centers were established in 1961;[23] a maternity law providing liberal paid leave for pregnant women was enacted in 1963;[24] and educational opportunities were created that helped women advance into new areas of work.[25] All these material supports were provided to the population free of charge, and they enabled the FMC to encourage significant numbers of women to enter the paid work force. In 1964, a Secretariat of Production was created within the FMC to examine the issues concerning the incorporation of women into the work force and to develop additional strategies for incorporation. Slow, steady progress was achieved in the 1960s, largely as a result of incorporating into new jobs women who had previously worked as domestics.

A surge in women's employment resulted from the great "ten ton sugar harvest" planned for 1970, which required a massive mobilization of the entire population, men and women, into productive work.[26] In the late 1960s the Confederation of Cuban Workers (CTC), the national trade union organization,[27] and the Ministry of Labor responded to the need to incorporate more women into the work force to reduce the labor shortage. In 1968, the Ministry of Labor adopted a preferential hiring program for women under which certain jobs, particularly in the textile industry, were set aside for women.[28] In 1969 and 1970, more than 100,000 women entered the production forces in both paid and voluntary work.[29] For the majority of women, this was to be their first work experience outside the home.

The following year the *Frente Feminino*, or Women's Front, was organized as a secretariat within the CTC to monitor the progress and address the needs of women in the workplace.[30] The Front, renamed the Department of Women's Affairs in the early 1980s,[31] has become one of the most active groups within the CTC and a powerful voice for women. Each work center elects a delegate to the Front. Delegates are elected not just by women, but by all workers in the work center. As a result, a small number of men are elected delegates. The rationale for not keeping the Front exclusively female is that the goal of women's equality is shared by society as a whole.

The national priority given to free education and expanding women's participation yielded dramatic results in the 1960s. Illiteracy in Cuba dropped from 23 percent to less than 5 percent. By 1970 young women made up 55 percent of high school students and 40 percent of those attending institutions of higher education.[32] The professions were immediately opened to women who took advantage of the opportunities. Nearly one-half of Cuban medical students in the mid-1960s were women.[33] By 1971, the percentage of women in the labor force had reached twenty-three percent nationwide with even greater increases in rural areas.[34]

Some observers argue that the advances in providing day-care and liberal maternity benefits were promoted not to help women but rather to push them into unfilled jobs.[35] This criticism is unfair. Although socialism, as well as capitalism, requires a productive work force, Cuban women were never forced to work nor penalized for not working. Moreover, the changes in Cuba went far beyond what was necessary simply to get women into assembly lines. Although the majority entered jobs traditionally held by women,[36] Cuban women were given opportunities to and did enter a wide variety of professions. The revolution gave Cuban women unprecedented financial independence and options.

This progress, however, did not reflect societal acknowledgment of women's equality. Women remained barely visible in the ranks of leadership outside their own organizations. Nevertheless, the first steps in the process through which advancement into leadership positions could be achieved had been taken. Moreover, Cuban women now had national organizations supported by the revolution through which they could address their concerns in society and in the workplace.

Women's Organizations

A creation of the revolution, the FMC was recognized in the 1976 Constitution as one of the mass organizations charged with "fulfill[ing] the state functions ... according to the Constitution and the law." The "state functions" are not specified, but the FMC, because it has traditionally worked with the family, has taken a significant role in the implementation of some state policies, such as crime prevention and efforts to increase school attendance. From 1960 to 1975, the Party leadership exercised considerable guidance over and gave direction to the activities of the FMC. Since then, the Party has continued to provide direction, but the content of Party policy with respect to women's issues became increasingly influenced by information and proposals made by the FMC. Today, other centers are also engaging in discussion and development of policy concerning women, such as the Cuban Society of Civil Law and academic institutions.

From the 1970s until the late 1980s, as the goal of women's equality became more clearly defined by the FMC, the FMC took greater initiative in defining issues and proposing solutions for adoption by the Party and the legislative bodies. In fact, it centralized virtually all research and policy development in the area of women's issues outside of the CTC where the Women's Front played a major role. As noted above, other groups and institutions are becoming increasingly involved, thus eliminating the previous quasi-monopoly of the FMC over women's issues.

FMC decisions and projects have been undertaken in the specific context of social, political, and economic policies of the revolution at a given time. In 1975, the First Congress of the Party defined the "immediate task" of the FMC to be: "to intensify—together with the rest of the political and mass organizations—the fight for the creation of the objective and subjective conditions which permit the full exercise of equality of women."[37] Within that context, the FMC has played the role of communicator of state policy, initiator of policy recommendations, and implementor of programmatic work.

Among the work undertaken by the FMC has been the recruitment of women into the Territorial Troop Militia, a voluntary civil defense force. Women now comprise 48 percent of this force.[38] The FMC also continues to organize the Militant Mothers for Education (which fosters parental involvement with children's education), health brigades and cultural activities. Some of these activities are undertaken with the Committees for the Defense of the Revolution (CDRs). In addition, the FMC as an organization is concerned with many issues of importance to women, including sex education, teenage pregnancy, physical fitness, and nutrition. The organization has also led a child support campaign to get fathers to fulfill their legal obligations. For years the FMC supervised publication of two magazines, *Mujeres* and *Muchacha,* which have now been merged due to shortages of paper, as well as the production of television programs for women. Currently, the FMC has launched a new project: the "Casa de la Mujer." These *casas* are neighborhood centers where women can meet to discuss issues and also go to receive counseling and legal support. Two such *casas* were established in Havana in 1992.

Membership in the FMC is voluntary and in the late 1980s included 83.5 percent of Cuban women starting at age fourteen.[39] The organization grew rapidly. In 1961 there were approximately 17,000 members.[40] Within two years, by the date of its first congress, more than 350,000 Cuban women had joined.[41] Though initially supported financially by the state, it is now primarily self-financed, mainly from membership dues.

The structure of the FMC parallels the pyramidal scheme of the national political institutions. The base level consists of small delegations that are grouped into *bloques* roughly corresponding to a neighborhood. These *bloques* elect delegates to municipal, provincial, and national committees. Issues are raised at all levels for discussion and action, but policy is made at the national level. Although the full congress, which is attended by several thousand women, only meets every five years, the national plenary meets annually to discuss issues and to direct the work of the organization.[42]

In recent years, the FMC has lost a great deal of its base and influence as other institutions have become involved in women's issues. The FMC came under considerable attack during the public discussions leading up to the Fourth Party Congress. Although no one questioned the need to continue to advance women's equality, some posited that it was no longer necessary to have a separate organization because the FMC's work was duplicative of the CDRs and the trade unions. There were also suggestions that it had lost touch with the new generation of women. Many of the most dynamic young women work within the Union of Communist Youth (UJC) or in other spheres. The FMC continues actively to represent Cuban women in international institutions and networks of women's organizations.

Like the FMC, the Department of Women's Affairs of the CTC, initially had a national structure with councils at the national, provincial, municipal, and work-center levels of the trade unions.[43] Today, it functions only at the national level. It is not, however, a membership organization, and delegates are elected by members of the CTC.[44] Some have said that the Department of Women's Affairs represents the interests of women workers, while the FMC

represents housewives.[45] Although the characterization is an exaggeration because the FMC does address workplace issues, the Department has taken an
aggressive approach to promoting women's equality in the workplace.[46]

The two primary functions of the Department are to deal with women's
concerns in the workplace and to monitor hiring and promotion decisions. It
also supervises courses given to women to increase their work qualifications
and holds seminars to explain to women the laws that affect them.[47] Furthermore, the Department investigates claims of discrimination and has begun analyzing the effect of incentive systems on women.[48] The principal focus of its
current work is to increase the promotion of women into management positions and to assure that women's jobs are not disproportionately affected by
work force reductions.[49] The success of women in moving into leadership positions at the local trade union level, in proportions higher than they represent
in the work force, is evidence of the strength of the Department.

Defining Goals and Confronting Obstacles

Both the FMC and the Department of Women's Affairs concern themselves
with women from all sectors of society—the well educated as well as the newly
literate, professionals as well as production workers. This equal concern is
consistent with the socialist content of the women's movement and under-
scores the attention given to the elimination of class bias in the search for
women's equality in Cuba.

The emphasis of the FMC's work during the 1960s had been almost entirely on getting women out of the house and into some kind of participation–
into educational programs, into voluntary service, and into the work force.
These efforts caused direct confrontation with entrenched notions of the traditional role of women as circumscribed by home and family. Success in
breaking down these social and psychological barriers generated a new consciousness among many women, who began to seek not just opportunities for
participation but conditions that would lead to equality. Although Cuban
women rapidly gained equal access to higher education and the professions after the revolution, equality in the workplace and in leadership were not as
readily achievable. Women's organizations recognized that the gains made by
women were not permanent as long as they were not accompanied by a real
societal transformation of consciousness.

One indication of the problem was the large number of women leaving the
work force. Although more than 700,000 women joined the labor force from
1969 to 1974, more than 500,000 simultaneously dropped out.[50] Thus, the
net increase during these years was fewer than 200,000.[51] Concern over the
impermanence of female workers was heightened by the economy's growing
demand for workers.[52] The FMC and the Department of Women's Affairs
studied the problem to find out why the female labor force was so unstable.
The major problems were not difficult to identify and were listed by the Sec-

ond Congress of the FMC: "[p]ressure of home and family, [inadequate] services, lack of economic incentive, lack of minimal conditions of hygiene and protection at work sites, lack of political work with the newly incorporated women on the job, [and] a lack of understanding concerning women's role in society."[53]

Women's participation in social and economic activities outside the home did not relieve them of responsibility for *all* the household chores and care of their children. In Cuba, as elsewhere, housework was traditionally women's work exclusively. A survey of 251 working women in 1975 showed that they spent "an average of 13 hours a day on job-related or household activities, and eleven and a half hours on weekends, due to the accumulation of housework."[54] This double duty burdened women with what has been called the "second shift."

The Cuban film *Portrait of Teresa,* made in 1976, vividly portrays the pain and frustration of a young woman trying to respond to the multiple demands of job, family, and self.[55] There is no happy ending. Teresa's struggle, universal to working women, is all the more difficult in an underdeveloped economy. Material conditions in Cuba had not advanced to the extent that services, convenience goods and foods, or electric appliances (*eléctrico domésticos*) such as washing machines were readily available. Teresa is shown rising at dawn to hand wash the family laundry, prepare breakfast for husband and children, dress the children and get them off to school before she goes to work. More housework awaits her return from work. She has little time for her husband, who does not do any household chores, and he courts the attention of a young, single woman.

In addition, because the economy was struggling to provide basic goods, a family could buy few consumer items with excess income. Therefore, if the husband worked, the wife had little economic incentive to work as well. Equally important, attitudes about the role of women in society had not advanced very far. Most men, as well as women, continued to hold "old-fashioned" beliefs about women as participants in economic and political activity.[56]

Continued economic growth could ameliorate the material conditions that hindered women's participation, but only a full-scale assault on subjective attitudes could effect the radical change necessary to women's development. Change would require the commitment of the entire society. That commitment did not originate with the population; rather, it was initiated by the governing leadership, which marshalled the nation's institutions to support the goal of women's equality.

In large measure, the failure of the FMC and other institutions early on to articulate and define the goal of women's equality impeded progress in the steady incorporation of women into productive work. In the mid-1970s, critical years in the political and economic development of the revolution, the

FMC, the CTC and the Party each addressed the question of women's equality and the necessity of eradicating the conditions that kept women in an unequal status. The central theme of the Second Congress of the FMC, held in March 1974, was not simply the incorporation of more women into productive service but the "struggle for women's equality." The First Congress of the Cuban Communist Party in 1975 took up this theme and embraced women's equality as an objective of the Cuban Revolution: "[T]he participation of women in society must be in absolute equality with men, and so long as any vestige of inequality remains, it is necessary to continue working to achieve this objective of the revolution."[57] Recognizing the historical double exploitation of women, the Thirteenth Congress of the CTC in 1973 also approved a resolution on the full equality of women.[58]

Rhetoric was translated into far-reaching legislation, which the FMC had a role in shaping by initiating proposals, reviewing drafts, and recommending changes. Both the Family Code[59] and Constitution, enacted in 1975 and 1976 respectively, declare the equal status of men and women in Cuban society. Although the direct impact of these laws on the achievement of women's equality has been mixed, yielding both advances and disappointments for women, the laws have had broader significance by not only codifying the commitment to equality but, most importantly, by articulating an ideal against which progress could be measured.

The Constitution

The Constitution of 1976 specifically prohibited discrimination on the basis of sex: "Discrimination because of race, color, sex or national origin is forbidden and is punished by law. The institutions of the state educate everyone, from the earliest possible age, in the principle of equality among human beings."[60] In addition to prohibiting discrimination, the Constitution expressly granted women "the same rights as men in the economic, political and social fields as well as in the family,"[61] and incorporated as law the equal relationship of men and women in marriage codified in the Family Code.[62]

Further, the Constitution set out the state's obligation to support women's integration into the work force:

> In order to assure the exercise of these rights and especially the incorporation of women into socially organized work, the state sees to it that they are given jobs in keeping with their physical makeup; they are given paid maternity leave before and after giving birth; the state organizes such institutions as children's day care centers, semi-boarding schools and boarding schools; and it strives to create all the conditions which help to make real the principle of equality.[63]

Although intended to be supportive of women's equality, the provision reflects paternalism which perpetuates unequal treatment based on physical capacity and child-rearing responsibilities.

After years of debate, this article was amended in July 1992 to eliminate explicit differentiation between men and women. The new provision states:

> Women and men enjoy the same economic, political, cultural, social and family rights. The State guarantees that women will be offered the same opportunities and possibilities as men to the end that women achieve full participation in the development of the country.[64]

The Constitution maintains the state's commitment to providing cay care, but expresses it in gender neutral terms:

> The state organizes institutions such as day care centers, boarding schools, homes for attention of the elderly and services which help the working family in carrying out their responsibilities.

The 1992 constitutional modifications also explicitly grant both men and women equal employment opportunities.[65]

Cuba's Constitution designates the National Assembly, not the courts, as the arbiter of legislative constitutionality. Thus, to redress legislation that is discriminatory or contradictory to the Constitution, women must seek action from the National Assembly or from administrative bodies to which the National Assembly has delegated authority. In the few instances where the FMC has sought changes in legislation or regulations which were discriminatory it has been generally successful. Individual acts of discrimination, such as workplace discrimination, may be challenged in workplace assemblies, in the newly established base organs of labor justice, or in the courts.

The Social Sphere: Home, Marriage and Family

Since household work remained women's responsibility, the FMC and the Party initially sought to ameliorate the burden by increasing day care services, increasing the availability of washing machines, and making food shopping more convenient. These measures, however, did not address the real problem: Men did not share child-care responsibilities or the housework. In 1975, the husband's obligation to share household responsiblities became law with the enactment of the Family Code. Although this obligation was not legally enforceable, making divorce the only legal recourse, the adoption of the Family Code did focus attention on the problem.

Changes in family law since the revolution, which is more fully discussed in Chapter six, has had a significant impact on domestic relations. The Family Code establishes equality in the marital relationship with respect to property and provides for alimony only on the basis of objective need. Both parents are responsible for child support. Yet old habits are difficult to shed. With little or no attention given to psychological and emotional factors which keep women in subordinate relationship to men, little progress has been made in developing equality in the home.

The Economic Sphere: Employment and Work Conditions

1. Affirmative action and preferential treatment for women. Cuba has implemented preferential programs to advance the employment of women. These programs have had varying success. The preferential hiring program of the late 1960s was abandoned in 1973 when it was shown that few qualified women applied to fill the positions allotted. A second plan, Resolution 511, was approved in 1980.[66]

Pursuant to Resolution 511, women were given preference for almost 500,000 designated positions.[67] The managers of enterprises designated these positions with the approval of the workers' councils. The FMC was to be consulted on the positions selected. Since many more women had received education and training in the interim years, more qualified women existed to take these positions than before. A special commission, comprising representatives from the State Committee on Labor and Social Security, the CTC, and the FMC, was established in 1981 to oversee implementation of this program.[68] According to the FMC, in 1985 women occupied the vast majority of the reserved positions.[69]

Women have not been the only beneficiaries of affirmative action measures. Faced with the growing dominance of women in some areas of higher education, Cuba has at times embarked on a preferential program for men. Women's success in gaining entrance to professional schools such as medicine and law had been so great that they constituted 60 to 70 percent of incoming students in 1984.[70] In 1985, medical schools instituted special quotas to maintain a proportional balance of men and women, though women continue to hold a slight edge.[71]

2. Impact of economic reform. At the same time the Family Code and 1976 Constitution were adopted, other major institutional and legislative changes were occurring in Cuba that reorganized its economic and political structure. These changes have had a profound impact on women's rights and on the organization of social and economic institutions in general.

The First Congress of the Communist Party adopted sweeping reforms in the structure of economic institutions to enhance efficiency. Under the new system, decentralized management in semi-autonomous enterprises replaced centralized management of production.[72] The FMC nervously viewed the change as a setback for women because it thought that centralized agencies that contracted employment could more effectively implement programs of preferential placement. The FMC feared that enterprise managers, responsible for profitability, would use efficiency as an excuse to discriminate against women in selecting personnel.[73]

Decentralization was only implemented in 1980 and took time to function as planned. The evidence since 1980 bore out the fears of discriminatory practices, and in 1985 the FMC cited instances of injustice and discrimination against women.[74] Decentralization, however, made specific discriminatory conduct more identifiable, and local management became individually accountable for discrimination in hiring and promotion decisions.[75] Thus, unlike infractions of familial duties under the Family Code, the laws prohibiting discrimination are readily enforceable. The FMC has called for that enforcement.

Many women, however, did not make claims to vindicate their rights. As the FMC noted, many women, as well as men, did not know their rights or how to enforce them.[76] At the Fourth National Congress, the FMC resolved to correct this problem. While there are no statistics on the numbers of complaints brought, informal accounts suggest that women are beginning to bring such complaints. New structures for resolving workplace disputes, which were established in May of 1992, will help individuals redress such grievances. Moreover, as workers in general have more input into working conditions, management policies and planning decisions,[77] women will have more influence in the workplace, enabling them to combat discrimination and call management to account for its failure to hire and promote women.

Measures designed to stimulate productivity have had a less visible, but equally discriminatory, effect. In the past, exemplary workers who overachieved production quotas and worked voluntarily on weekends were rewarded with household appliances such as washing machines, which were in short supply.[78] Married women or single women with children, who most needed these appliances, could not easily put in extra hours or volunteer time and also perform household duties. Women were, however, given credit of time and a half when they did volunteer, thus, giving some, though inadequate, recognition for the hours spent caring for home and children. Yet it is difficult to imagine how women could find the time to volunteer at all.

In addition, until recently, women were given excused absences from work to take care of sick children while men were not.[79] Although intended to be helpful, these measures actually undermine women's advancement since they reinforced the unequal sharing of child care and also require women to be absent more frequently than men, hindering women's chances of employment and promotion. As a result of FMC pressure, this rule was changed to give the management discretion in granting excused absences to men and women.

Cuba's economic situation inevitably affects women's opportunities. The slowing of the Cuban economy and the growing international economic depression put women's progress in doubt in 1980. The Main Report of the Third Congress of the FMC suggested that, under the circumstances, further incorporation of women into the work force might have to be delayed.[80] Remarks by Castro indicate that consideration had been given in 1980 to stalling women's progress in favor of giving jobs to young men who were just joining the labor force.[81] Fortunately, the projections of unemployment proved incorrect. The Cuban economy continued to grow, and women continued to enter the work force in impressive numbers.[82] The proposal favoring employment of young males over women, however, indicated that, despite rhetoric and legislative dictates supporting women's equality, the predominantly male leadership had considered subordinating the progress of women in times of economic difficulties.

This kind of trade-off was strongly rejected at the FMC congress in 1984. In response to the practice of some enterprise managers to use efficiency as a rationale for not hiring or promoting women, the FMC quoted a remark made by Fidel Castro at the FMC's previous congress: "We cannot be guided only by strictly economic criteria without taking into account the question of social justice. We are not capitalists, we are socialists and we want to be communists."[83] Thus, the Fourth Congress denounced subordination of women's equality to goals of efficiency and productivity. Instead, the congress addressed the causes of higher absenteeism among women and proposed solutions.

The "special period" created by the economic crisis that began in 1990 has taken its toll on employment opportunities and individual development for everyone in society. There are fewer professional positions available and many university departments have shrunk, the major exceptions being in the sciences, law, and economics. The crisis prompted the FMC and the CTC to undertake measures to protect women's participation in the work force, particularly in the textile industry, which was hard hit by parts and energy shortages. Unlike men, women who have child-care responsibilities cannot easily take temporary agricultural jobs, although some do. Yet in terms of promotion, women have fared well relative to men and head some of the most important institutes, such as the Academy of Science and the Finlay Institute.

3. Equitable pay. Although concentrated in some areas of traditional work, Cuban women have not been locked into "feminine" jobs and locked out of nontraditional jobs as the result of preferential treatment. Women continue to break into new areas of work at both the production and professional levels. Nor has the growing proportion of women in certain fields resulted in a devaluation of that profession in terms of wages.[84] For example, women will soon constitute more than half the lawyers in Cuba and are as likely to specialize in criminal law or economic law as they are to specialize in domestic relations law. Yet salaries for lawyers have increased steadily and are currently based on productivity, not the area of specialty.[85] Similarly, traditional areas of women's work are not paid less, on the average, than nontraditional work. For example, women constitute a large proportion of health technicians. The entry-level salary for nurses is equal to that of all other skilled technicians.[86]

4. Benefits and paternalism. Cuba has one of the most advanced maternity leave laws in the world. The Working Woman Maternity Law adopted in 1974, which extends the benefits provided by the previous law of 1963, demonstrated the extraordinary amount of concern and care for pregnant women and their babies in Cuba.[87] Fully paid maternity leave was extended from twelve to eighteen weeks.[88] In 1992, paid leave was extended an additional twelve weeks at 60 percent pay. Additional non-paid leave up to one year after childbirth may also be taken with a guarantee that the woman can return to her original position.[89] Women are also given one day of paid leave a month to visit a clinic for prenatal care before birth and one day of paid leave a month during the child's first year for pediatric checkups.[90]

Maternity benefits, however, were initially coupled with paternalistic attitudes that affected women's opportunities. Because of their reproductive capacity, women received generous benefits, but they were also excluded from many kinds of work considered dangerous to female reproductive organs. The first such regulation, Resolution 48, adopted in the late 1960s, was overly inclusive and applied to all women whether they were of childbearing age or not.[91] Under this regulation women were prohibited from all jobs requiring heavy lifting. The regulation prohibited women from entering many nontraditional jobs. As a result of women's complaints about the discriminatory nature of the regulation, Resolution 48 was replaced in 1976 by Resolution 40, which perpetuated paternalism but the list of exclusions was substantially reduced.[92]

Finally, in 1977, the National Assembly approved a new occupational health and safety law that superseded Resolution 40 and permitted a woman to choose to work at jobs that previously excluded women, provided she obtained a certificate from her doctor indicating she was fit.[93] The Women's Affairs Department has been particularly aggressive in scaling back the number of positions not recommended for women and in protecting a woman's right to reject the recommendation.[94] As noted above, the 1992 constitutional modifications have eliminated language which gives preference to women for certain jobs.

Reproductive Rights

Even before the Cuban revolution, abortion was legal in many instances in Cuba. The former Social Defense Code exempted abortion from criminal sanction when it was necessary "to save the life of the mother or to avoid serious damage to her health" as well as in cases of rape or to prevent the transmission of a serious hereditary or contagious disease.[95] This relatively liberal law, which was given very loose interpretation by doctors for women who could afford their services, did not help low-income and poor women who did not have access to such services and often suffered at the hands of unskilled abortionists.

Outrage at the number of poor women who died or suffered serious physical harm from illegal abortions prompted Dr. Celestino Alvarez Lajonchere to campaign for the opening of free abortion services in Cuba in the early 1960s. His concern that women not die from illegal abortions led to an interpretation of the law that no woman be denied an abortion since illegal abortions posed potential "serious damage to her health" and were life threatening. In 1965, abortions were made available in the Calixto Garcia Hospital to all who desired them, and in 1979, all criminal penalties for abortion were eliminated from the Cuban Criminal Code.

There is one area, however, in which inconsistency persists in the law: parental involvement in the case of minors. Ministry of Health regulations require parental consent where the young woman is under 16, but this is rarely required in fact. On the other hand, health workers report that at times it is the parents who insist on the abortion contrary to the wishes of the young woman. No consistent approach has been developed to deal with such cases.[96]

Since 1965, when abortion services were first made freely accessible in Cuba, the number of abortions has grown to almost match the number of live births. Recent statistics show that for ten births there are nine abortions and that almost one-third of abortions involve women under the age of twenty. Although there has been a decline since 1989, studies suggest that the decline is only apparent as more and more women who believe they are pregnant seek a menstrual "regularization," a procedure by which menstration is brought on by extraction. This procedure is not technically considered an abortion, but it seems to be used frequently for the purpose of ending an unwanted pregnancy.

As the number of abortions has increased, the birth rate in Cuba has declined to below replacement levels and in 1989 stood at 1.82 children per female, the lowest in Latin America. This low birth rate is not due to increased infertility, but rather to the choice of Cuban women to have fewer children. For many, this choice means terminating unwanted pregnancies. Although abortion is not a substitute for contraception for most women, abortion has become so commonplace that its availability may impede greater use of other forms of pregnancy prevention.

According to one joint study by Dr. Sonia Catasus of the Center for Demographic Studies and Dr. Luisa Alvarez of the Ministry of Health, there are many social and economic factors that influence a woman's choice to terminate a pregnancy.[97] Changes in sexual behavior have led to increased sexual activity outside of wedlock or stable relationships, particularly for adolescent women. Women who become pregnant in such circumstances are more likely to terminate the pregnancy than women in stable relationships. Poor housing conditions and lower income are also linked to higher abortion rates. The likelihood of a pregnancy being terminated is higher when the family unit living together is a nuclear family as opposed to an extended family, suggesting that women who have greater family support networks are more likely to bring a pregnancy to term.

Most women do use some form of contraception, pills and IUDs being the most popular. Why then are there so many unwanted pregnancies? The following are among the responses given at a forum held at the UNJC in 1992:

(1) lack of education among women who do not use contraceptive methods; (2) some women seek birth control devices only after having their first abortion; and (3) these devices can and do fail. In addition, because these devices themselves pose health risks, some women cannot use them at all. Moreover, in the case of pills, the supply has sometimes been irregular because of dependency on imports. Interruption in the taking of birth control pills increases the chances of unwanted pregnancy. Cuba is now beginning to manufacture its own birth control pills in order to better assure steady supplies.

As in most societies, the prevention of pregnancy is still generally viewed as the woman's responsibility. Although use of condoms is increasing as the result of educational efforts concerning venereal disease and AIDS, unfortunately condoms must still be imported and supplies are threatened by hard currency shortages as well as by the effects of the U.S. trade embargo, which makes finding sources more circuitous and expensive.

Although Cuban women no longer suffer the harm of illegal abortion, abortions themselves, and multiple abortions in particular, pose health risks. The growth in the number of abortions has alarmed many doctors and specialists. Yet the focus in Cuba is not to limit access to abortions but to find ways to reduce the number of unwanted pregnancies. The Cubans present at an interdisciplinary forum held at the National Union of Cuban Jurists in May 1992 unanimously agreed that abortion is foremost a health issue requiring that abortion services be available and that a woman's right to decide when to have children never be challenged.

Integration into Leadership

In addition to establishing women's rights to equality, the Constitution established a new political structure and institutions that opened opportunities for women, as well as men, to participate in decision making by electing and being elected delegates to the Popular Assemblies. In the 1985 elections, women took 11.5 percent of the delegate positions in the municipal, 21.4 percent in the provincial, and 22.6 percent in the national assemblies.[98] Although these figures represent an increase over the previous elections,[99] the FMC as well as the Party expressed great dissatisfaction with the results.[100] Women made no progress in the first direct elections of members of the National Assembly held on February 24, 1993, receiving 22.75 percent of the delegate positions. None of the seven executive positions was filled by a woman; only five women were elected to the thirty-one member Council of State.

In addition, although the number of members of the Cuban Communist Party more than doubled between 1975 and 1980 as a result of its reorganization,[101] and membership among workers expanded,[102] women's membership in the Party, increased very slowly from 14.1 percent in 1974 to 21.9 percent in 1984.[103] The percentages roughly mirror growth in women's representation in the National Assembly.[104]

Clearly, the advance of women in employment and education has not been reflected in the nation's leadership. Although women have made progress in Party membership, election to the People's Assemblies and appointment to middle-management positions, progress has been frustratingly slow in the area of upper-level management and national leadership positions.

For example, in 1985, in the central state agencies, which include ministries, state committees and national institutes, women made up less than 5 percent of the presidents or ministers and occupied 10 to 12 percent of director and assistant director positions.[105] Women did, however, represent 29.3 percent of the managers, and 40.5 percent and 41.3 percent respectively of the assistant managers and administrators.[106] Similarly, in the CTC, women held only 17.7 percent of leadership positions on the national level, but more than 45 percent of such positions at the base level.[107] It is interesting that fellow workers have more confidence in women's ability to provide leadership than do the national labor leaders.

The Party leadership, as well as the leadership of the mass organizations, have frequently expressed dissatisfaction with these figures. In direct response to the demands of the FMC for the promotion of more women into leadership, the Third Congress of the PCC adopted a policy of assuring that women will be represented in the Political Bureau and Central Committee of the Party in numbers corresponding to their proportional membership in the Party. In the Central Report to the Congress, Fidel Castro noted progress toward women's equality but urged continuation of "our determined struggle to implement the Party's policy for the total emancipation of women."[108] He further declared that its achievement "[a]bove all ... requires constant, effective ideological effort, largely educational, and an unflinching struggle against the prejudices and discriminatory attitudes that still block the full development of women's potential, both at home and in their professional and social life."[109] Further, in his closing speech at the Congress, Castro noted that reliance could not be placed on antidiscrimination laws alone to bring about full equality: "The correction of historic injustice cannot be left to spontaneity. It is not enough to establish laws on equality and expect total equality. ... It has to be the work of the Party, because we need to straighten out what history has twisted."[110] As a result, the percentage of women elected to the Central Committee by the Third Congress of the Communist Party increased from fourteen to eighteen percent.[111]

Further advancement of women was not on the agenda of the Fourth Party Congress. Other issues, specifically economic and political reform, critical to the very survival of the revolution, took precedence. Despite the elevation of many younger members to leadership in the Party, the percentage of women in the Central Committee did not change. Three women now sit on the Political Bureau which numbers twenty-five. Of significance, the FMC no longer has a representative on the Political Bureau. Vilma Espín, the only woman previously a full member, was removed. Espín still retains her seat in the Central Committee as does Yolanda Ferrer, who is also in national leadership of the FMC.

From Goals to Rights

Although disappointed with the pace of change, the FMC has never adopted a separatist approach to women's rights; instead, it maintains the view that women's equality is inseparable from the advancement of the society as a whole. At the Fourth Congress, the FMC concluded:

> All the advances which we report here, are the result of a certain conception that, in an underdeveloped country like ours, women must fight for their own liberation at the same time they fight for the liberation of the nation and society, and that later, when they have produced transformations in the socioeconomic structures, it is necessary to continue struggling for equality between women and men in all aspects of life.[112]

In fact, members sometimes state that it is a "women's" not a "feminist" organization, meaning that they do not concern themselves with women's rights divorced from comprehensive social change. This is a recurrent refrain heard by visitors to the FMC's headquarters in Havana. The phrase is used often to distinguish their approach from what they perceive to be the pervasive approach among North American feminist groups: a struggle for women's rights separate from revolutionary change.[113]

Although the FMC has not taken a confrontational stance vis-à-vis the male leadership, deeming such a stance divisive, the 1984 Congress of the FMC took a decidedly more aggressive stance toward achievement of equality. The tone of the Congress exhibited the FMC's growing impatience with the tempo of progress and with conditions that perpetuate discrimination. For the first time, the FMC spoke in terms of present rights, not simply goals, that were not being respected.

For example, the 1984 Congress specifically called for equality in promotions, not preferences, and an end to discriminatory practices that are contrary to the guarantees of the Constitution. The Congress urged action to eliminate these practices and to make accountable those guilty of discrimination. "[T]he errors and arbitrary decisions that are made must be rectified, even if they involve only one case. There is no room for discrimination in our society, and those who act against the revolutionary laws should be punished."[114] The Congress also recognized the need to educate women workers of their legal rights and to encourage them to file complaints to protect those rights.[115] Thus, while noting the impressive progress of women, the Congress focused more sharply on the persistent obstacles to women's equality and explicitly recognized that to overcome these obstacles it was going to have to take a more activist role in relationship to its own work, the CTC, the Party, and other organizations and institutions.[116]

Moreover, the FMC, aware of the relationship between law and equality, undertook a study of laws and customs that perpetuate inequality and reinforce attitudes about women's place in society as chief caretaker and homemaker. For example, hospital regulations permitted only women to care for family members who were hospitalized.[117] Consequently, women performed this task and in the case of prolonged illness could be absent from work for substantial periods of time. These absences, forced on women by discriminatory practices and rules, diminished women's chances of being hired or promoted.[118] The FMC successfully urged that these hospital rules be changed and pressed for more equitable application of work rules to eliminate discrimination.

The FMC also recognized the necessity of continued ideological work to convince both men and women of the importance of sharing these tasks: "[W]e should remember that, sometimes, women themselves don't accept men's participation in these tasks. These concepts from the past should be changed. ... Naturally, all this means that ideological work should be strengthened, since men's absences from work for these reasons aren't understood yet in many places."[119] Thus, the organization views progress as an ideological problem, not only a legal problem.

The 1984 Congress demonstrated two important advances made by the FMC. First, in the last decade the FMC had sharpened its analysis of the objective factors limiting women's equality, and it demonstrated its ability to effect change based on its analysis. Second, the FMC recognized the need to heighten women's awareness of their complicity in the perpetuation of entrenched "machismo."[120] The FMC has yet, however, to develop a comprehensive analysis of the contradictions between women's aspirations for economic and political equality and the enduring inequality in social relationships between Cuban men and women. Germaine Greer has observed that Cuban women have not redefined their relationships with men to match their emergence into economic and political life, but continue to rely on men for emotional satisfaction and self-esteem. "Cuban feminism," she reports, "shows no signs of any attempt to reduce women's psychic dependence upon their success in heterosexual relationships by strengthening camaraderie among women or teaching them that in order to live with men they must learn to live without them."[121]

Moreover, some activities of the FMC itself may actually impede establishing equality between men and women. The FMC organizes the Militant Mothers for Education and the mothers' advisory councils for the day-care center. The focus on women's involvement in these activities perpetuate the role of women as primarily responsible for child rearing and do not promote the involvement of men, a key link to breaking down stereotypes for this and the next generation.

Perhaps because it failed to struggle with these issues and contradictions, the FMC has lost considerable strength in the past few years. Nor has it adjusted to change. Proposals for reform of its structure were prepared for its Fifth Congress, which took place in March of 1990, but the agenda was derailed by the economic and political crisis heralded by both the crumbling of the eastern European bloc and intensified hostility from Washington. The decline of the FMC, however, has not deprived women of vehicles for voicing concerns or for addressing women's issues. Women will likely benefit from the diversity of forums in what had previously been a camp virtually monopolized by the FMC. Moreover, the growing number of women in the legal profession, which itself is becoming more active in influencing legal policy, ensures an expanded role for women in Cuba in the future.

Conclusion

Cuban women have found their voice within the revolution. With statute and law to back up their demands, women are no longer simply pursuing the "goal" of women's equality, but are demanding eradication of barriers and enforcement of their legal rights. The representation of women in policy making positions, although not proportional, is substantial and slowly increasing. Furthermore, the process of democratization strengthened by recent constitutional modifications enhances the chances for equal sharing of power between men and women.

Cuban women could not have come so far, however, without a national commitment to women's equality—a commitment which, thus far, has not sacrificed equality on the altar of "efficiency." Yet neither equality of opportunity, supportive legislation nor further democratization guarantees the revolution in consciousness essential to full realization of equality. Paternalism and machismo persist as formidable barriers to change. The day is yet to come when Cuba has a party, leadership and government of men and women.

Racial Equality

There is a paucity of literature on race relations and racial discrimination in Cuba, both pre- and post-revolution. Thus, it is very difficult to measure with any precision the depth of racial cleavage or the progress toward equality that has actually been achieved as a result of the revolution. According to the 1981 census, 66 percent of the population was defined as "white," 22 percent as "mixed," and 12 percent as "black,"[122] but there are no statistics on the racial composition of political institutions, professions or other sectors. What can be stated unequivocally, however, is that the revolution did not merely pay lip service to the goal of equality as previous governments had done. It undertook to dismantle institutional racism and actively pursued a policy of racial equality.

Cuba did not abolish slavery until 1886, placing it second to Brazil as the last countries in the hemisphere to do so. Although Cuba never experienced the persistent, virulent racism that is so much a part of U.S. history, black Cubans did suffer violent repression in the early years of the Republic. Despite their substantial role in the war for independence, blacks suffered discrimination at the hands of, first, the U.S. military government[123] and, then, the elected government which deprived them of equal participation in the political and economic life of the new republic.[124] In fact, some commentators observed that blacks were better treated during the colonial period than in the early years of independence.[125]

As a result, blacks organized an association of black voters in 1907 that became the Partido de los Independientes de Color in 1910. But this effort was also frustrated by legislation designed to destroy the black political movement. The party was banned as were its newspapers. Lourdes Casal has described the devastating impact of government response to the movement:

> [T]he Morúa Amendments to the Electoral Reform Law of 1910 closed the door of legality to the organization of parties along race lines and eventually led the Independientes to take arms against the José Miguel Gómez Administration. The ensuing racial war, still insufficiently studied, led to a nationwide extermination of blacks of quasi-genocidal proportions.[126]

Some 3,000 blacks were killed. According to Casal, "[The] black Cuban community never recovered from the heavy losses inflicted upon its most race-conscious male leadership."[127] Since then, the affirmation of black racial identity has found no expression in organized politics. Moreover, in general, blacks were increasingly excluded from opportunities in the higher-paid trades and continued to constitute the poorest sector in Cuba, particularly in urban areas.[128]

Although prior constitutions each contained a general provision declaring all citizens equal before the law, none specifically proscribed racial discrimination until the 1940 Constitution was adopted. The 1940 Constitution contained two sections specifically relevant to race. Article 10 declared that

> the citizen has the right. ... [t]o reside in his country without being the object of any discrimination ... on basis of race, class, political opinions or religious belief.

Article 20 states, in addition to repeating former provisions concerning equality of citizens before the law, that

[a]ll discrimination based on sex, race, color or class, and any other motive harmful to human dignity is declared illegal and punishable.

To enforce this provision, a 1955 amendment to the Social Defense Code of 1936 made acts of discrimination on the basis of "sex, race, color or class" punishable by fine.[129]

None of these provisions, however, was enforced. Racial discrimination was so openly practiced right up to 1959 that even Batista was reportedly denied admission to some of Havana's exclusive clubs because he was mulatto. Many recreational facilities as well as jobs were known to be closed to blacks. Moreover, the Social Defense Code itself contained provisions which expressly discriminated on the basis of race. For example, Article 571 (Violations of the Public Order) punished as a misdemeanor the practice of certain religious cults of African origin. Also, anyone who went out on the street, without special permission to form part of a *comparsa*, or *conga* or other "dance of an African character," was chargeable with a misdemeanor. These provisions were not repealed until the Criminal Code of 1979 was adopted.

As was the case with respect to gender equality, racial equality was not expressly included among the goals for which the revolutionaries fought. It, too, went unmentioned in Castro's speech in his defense after the assault on the Moncada Garrison in which he detailed the injustices that prompted rebellion. However, elimination of racial discrimination quickly became a permanent part of the program for the new society.

In the early months after the defeat of Batista, Castro openly and directly denounced racial discrimination in unequivocal terms. In March 1959, he declared:

> One of the battles which we must prioritize more and more every day ... is the battle to end racial discrimination at the work place. ... There are two types of racial discrimination: One is the discrimination in recreation centers or cultural centers; the other, which is the worst and the first one which we must fight, is racial discrimination in jobs.[130]

The closing of private schools in 1961 and the public investment in public education were extremely important to the process of rectifying racial inequality. Even in special secondary schools set up by the new government for the brightest students, a policy of regional representation helped increase the numbers of black youths attending. Race has not been taken into account as a factor in admission to schools at any level and educational opportunities have been available on an equal basis, but social factors rooted in the vestiges of past discrimination may continue to impede black youth. Although certainly not a small minority, blacks do not appear not to be proportionately represented in university programs. Numerous programs have been designed, however, to assure that children attend school, and many of the families that received this attention were among the poorest and therefore more likely to be black.

As evidence of progress, increasing numbers of blacks and mulattos enter university and the professions and have become more visible in high-level positions in governmental and non-governmental institutions. At the last General Assembly of the *bufetes colectivos,* for example, the numbers of black and mulatto lawyers present made up nearly half the assembly, and there is an increasing number of black judges at all levels of the judiciary. Similar advancement is found in other professions, such as medicine and the sciences.

Blacks also benefitted from the elimination of the private rental of housing and efforts to improve housing conditions. Immunization projects, sanitation services and the development of a national health service have substantially improved health conditions. Thus, since the black population as a whole was among the most disadvantaged in pre-revolutionary Cuba, it benefitted disproportionately to other sectors. It is not surprising, therefore, that support for the revolution among blacks was reportedly higher than among whites. Maurice Zeitlin reports in a 1962 survey that 80 percent of black industrial workers as compared to 67 percent of white workers expressed support for the revolution.[131]

The government policy of non-racialism also had an influence on social attitudes. While the persistent and acute housing shortage has not enabled the eradication of run-down, marginal neighborhoods in Havana (which are primarily black), most neighborhoods are becoming increasingly integrated with respect to both race and profession. Inter-racial marriage, which was never a rarity in Cuba, began to increase markedly after 1959[132] and has become widely accepted as normal among most Cubans, with resistance among some members of the older, more conservative, generations.

The 1976 Constitution, like the 1940 Constitution, contained a provision prohibiting discrimination on the basis of race, color or national origin. In addition, however, it also imposed an affirmative duty on the state to educate "everyone, from the earliest possible age, in the principle of equality among human beings."[133] Also, the Constitution enumerated certain specific rights to all without respect to race, color or national origin.[134] Among these rights are equal pay for equal work, access to jobs based on merit and ability, access to all educational institutions and medical care. These rights are maintained in the 1992 Constitution. The protected categories, however, were modified only to replace "color" with "color of skin," and to add religious beliefs.[135]

With the adoption of the 1979 Criminal Code, the criminal sanctions for racial discrimination were broadened and strengthened. Article 349.1 imposes sanctions of six months to three years and/or a fine on "anyone who discriminates or promotes or incites discrimination, with expression or offensive intent against one's sex, race, color or national origin or who obstructs or impedes enjoyment of rights of equality." The same sanction is imposed against anyone who disseminates ideas based in racial superiority or hatred or commits acts of violence or incites commission of such acts.[136] These provisions are consistent with Cuba's ratification of the United Nations Convention on the Discrimination of Apartheid and All Forms of Racism.

There is no information available regarding any individual cases of race discrimination or enforcement of these laws. Unlike gender cases, where individual cases of job discrimination have been prosecuted or reported in the press, often leading to redress of the discriminatory conduct, complaints based on race have not been reported. If such incidents take place at all, they are probably rarer than cases of work place discrimination against women.

Although black Cubans have become more fully integrated into the political and economic life of the country, striking disparities persist. In an unprecedented recognition that correction of "historic injustices cannot be left to spontaneity," Castro exhorted the Party at its 1985 Congress to undertake affirmative measures to promote youth, women and blacks. The acknowledgment of persistent racial disparity came as quite a surprise, as Cuba had never admitted any failings in promoting a color-blind society. Unlike gender equality, which was the focus of much attention, this was the first time that Castro, or any other leader, publicly acknowledged the need for affirmative measures to eradicate the vestiges of Cuba's long history of racial discrimination.

While black Cubans have had the same educational and employment opportunities as all Cubans and are found in increasing proportion in all professions and economic sectors, observers could not help but notice the small numbers of blacks in leadership posts. It was not readily apparent how such an affirmative action program would work as an increasingly large proportion of the Cuban population is racially mixed. No explicit program of implementation was announced. From conversations with members of local CDRs and trade unions, however, it seemed that the pronouncement had some effect and that elections to offices in these organizations reflected greater consciousness of race, at least in the short run. For example, in one CDR election, an active member was nominated for president. After the nominator presented a lengthy list of his many qualifications, she added, "Also, he is a black!" which was greeted with laughter. He was elected.

There are increasing numbers of Cubans of African descent represented in the highest levels of the government and Party. In 1989 the Central Committee membership was 28.4 percent black or mulatto (self-defined).[137] Because there are no statistics available by race it is not possible to give an accurate account of the ethnic makeup of the National Assembly, but, according to Casal, the combined black and mulatto representation in 1978 was approximately 38 percent, compared to 9 percent in the 1943 Congress.[138] Nevertheless, the number of blacks among the very top cadres is disproportionately small compared to the population. For example, after the 1991 Party Congress which elevated more women and young party members to the Political Bureau, non-whites continued to make up less than 15 percent.

There is increasing recognition that historic economic factors have left black Cubans among the poorest sectors, even today when opportunities are opened to all regardless of race. Because of these factors, blacks have had less chance of gaining the privileges of the professional class or of the higher-level bureaucrats (who have access to travel and other perks, even if minimal by U.S. standards). Criminal activity, such as theft and inter-personal violence, remains higher in black sections than others. Thus, blacks are over repre-sented in the prison population.

This is not the result of a system that denies equal opportunity or that fails to encourage full participation. Rather, it reflects failure to recognize and ad-dress the effects of past inequities. The current condition of economic scarcity can only exacerbate the situation. Despite government efforts to distribute goods equitably, the thriving black market offers scarce goods to those who have more money. For the lowest-paid workers and the growing numbers now living on pensions as a result of lay-offs, such goods are only obtainable by participating in illegal and black market activities.

The issue of racial identity as a differentiating characteristic in Cuban soci-ety is fraught with tension and contradictions. Cuban culture and national identity are bound up with the intertwining of its Spanish and African origins. While Afro-Cuban religions were repressed to different degrees throughout Cuban history until 1979, Afro-Cuban music, art and other cultural manifes-tations have been infused in the Cuban cultural identity for decades. Castro himself gave recognition to this dual heritage when he described Cubans as a "latino-african people." As Casal has noted, Cuba after the revolution has evolved into a "true *mestizaje*, of the complex interactions of two powerful cultural traditions."[139] This fusion, as well as the socialist ethic of collectivity and the apprehension of creating racial antagonism, works against the political expression of separate racial identity.

Subtle forms of bias linger in the national culture. Bias is visible in the way in which the visual media portray black and mulatto Cubans. In general, the main characters in movies are white, and while blacks and mulattos are not rel-egated to stereotypes, they infrequently appear as the protagonist. Moreover, couples in movies are typically of the same race, which is at odds with Cuban society where intermarriage is commonplace. This portrayal appears to reflect an attitude in which "blackness" continues to be undervalued. In Cuban id-iom, the term "negrito" may be used to describe a person with affection in an almost folkloric sense, but it also may be used to identify those who commit petty crimes. There is no comparable term to identify a white person. These remnants of prejudice and bias, which impede the full realization of a non-ra-cial society, remain absent from the national discourse on racial equality.

It is this silence on the issue of race in Cuban society that differentiates it from the issue of gender equality. Although it is against revolutionary policy to discriminate against women, some forms of different treatment have been permitted in recognition of biological differences and there is continuing public discussion about the affects of such differentiation. There is also considerable public dialogue on the struggle against machismo. However, once the government dismantled institutional racism, racial bias and inequality was expected to disappear and any discussion of its continued existence, even in subtle forms, touches a sensitive nerve. Until Cubans are able to publicly recognize the issue and discuss it openly without creating antagonism, Cuban society will not overcome the vestiges of its past.

Notes

1. The exception is the followers of Jehovah's Witness who have not been permitted to practice freely because their beliefs oppose service to the state, particularly military service.

2. The limitations on participation included exclusion from membership in the Party, and, thus, high ranking positions in government. In addition, religious holidays are not observed in Cuba, and workers are expected to work whenever a holiday, such as Christmas, falls on a work day. Although workers can be excused from work for religious purposes, they do not receive pay for the time off.

3. Speech by Fidel Castro at the Second Congress of the Federation of Cuban Women (November 19, 1974), in *Second Congress of the Federation of Cuban Women, Central Report* (1975), p. 276. [Hereinafter cited as *Second Congress FMC.*]

4. The phrase was first used by Fidel Castro in a speech given at the Fifth National Plenary of the Federation of Cuban Women (FMC) in 1966. Fidel Castro, "The Revolution within the Revolution," in *Women and the Cuban Revolution* (New York: Pathfinder Press, 1981), Elizabeth Stone, ed., p. 48. It has since been repeated in the literature of the FMC and has even appeared on billboards and posters in Cuba.

5. The reports on the percentage of women employed in the late 1950s vary from 13 percent to 17 percent, representing 200,000 to 260,000 women. Alfred Padula and Lois Smith, "Women in Socialist Cuba, 1959–84," in *Cuba: Twenty-Five Years of Revolution, 1959–1984* (New York: Praeger, 1985), Sandor Halebsky and John M. Kirk, eds., p. 80 (report that 17 percent of women were employed in 1959); Carmelo Mesa-Lago, *The Economy of Socialist Cuba* (Albuquerque, N.M.: Univeristy of New Mexico Press, 1981), p. 188 (reports 13 percent in 1958).

6. Some authorities estimate the percentage of women working as domestic servants at 70 percent. Padula and Smith, p. 80; Margaret Randall, *Women in Cuba: Twenty Years Later* (New York: Smyrna Press, 1981), p. 23.

7. Padula and Smith, pp. 80–81.

8. In 1958, 28 percent of the labor force, more than 600,000, were either unemployed or underemployed. Carollee Benglesdorf and Alice Hageman, "Emerging from Underdevelopment: Women and Work," *Cuba Review* (September 1974), p. 4. This entire issue of *Cuba Review* is devoted to women in Cuba.

9. Several groups of feminist activists in the 1920s and 1930s worked for the right to vote and employment benefits. Cuban women won the right to vote in 1934 as well as some benefits. One achievement of these activists was the very progressive statement on women's equality inserted in the 1940 Constitution. These achievements, however, were primarily paper victories, and the women's rights won were minimally enforced. Nor was any effort made to provide opportunities for poor and working class women who did not have access to education or employment. See K. Lynn Stoner, *From the House to the Streets* (Durham, N.C.: Duke University Press, 1991).

10. Vilma Espín, who married Raúl Castro in the year before Batista's defeat, became the first president of the FMC and remains its president today.

11. Randall, p. 125.

12. Ibid. Details of the origin and conception of the FMC are scarce and hardly mentioned in the literature. Apparently the founding members came primarily from the same groups which joined to overthrow Batista. The Cuban Revolution was fought by a loose coalition of political groups which included the 26th of July Movement headed by Fidel Castro, the Revolutionary Directorate (primarily a student movement), and the Popular Socialist Party (PSP), which was the old Communist Party. William LeoGrande, "Party Development in Revolutionary Cuba," *Journal of InterAmerican Studies & World Affairs* 21 (1979), pp. 457–458.

13. Randall, p. 130.

14. *Primer Congreso Nacional de la Federación de Mujeres Cubanas, Memoria* (1962), p. 52. All the mass organizations, like the FMC and the Confederation of Cuban Workers (CTC), as well as the Communist Party of Cuba, hold national congresses of their members. Since 1975, the interval between congresses has been regularized to every five years. The FMC generally holds its congress in the year preceding the Party congress.

15. Leo Huberman and Paul M. Sweezy, *Socialism in Cuba* (New York: Monthly Review Press, 1969), pp. 62–63. In 1964, almost 2.5 million children under age fourteen were vaccinated against polio. An additional 1.4 million children under age six were vaccinated in 1966. Ibid. The FMC continues to implement vaccination programs in Cuba.

16. On April 15, 1961, an invasion force of Cuban expatriates landed at the Bay of Pigs. The invasion was planned by the CIA and approved by President Kennedy, who was misinformed by some of his advisors about the potential for success. It was believed that large numbers of people in Cuba would quickly join the invading forces to overthrow the revolutionary government. The invasion was defeated within a few days. For a thorough account of the planning, execution, and defeat of the Bay of Pigs invasion, see Peter Wyden, *Bay of Pigs* (New York: Simon and Schuster, 1979). Many women went to the battlefront to carry supplies to the troops and to care for the wounded. Vilma Espín, "The Early Years," in Elizabeth Stone, ed., pp. 43–45.

17. Padula and Smith, p. 82. As a result of the campaign, a little over 700,000 people were taught to read and write. The illiteracy rate in Cuba dropped from 23.6 percent to about four percent. Huberman and Sweezy, p. 27. Fifty-five percent of those taught to read and write were women. *Second Congress FMC*, p. 101. For an account of the literacy campaign, see generally Jonathan Kozol, *Children of the Revolution* (New York: Delacorte Press, 1978).

18. See Padula and Smith, pp. 80–81; Randall, p. 24.

19. *Women and Revolution,* p. 11; Isabel Larguia and John Dumoulin, "Women's Equality and the Cuban Revolution," in *Women and Change in Latin America* (South Hadley, Mass.: Bergin and Garvey, 1985), June Nash and Helen Safa, eds., pp. 344, 348. The authors report that many of these women came from homes where their parents "would often frown on their even learning to read and write." Ibid.

20. Heidi Steffens, "FMC: Feminine, Not Feminist," *Cuba Review* (September 1974), p. 22.

21. Benglesdorf and Hageman, p. 5.

22. *Women and Revolution,* pp. 11, 41–42.

23. Day-care centers (*círculos infantiles*) were first started by the FMC in 1961. The FMC trained women to work in the centers; many were former domestic servants. *Second Congress FMC,* p. 104. The number has grown slowly since then due to economic constraints; as of 1984, 838 day-care centers existed. *Cuarto Congreso de la Federación de Mujeres Cubanas, Informe Central* (1984), p. 53 [hereinafter *Cuarto Congreso FMC*]. Day care was initially free, but by 1970 the government began charging a maximum of 25 pesos per month for day-care services dependent on ability to pay. The actual cost for one child at the time was about 100 pesos a month. Padula and Smith, p. 85. Today, there are about 1,000 day care centers and charges range from 0–40 pesos.

24. Ley No. 1100 (Ley de Seguridad Social), March 27, 1963. The Working Woman Maternity Law of 1974 expanded the benefits provided by this earlier law. Ley No. 1263 (Ley de Maternidad de la Trabajadora), *Gaceta Oficial Ext.,* January 16, 1974.

25. *Second Congress FMC,* pp. 104–105. During the first fifteen years of the revolution, the number of students enrolled in schools of higher education increased more than five-fold from 15,000 to 83,800. Marvin Leiner, "Cuba's Schools: 25 Years Later," in *Cuba: Twenty-Five Years,* pp. 27, 31. Education at all levels in Cuba is free, even adult education programs, and students receive additional support in the way of room and board. Ibid. By 1983, Cuba ranked 20th among 142 countries in the percentage of women enrolled in university programs. Ibid.

26. Benglesdorf and Hageman, p. 3.

27. For an analysis of the trade union movement in Cuba since the revolution, see Marifeli Pérez-Stable, "Class, Organization, and Conciencia: The Cuban Working Class After 1970," in *Cuba: Twenty-Five Years,* p. 291.

28. *Women and Revolution,* pp. 13–14. Resolution 47, which set forth the program, was repealed after the CTC voted in 1973 to end it. It had become clear that despite educational and training programs there were still not enough women in the work force to fill all the jobs set aside.

29. Padula and Smith, p. 84.

30. Very little literature on the Women's Front exists. For a brief description, see Carollee Benglesdorf, "The Frente Feminino," *Cuba Review* (September 1974), p. 27.

31. Interview with Esther Lidia Chinea, National Director of the Department of Women's Affairs of the CTC, Havana, December 27, 1985. According to Chinea, the change was made because the name "Front" was too confrontational in tone and inconsistent with the principle of women's solidarity with the revolution.

32. Benglesdorf and Hageman, p. 5. Almost half of the 15,000 students enrolled in state-funded universities were women in 1956–57. Marcia Dolores Ortiz, *Cuban Women in Higher Education* (Havana, 1985), pp. 20–21. Fewer than 20 of these, how-

ever, were enrolled in engineering or the sciences. During the 1984–85 school year, of more than 240,000 students enrolled in Cuba's universities, approximately half were women. Ibid., p. 22. Moreover, approximately half of the students enrolled in schools of technology, sciences, economics, and medicine were women. Ibid., p. 23.

33. *Women and Revolution,* p. 11. As of 1984, women comprised well over half of Cuba's medical students. Ortiz, p. 23.

34. Benglesdorf and Hageman, p. 8, note 7. The figure is even more impressive when one considers the difficult challenge of expanding production and absorbing the large numbers of unemployed men in an underdeveloped country faced with an almost total hemispheric economic blockade imposed by the United States and its Latin American allies in 1961.

35. See, e.g., "'La Silenciada,' Cuba: Paradise Gained, Paradise Lost—The Price of 'Integration,'" in *Sisterhood Is Global* (Garden City, N.Y.: Anchor Press/Doubleday, 1984), Robin Morgan, ed., p. 169.

36. Benglesdorf and Hageman, p. 7 (chart showing large percentages of women who worked in textile production [80 percent], health services [60 percent], and education [55 percent]).

37. *Plataforma Programática del Partido Comunista de Cuba* (Havana: Editora Política, 1982), p. 147.

38. Karen Wald, "Cuban Women: Still a Long Way to Go," *Cubatimes* (May-June 1985), p. 15.

39. *Fourth Congress FMC,* p. 9.

40. *First Congress FMC,* p. 6.

41. Ibid.

42. Ministerio de Justicia, *La Mujer en Cuba Socialista* (Havana: Editorial Orbe, 1977), pp. 5–18.

43. Chinea interview.

44. Benglesdorf and Hageman, p. 28.

45. Ibid.

46. Chinea interview.

47. Ibid.

48. Ibid.

49. Ibid.

50. *Tesis y Resolución: Sobre el Pleno Ejercicio de la Igualdad de la Mujer* (Havana: Instituto Cubano del Libro, 1976), p. 16 [hereinafter cited as *Tesis*]. This thesis on women's equality was presented to and adopted by the First Congress of the Party in December 1975.

51. Ibid.

52. Benglesdorf and Hageman, p. 6. A vagrancy law went into effect in March of 1971. Although the statute states in article 2 that "[a]ll citizens who are physically and mentally fit have the social duty to work," and includes all such women between the ages of seventeen and fifty-five, only men are legally accountable for not working. Benglesdorf notes:

The law stops short of making it a crime if women do not work. But its direction is clear. The discussions it provoked made this obvious. *Granma* of March 14,

1971, reported that during the discussions of the law, one of the changes proposed, but not adopted, was "that it be applied to single women who neither work nor study." Some work centers recommended that the full weight of the law be applied to women. Generally, however, it was recognized that the material conditions did not yet permit such an application. Ibid.

53. *Second Congress FMC,* p. 116.

54. *Tesis,* pp. 15–16.

55. Cuban film has consistently played an important role in heightening societal consciousness of women's burdens and frustrations in the Cuban Revolution. Examples of such films include *De Cierta Manera*, which candidly portrays the frustration of a school teacher whose consciousness and aspirations have advanced beyond the people she serves. The film also deals with manifestations of machismo among Cuban men. A 1983 film, *Hasta Cierto Punto,* is a painfully honest look at the complexity of the male/female relationship in contemporary Cuba. A popular film in Cuba and winner of first prize at the Latin American Film Festival in Havana, the film demonstrates a perceptive and sophisticated consciousness of the issues. Less can be said of television and magazine images of women, which tend to reinforce traditional images of women as homemakers and love objects. A number of television programs, however, have dealt with the subject of machismo and equality.

56. *Women and Revolution,* p. 15. Stories abound from the 1960s and 1970s of husbands appearing at job sites or FMC or CDR meetings and demanding that their wives return home.

57. *Tesis,* p. 9. This thesis as well as other reports presented at the Congress were discussed at length in the year preceding the Congress at workplaces, schools, military units, and mass organizations. Randall, p. 33.

58. "Resolución Sobre la Mujer Trabajadora" in *Trece Congreso de la CTC* (Havana, 1973), pp. 152–54. The CTC Congress resolved to (1) contribute to women's full and dignified access to whatever type of work as a right and duty conferred by the socialist society; and (2) realize the incorporation of women into work with full equality with men. Ibid.

59. Código de la Familia (1975), *Gaceta Oficial,* February 15, 1975. The Family Code was approved by popular referendum in November 1974. It was officially enacted by the Council of Ministers on February 14, 1975, and became effective on International Women's Day, March 8, 1975.

60. Constitución de la República de Cuba (1976), Art. 41.

61. Ibid., Art. 43.

62. Article 35 of the Constitution states: "Marriage is the voluntary established union between a man and a woman ... It is based on full equality of rights and duties for the partners, who must see to the support of the home and the integral education of their children through a joint effort."

63. Ibid., Art. 41.

64. Constitución de la República de Cuba (1992), Art. 44. This article further provides: "To assure healthy births, the state grants women maternity leave, before and after birth, and insures that women may be given work positions compatible with her function as mother.

"The state makes an effort to create all the conditions which facilitate the realization of the principle of equality."

65. Ibid., Art. 8(b).

66. Resolución 511 (September 13, 1980) (State Committee on Work and Social Security).

67. *Fourth Congress FMC,* p. 37.

68. Ibid., p. 37. Expressing concern for the success of the program, the Main Report of the Fourth Congress declared it "absolutely necessary" that the FMC take a more active role in the Commission's activities in the future. *Draft Thesis IV,* p. 18.

69. *Fourth Congress FMC,* p. 37.

70. Fidel Castro, "Speech given at the Fourth Congress of the FMC, March 8, 1985," in *Granma,* March 24, 1985, p. 4, col. 3.

71. Ibid.

72. For an explanation of the new economic system and the structure of semi-autonomous enterprises, see Andrew Zimbalist, "Cuban Economic Planning: Organization and Performance," in *Cuba: Twenty-Five Years,* p. 213.

73. *Tercer Congreso de la Federación de Mujeres Cubanas, Memorias* (Havana, 1984), pp. 72–73 [hereinafter Third Congress FMC].

74. *Draft Thesis IV,* pp. 12–13, 17.

75. In 1980 a new disciplinary code was enacted governing conduct by enterprise managers and directors. Decreto-Ley No. 36 (Sobre la Disciplina de los Dirigentes y Funcionarios Administrativos Estatales), March 29, 1980. Although the law does not specifically cover discrimination in hiring and promoting women, Article 5(j) provides that it is an infraction of discipline for a manager or director to hire or promote workers in a manner inconsistent with the social interest. In addition, Chapter V, Article 41, of the Cuban Constitution prohibits discrimination on the basis of sex.

76. Fourth Congress FMC, p. 43.

77. See Zimbalist, p. 221. For example, workers now participate in discussions of annual work plans in their enterprise. They also participate in monthly assemblies where they discuss work conditions, production progress, workers' education, and other issues of worker concern. Worker delegates are elected to the enterprise management council to represent workers' views. Ibid.

78. Ibid., pp. 219–220. Prior to 1990, these goods were also available on the parallel market.

79. *Draft Thesis IV,* pp. 13–16.

80. The FMC noted that the pace of women's incorporation into the labor force would necessarily slow because of economic conditions and suggested that "the further incorporation of women will depend, primarily, on her skill and training and will come about slowly in accordance with the country's economic development." *Third Congress FMC,* pp. 72–73.

81. Castro, "Speech at Fourth Congress."

82. More than 240,000 women entered the work force between 1980 and April 1984. Draft Thesis IV, p. 9.

83. *Fourth Congress FMC,* p. 44.

84. This is a common phenomenon in the United States, for example. See, e.g., *County of Washington* v. *Gunther,* 452 U.S. 161 (1981); *American Federation of State,*

County & Municipal Employees v. *State of Washington,* 578 F. Supp. 846 (W.D. Wash. 1983). In Cuba, salary schedules covering broad categories of work are legislated by the State Committee on Social Security and Labor. Salaries are not negotiated individually or by local trade unions with the management of a particular state enterprise. The unions do, however, have some say in overall salary schedules.

85. "Informe de Rendición de Cuenta de la Junta Directiva Provisional a la Asamblea General de Bufetes Colectivos," in *Memorias de la Sesión Constitutiva de la Asamblea General* (Havana: Organización Nacional de Bufetes Colectivos, 1985), pp. 23–25.

86. Compare Resolución 693 (April 15, 1981) (CETSS) with Resolución 741 (June 1, 1981) (CETSS) (salary schedules of technicians and nurses). In 1981, the starting salary for nurses, depending on classification and experience, ranged from 148 to 231 pesos. Starting salaries for technicians in 1981 ranged from 111 to 198 pesos monthly. For medical school graduates the starting salary for the first two years was 231 pesos a month.

87. Cuban women received maternity benefits by law as early as 1934, but these benefits were limited and the law largely unenforced. Perreira interview; Ministry of Justice, "Forward" to *Working Woman Maternity Law* (Havana: Editorial Orbe, 1975), p. 3.

88. Ley de Maternidad de la Trabajadora (1974), Art. 2, *Gaceta Oficial,* January 16, 1974. Women are obliged to stop working in their 34th week of pregnancy.

89. Resolución No. 2 (1974), Art. 14 (Ministry of Labor). This resolution contains regulations for implementing the Maternity Law.

90. Ley de Maternidad de la Trabajadora (1974), Arts. 12–13.

91. *Women and Revolution,* pp. 13–14.

92. Resolución 40 (1976) (Ministry of Labor). The list was still shockingly long and overly inclusive in barring women from such jobs as all work below water or more than five meters above ground on scaffolds, and all work operating offset machines in book factories. It drew criticism from the FMC at its Third Congress in 1980: "Resolution 40 still suffers from many of the defects of the previous regulations which are presently being revised to correspond to the reality of women today in our country." *Third Congress FMC,* p. 78.

93. Ley de Protección y Salud (1977). This law was incorporated in the Código de Trabajo (1985), Chapters 7–8, *Gaceta Oficial Ext.,* April 24, 1985.

94. Chinea interview; Ora Schub, unpublished notes of interview with Digna Cires, Director of Women's Department of the CTC, Havana, September 14, 1985.

95. Código de Defensa Social (1936), Art. 443.

96. This information is based on the author's participation in discussions held at the First Interdisciplinary Forum on Abortion, held at the National Union of Cuban Jurists in Havana, Cuba, May 30, 1992.

97. Luisa Alvarez Vazquez and Sonia Catasus, "Consideraciones Sociodemográficas sobre el Aborto," paper presented at the First Interdisciplinary Forum on Abortion, Havana, Cuba, May 30, 1992 (photocopy).

98. *Fourth Congress FMC,* p. 48. Elections were not held in 1990 as expected because of changes in electoral procedures proposed by the Fourth Congress of the PCC, which itself was not held until October of 1991.

99. The corresponding statistics in the elections of 1980 were: municipal, 7.2 percent; provincial, 17.8 percent; and national, 21.8 percent. "Tesis: Participación de la Mujer en la Vida Económica, Política, Cultural y Social del País," in *Third Congress FMC,* p. 84.

100. *Fourth Congress FMC,* p. 48; *Second Congress PCC,* p. 377. Although the Cubans are not satisfied with these figures, the results are very impressive when compared to the number of women elected to the United States Senate (2 percent) and the House of Representatives (approximately 5 percent) as of 1986. 1985–86 Cong. Index (CCH) 11,001–02, 25,303–06.

101. William LeoGrande, "Party Development in Revolutionary Cuba," *Journal of InterAmerican Studies & World Affairs,* Vol. 21 (1979), pp. 473–477.

102. In December 1975 Party membership totaled 211,642 compared to 434,143 in 1980. *Second Congress PCC,* p. 77. The percentage of production and service worker members in the Party rose from 36.3 percent to 47.3 percent during the same period. Ibid. p. 78.

103. *Fourth Congress FMC,* p. 51.

104. Party membership is not a requirement for election to the National Assembly although most delegates are also party members.

105. *Fourth Congress FMC,* p. 21.

106. Ibid.

107. Ibid., p. 23.

108. "Third Congress of the Communist Party of Cuba, Main Report," published in *Granma Weekly Review,* February 16, 1986, p. 1, col. 2.

109. Ibid. p. 12, col. 3.

110. Closing speech by Fidel Castro, Third Congress of the Communist Party of Cuba (February 10, 1986) (unofficial translated transcript). The analysis of historic discrimination was also applied to Black Cubans who are underrepresented in positions of leadership. Ibid.

111. Greer, p. 286.

112. *Fourth Congress FMC.*

113. Perreira interview; Steffens, p. 22.

114. *Draft Thesis IV,* p. 18.

115. Article 5 of Decreto-Ley No. 36 stipulates that it is an infraction of discipline on the part of enterprise managers to hire or promote employees for reasons of friendship or kinship or for any reason inconsistent with the social interest in applying correct criteria. Decreto-Ley No. 36 (1980), Art. 5(j). No body of discrimination law has yet evolved in Cuba. Therefore, no articulated standards for proving liability exist.

116. *Fourth Congress FMC,* pp. 45–46.

117. In Cuba, relatives are required to assist hospital staff in caring for sick family members. They carry out such nonmedical tasks as bathing and feeding. Wald, pp. 12–13.

118. This problem was specifically noted at the 1984 FMC Congress. *Draft Thesis IV,* pp. 13–15.

119. Ibid. p. 14.

120. Ibid., pp. 14, 25.

121. Greer, pp. 288–89.

122. Jean Stubbs, *The Test of Time* (London: Latin American Bureau, 1989), p. v.

123. Louis A. Pérez, *Cuba Under the Platt Amendment* (Pittsburgh, Penn.: University of Pittsburgh Press, 1986), p. 149; Lisa Brock and Otis Cunningham, "Race and the Cuban Revolution," *Cuban Studies,* Vol. 21 (Winter 1991–1992), p. 175.

124. Pérez, pp. 149–50.

125. Ibid.

126. Lourdes Casal, "Race Relations in Contemporary Cuba," in *The Cuba Reader* (New York: Grove Press, 1989), Philip Brenner, et al., eds., p. 474.

127. Ibid.

128. Ibid. pp. 476–477; Jorge I. Domínguez, *Cuba: Order and Revolution* (Cambridge, Mass.: Harvard University Press, 1978), pp. 75–76 and Appendix B.

129. Código de Defensa Social (1936), Art. 213(Bis), added by Decreto-Ley No. 1933 of January 22, 1955, Article One, *Gaceta Oficial,* January 24, 1955.

130. Fidel Castro, "Discurso del 22 marzo de 1959," *Revolución* (March 23, 1959), pp. 24–27.

131. Maurice Zeitlin, *Revolutionary Politics and the Cuban Working Class* (Princeton, N.J.: Princeton University Press, 1967), p. 77. See also, Brock and Cunningham, p. 175.

132. Casal, p. 479.

133. Constitución (1976), Art. 41.

134. Ibid., Art. 42.

135. Constitución (1992), Art. 43.

136. Código Penal (1979), Art. 349.2.

137. Nelson Valdés, "The Changing Face of Cuba's Communist Party," in *The Cuba Reader* (New York: Grove Press, 1989), Philip Brenner, et al., eds., p. 176.

138. Casal, p. 483; Domínguez, p. 226.

139. Casal, p. 484.

6

Family Law

Like the former Marxist regimes of Europe, the Cuban government has not attempted to socialize family functions significantly. To have done so would have been so at odds with the deeply rooted culture of patriarchy and so socially disruptive as to endanger other goals of the revolution. Although measures were taken early on to assist families economically and to formalize consensual unions, it was not until the mid-1970s, that the government undertook to define the socialist family, its role in society and the rights of its members. Rather than weaken the nuclear family, the revolution aspired to recreate it as the basic unit of the new socialist society.

The socialist Family Code adopted in 1975 was conceived as an instrument to cultivate an ideal family based on mutual affection and "absolute equality" between spouses and elimination of all discrimination applied to children, whether "legitimate" or not or adopted.[1] It not only explicitly rejected the bourgeois family norms that maintained patriarchy and the subordination of women, it attempted to transform the marital relationship into one of true equality. Central to the Cuban concept of marriage is that men and women not only have equal rights with respect to property, but they each undertake obligations to contribute equally to the maintenance of the home and the care of children. This attempt to establish gender equality in the family is distinctly feminist in approach and distinguishes Cuban law and policy from that of other contemporary socialist countries.

As the revolutionary agenda unfolded, Cuban families were strained by the trauma of radical social transformation. The former social and political influence derived from family ties among the propertied classes evaporated with the nationalization of most private enterprise. Moreover, social upheaval led to deep family divisions. Many families were torn apart as members of the upper and middle classes emigrated in vast numbers in response to the socialization of the economy, the introduction of a new political order and the impact of the U.S. trade embargo, which created scarcities of consumer goods.[2] In

123

addition, although the marriage rate increased in the first decade after the revolution as a result of eased regulations to formalize consensual unions,[3] the divorce rate soared as adjustments to radical social changes shook family bonds.[4]

In the early 1960s, the Cuban Roman Catholic Church together with help from the Spanish clergy and governmental and non-governmental agencies in the United States spread fear among the middle and upper classes that the new government was going to interfere with guardianship of children and destroy the family.[5] Parents were urged to send their children unaccompanied to the United States to prevent the revolutionary government from sending them off to the godless Soviet Union for indoctrination. As a result of this project, dubbed Operation Peter Pan, thousands of parents were convinced by such propaganda to separate from their children, thinking it would be only a matter of months before the regime would be toppled. In the United States, these children were housed, fed and sent to schools. They remained separated until their parents emigrated to the United States, and for many the separation was a traumatic experience causing deep wounds within the family.[6]

Although the government lifted some economic burdens from families by providing important services in the areas of health care, day care and education and by assuring housing, it also recognized that the state could not replace the family in the primary role of raising children, looking after their everyday needs as well as ethical and intellectual development. Some measure of responsibility is borne by educational institutions, but even these are not viewed as an adequate substitute for parental affection and guidance. Having lifted some burdens, however, the government has imposed others by encouraging volunteer work as well as political participation, taking parents away from the home and limiting time with children. Moreover, the integration of women into political and social activities has forced re-examination of the traditional role of women in the family and put strains on emotional bonds still shaped by inequality in sexual relations.

The social and political contradictions inevitably affected the family. To create the "model" socialist family required a stable base, but the event of the revolution itself as well as rapid economic and social transformations and the persistence of patriarchal customs opposed that stability and frustrated the project.

The Pre-Revolutionary Family

There has never been a "typical family" in Cuba. Ever since the colonial era, family characteristics varied by both class and race, and rural family patterns differed from those of urban families.[7] Upper-class families before the revolution most closely mirrored the traditional patriarchal family of the colonial period,[8] but even the bourgeois family did not conform to traditional religious teaching. Married men frequently formed extra-marital relationships with women with whom they maintained a household and had children. Informal marriages, or consensual unions, were common among both the urban and rural poor. Regardless of class, however, household membership extended beyond the "nuclear" unit to include grandparents, grandchildren, and other relatives. In the case of the upper class, the extended family included resident servants as well.

Pre-revolutionary Cuban family law was derived from the strongly patriarchal Spanish Civil Code that governed domestic relations in Cuba from 1868 until 1950,[9] and it bore little relation to the complex reality of sexual relations and filiation. The legal institution of marriage was really a small enterprise run by men to serve their everyday needs and to produce heirs. In fact, anyone not capable of procreation was prohibited from marrying.[10] Although the law provided for financial support for married women and their children who served those interests, it afforded them no rights and conserved their dependence on fathers and husbands.

Wives served both as the reproductive vessel and as managers of the household. Although upper- and middle-class families were likely to employ servants, women did not as a result freely engage in social, economic or political activities that would take them outside the home. They were expected either to do the household chores or to supervise the servants who did them. A small number of women, however, did receive higher education and became teachers and professionals.[11]

Under the Civil Code, a married woman was completely subordinated to her husband, who was designated the sole administrator of the marital property, as well as the protector and legal representative of the wife, who was obliged to obey him.[12] A double standard of sexual morality was strictly applied. Social norms dictated that women be virgins until marriage and remain absolutely faithful to their husbands. So prized and to be protected was female virginity that an unmarried women was prohibited by law from leaving her family's home until she reached the age of twenty-three except for purposes of marriage, even though the legal age of majority for both men and woman was twenty-one.[13] Young men, on the other hand, were expected to prove their manhood immediately upon reaching puberty and to reaffirm it in subsequent "conquests" regardless of their marital status or that of the woman involved.[14] Although divorce was not legally recognized until 1918,[15] the Civil Code provided that couples could separate for cause. Pursuant to these provisions, the wife's adultery was always legitimate cause for legal separation, but the husband's adultery was cause only if it resulted in public scandal or neglect of the wife.[16] Thus, the law gave tacit approval to extra-marital relationships of men.

Changes in the law affecting traditional family relations began to occur well before the revolution. The first law providing for a legal divorce enacted in

1918 permitted divorce on specific grounds, including proof of incompatibility.[17] In addition, the Cuban Constitution of 1940, considered one of the most progressive in the hemisphere at the time, contained a provision prohibiting sex discrimination. Ten years later the domestic relations provisions of the Civil Code, which denied women even the semblance of equality in the marital relationship, were modified to eliminate some of the more blatant inconsistencies between the code and the equality provisions of the Constitution.[18] As a result, married women were specifically granted the right to administer property and to be their own representatives.[19]

However, these changes produced virtually no improvement in women's status since there was no societal support for their implementation.[20] Rather, social values and custom kept most women in the same situation as before. Further, the law was not only male- but class-biased; it only recognized rights and responsibilities within that minority of families consisting of husband, wife and legitimate children, which described primarily middle- and upper-class families. Women in the lower classes frequently did not have the benefit of formalized marriage or the resources to enforce their rights if they did. Many of the illegitimate children born to lower-class women were fathered by men from the upper classes, since it was dishonorable to "spoil" unmarried women of their own class.[21] Despite the large number of children born out of wedlock, they were not protected by family or inheritance law. Informal unions were also patriarchal and generally unstable, placing heavy burdens on women who labored under both the oppressiveness of machismo in domestic relations as well as social and political discrimination. Poor and rural women worked outside the home out of necessity, most frequently as factory workers, domestic servants and farm laborers.

Thus, the revolution inherited deeply entrenched patterns of patriarchy in family relations. Despite the embrace of socialism and the promotion of women's equality in education and employment in the early 1960s, nothing was done to overcome these patriarchal values so connected with women's subordination until 1975. The first effort the revolutionary government undertook in the early 1960s with respect to family structure was conservative in nature and centered on legitimizing the thousands of consensual unions. Teams of workers canvassed the cities and rural areas attempting to register births and to encourage formalization of informal marriages. It was not until women themselves began to react to the weight of having to shoulder both social and domestic responsibilities that attention was paid to the oppressive nature of the traditional family structure.

The 1975 Family Code

The Family Code, adopted in 1975, was far-reaching in its purpose to redefine the Cuban family and transform it into the "elementary cell" of society that would contribute to the development of new generations of socialists.[22] The socialist concept of the family rejects the idea of the family as a private contractual union, implicit in the former Civil Code. Consistent with Engels's argument in *The Origin of the Family, Private Property and the State,* which stated that only with the destruction of the bourgeois family structure, which was based on economic dependency, would true monogamous unions founded solely on love be possible, the Family Code defines marriage as a union based solely on mutual affection and "absolute equality."[23]

The primary role of the family in socialist Cuba—and hence the goal of family law—is to contribute to the development and upbringing of children in accordance with socialist values and to provide for the emotional needs of individuals.[24] Thus, by eliminating inequality and subordination in the marital relationship, the objective of the Code was not to destroy the nuclear family but to strengthen it so that it could better contribute to the moral and educational development of children.[25] The Code also establishes equality for all children, thus eliminating all distinctions in the rights of "legitimate" and "illegitimate" children imposed under previous law. The importance of the principles set forth in the Code were reinforced a year later by their restatement in the Cuban Constitution.[26]

Although interested in reviewing other socialist experiences, the drafters of the 1975 Code felt no compunction to copy the legislation of other socialist countries. The Commission on Juridical Studies, which had a hand in drafting the Family Code, studied the laws of the European socialist countries, which they published in Spanish translation in the late 1960s. Although these laws also characterized the family as the elementary unit of society based on mutual affection in which the spouses enjoyed equal rights and duties, none made women's equality a centerpiece of family law.[27] In contrast, the Cuban Family Code begins with the statement that the principle of equality "must be explicitly and fully reinforced" in all legislation, and its equality provisions are both more explicit and far-reaching.

Because provisions supporting women's equality were central to the Code, the FMC took a major role in its drafting. As with many pieces of major legislation in revolutionary Cuba, hundreds of thousands of tabloid copies of the draft were circulated among the population for discussion in the mass organizations: the Committees for the Defense of the Revolution, the trade unions, the Federation of Cuban Women, the National Association of Small Farmers, the Federation of University Students, the Federation of Students of Intermediate Education and a number of state and social agencies.[28] Recommendations for modifications were sent from these groups to the drafters for consideration for incorporation.

The process not only allowed for popular participation in the drafting of legislation, even if resulting modifications were minimal, but it also stimulated mass discussion of major policy decisions. In the case of the Family Code,

broad public discussion was of particular importance because the concept of
equality between men and women in domestic relations was completely contrary to tradition and not one easily accepted by the general population. The
final draft of the Code was adopted by popular referendum in 1974 and made
effective on International Women's Day, March 8, 1975.

In addition to its focus on equality in the marital relationship, the Code includes other important innovations. It gives legal recognition to informal
unions under certain circumstances, facilitates adoption procedures and extends family responsibilities with respect to financial support beyond the nuclear family. Although the Code has not fulfilled its objective of creating the
new socialist family, Cuban lawyers and policy makers are engaged in active
debate on ways to improve its effectiveness, and there are numerous proposals
for both modifications and enactment of a new code.

Equality in Marriage

Some aspects of the Code do not depart significantly from prior law. The legal
age for marriage without special consent is eighteen for both men and wom-
en,[29] but boys can be married at age sixteen and girls at fourteen with the consent of their parents, their guardian or a court.[30] The legal age for marriage
was an issue of great discussion in mass discussions prior to the adoption of
the Code, and many argued that the minimum age should be lower. Previous
law permitted boys and girls to marry at ages fourteen and twelve respectively
with consent of parents,[31] reflecting deeply held social beliefs that girls, in particular, were eligible for marriage at puberty. The new Code, however, maintains similar sex-based distinctions that are clearly less favorable to young girls,
who are more likely to be pressured into marriage at an earlier age than boys
because of persistent attitudes toward female sexuality.[32]

Similar to the requirement imposed under the former Civil Code, a marriage must be performed by a state official in a civil ceremony to be legally recognized.[33] Although civil, the marriage ceremony is not necessarily a cold,
perfunctory affair. Brides often wear traditional white gowns accompanied by
a wedding party. Ceremonies are now performed at *palacios de matrimonio,*
splendid old buildings which formerly housed private clubs of the upper classes, and the government provides the newly-weds with beer and other refresh-
ments for the wedding party. Couples may choose to have a religious ceremony as well, but only the civil ceremony will be given legal recognition.

Where the 1975 Code diverges most from the past is in its regulation of the
family relationship, a departure compelled both by ideology and practice. The
growth of women's participation in the economic and political life of the
country after the revolution represented an abrupt change from their established role as housewife and imposed enormous strains on family relations for
women who chose to participate. Of course, poor women generally had always worked outside the home to feed their children and constituted the

thousands of domestic workers. Rural women also engaged in productive farm work. At the same time, however, all women continued to be bound by traditional household and child-care responsibilities. The weight of these pressures kept many women from participation in the work force, and many who took salaried jobs in the late 1960s and early 1970s quickly left them and returned to the kitchen.[34]

Since Cuba did not socialize household tasks, the continued feminization of household responsibilities remained a formidable barrier to women's advancement as it has in most other countries, socialist or capitalist. A survey conducted by the Cuban Communist Party in 1975 found that employed women worked an average of thirteen hours a day from Monday through Friday and eleven-and-one-half hours a day on the weekends in order to fulfill the obligations of both job and home.[35] The initial government response to the double burdens of working women was to find ways of making housework easier. For example, programs to make grocery shopping more convenient and faster were instituted in the early 1970s. Working women were allocated special times to shop and were given priority in shopping lines.[36] But improved material conditions could not and did not provide an adequate solution. If women were to be fully integrated into productive work as well as leadership roles, family relationships would have to be restructured and family responsibilities shared.

The Family Code of 1975 attempted that reordering. As noted in Chapter five, while continuing to reflect the traditional value placed on the nuclear family as the norm for society, the Code eliminated features of the past patriarchal model that reinforced the subordination of women. Its major provisions declare the equality of men and women in marriage and the *duty* of both husband and wife to share in household chores and in the raising and support of their children. Thus, the Code reflects a national policy to change the traditional relationships between family members. Equality between husband and wife in marriage became a constant theme in the media, in educational materials and in popular discussion.

Although the 1950 amendments to the Civil Code gave women and men the same rights in marriage, the Family Code of 1975 affirmatively expressed and established equal rights and duties between the marriage partners. This equality extends not only to the right to own personal property and to administer marital property, to seek divorce and to exercise *patria potestad* (parental guidance and control) over children, but also to the equal legal obligation to care collectively for the home and children. The heart of the civil marriage ceremony consists of the reading of Articles 24–28 of the Family Code, which establish equality between the parties, their duty to be mutually loyal and helpful and to share in family responsibilities.

The mutual obligation to share housework is one of the most important issues related to women's equality and, not surprisingly, it was the most controversial provision in the Code. Article 26 explicitly states:

> Both parties must care for the family they have created and each most cooperate with the other in the education, upbringing and guidance of the children. ... They must participate, to the extent of their capacity or possibilities, in the running of the home and cooperate so that it will develop in the best possible way.

Moreover, the fact that a woman may not be employed does not relieve the husband of his duty to cooperate with housework. As provided in Article 27:

> The parties must help meet the needs of the family they have created with their marriage, each according to his or her ability and financial status. However, if one of them only contributes by working at home and caring for the children, the other must contribute to this support alone, *without prejudice to his duty of cooperating in the above-mentioned work and care.* (emphasis added)

Establishment of this collective family obligation to share household duties was explicit recognition of the fact that if women truly were to have opportunities to be fully integrated into productive work and leadership, men had to be integrated into housework.

The significance of these provisions is not that they create a legally enforceable duty to share housework. Enforceability of Articles 26 and 27 is doubtful. Rather, the Code codifies a desired societal norm and has become a tool for education and social change. The adoption of the Family Code and the continuing discussion it has fostered have altered the way many Cubans now view domestic relations. Although men did not pitch in with the laundry and cooking immediately, and the majority still resist, particularly among older generations,[37] the message was clear that the correct, revolutionary thing for a man to do is to share in housework.

This ideal of the marital relationship is promoted in education and through the mass media, and it is reportedly becoming an accepted way of life among younger couples, according to Rita Perrera, a member of the national staff of the FMC.[38] If the evolution of humor is any indicator of a trend, men's attitudes toward household responsibilities have changed. Perrera recounted that when the Family Code was first passed, men poked fun at others who helped in household chores such as washing dishes and laundry. Now, she says, many jokes are pointed at the men who do not do their share.[39]

Yet old habits die hard and many regulations, practices and customs persist that undermine equal sharing of household responsibilities. Women themselves often are accomplices in the perpetuation of sexist customs by not socializing children, particularly male children, into sharing household chores.[40] A number of Cuban observers have pointed out that in many cases, even if the woman resented the unshared burdens of housework, she lacks the will to demand her rights.[41] As a result, many women reportedly decline promotion or public office because they cannot bear more responsibilities.[42] Even women in high positions may not challenge tradition and try to both excel in their career and shoulder all the housework. The FMC specifically addressed the problem at its Fourth Congress held in March 1984 and further emphasized that it was incorrect to view the husband's role as one of "helping" the wife with the housework, rather it must be a matter of "sharing."[43]

Other social factors conspire against change in traditional attitudes. Many women who work outside the home entrust primary care of their children when not in day care to grandparents or other elderly family members or to neighbors who reinforce the behavioral patterns of past generations. In addition, because of the housing shortage, several generations frequently share the same dwelling. The mother-in-law, be it the wife's or the husband's mother, frequently does not encourage male children or the husband in doing housework and may even insist that they not do it.

The perpetuation of this traditional role for women has exacerbated burdens for women in the current economic crisis. Meals are harder to plan and prepare because of shortages. A lot of time is spent just finding and obtaining necessary supplies. Power blackouts limit time to do ironing and cleaning chores, and transportation difficulties lengthen commuting time to and from work. Such hardships may discourage women from seeking work outside the home at all.

Divorce

Under the previous Code, divorce could only be granted for cause.[44] Even mutual incompatibility as grounds for divorce had to be proven to the court. Under the new Family Code, a couple may mutually decide to divorce without having to show any cause to the court: "Divorce will take effect by common agreement or when the court determines that there are factors which have led the marriage to lose its meaning for the couple and for the children and, thus, for society as a whole."[45] Either party may initiate the divorce process,[46] which in non-contested cases takes only about a month from the time the demand is filed with the court for a judicial decree to issue dissolving the marriage. The divorce procedure is regulated by the Law of Civil, Administrative and Labor Procedure.[47]

The vast majority of divorces are non-contested or by mutual agreement. A divorce requires the services of a lawyer, but in cases where the divorce is by mutual agreement and there is no dispute over property or custody, the parties can be represented by the same lawyer before the court. Conceptual difficulties were raised, however, by the situation in which one party sought a divorce for cause and the other party denied the allegations. The very fact that one party wanted to dissolve the union itself suggested that the marriage had "lost its meaning for the couple." In such cases, the courts generally converted the process to one based on mutual agreement.[48] This practice was rejected by the Supreme Court of Cuba, and in 1977 it issued instructions to lower courts that required them to conduct a hearing in all contested divorces.[49] However, the instructions and decisions that are published do not illuminate how a court is to make the difficult determination of whether or not the marriage has lost its meaning for the couple and the children, and at least one commentator has observed that the lower courts continue to treat most cases as divorce by mutual consent.[50]

The issue whether cause must be proven, however, has sparked considerable debate among Cuban jurists. Several argue that marriage based on love cannot be regulated juridically at all and that the state, in fact, exercises little influence through divorce laws.[51] Most of the debate centers on the nature of the legal process by which couples may obtain a divorce—that is, if it must be approved judicially. Whether a divorce is obtained for cause or by mutual consent has no effect on the rights of the parties established in the divorce decrees, except to the extent that the cause shown may be one relevant to issues of custody. Even in cases where divorce is by mutual consent, one party may argue for custody based on the best interests of the child. Substantively with respect to the issue of divorce itself, however, the debate perhaps does become "theoretical"[52] as two lawyers argue because the courts are not likely to deny a divorce where one party insists on dissolving the marriage. The court cannot require one spouse to love the other. Yet most continue to believe that the courts have an important function to play in the divorce if there are minor children.[53]

The divorce rate in Cuba has more than tripled since 1959[54] and, in 1988, Cuba's divorce rate ranked third highest following the United States and the former Soviet Union.[55] The increase in divorce has been attributed to a number of factors including changes in the law that make it relatively easy and inexpensive to obtain a divorce, changed societal conditions that give women more social and economic opportunities and the increasing number of marriages of couples under the age of nineteen. The fact that women can enter the work force on virtually equal footing with men has profoundly changed women's attitudes toward marriage.[56] Women are no longer economically dependent on men, and their economic independence has given them the option to choose, decline or end a marriage. According to informal reports in the mid-1980s, the vast majority of divorce petitions are filed by women.[57] If true, what explains it? Is it because women are most oppressed by unequal division of labor in marriage, or because women no longer tolerate their husband's sexual infidelity, or because they seek the same sexual freedom for themselves?

At the same time, however, the limited nature of alimony provisions encourage, if not necessitate, that women pursue a career. If the couple has lived together for more than a year or has children, the court may award alimony to the "party who does not have a job and lacks other means of support."[58] But this support is temporary, lasting only six months if there are no children and up to a year if there are.[59] Only in cases where a spouse is physically or mentally unable to work may alimony payments be extended beyond the statutory period. Thus, a woman who does not suffer a disability and who is of working age[60] must support herself financially after divorce, regardless of whether she worked during the marriage.

In other circumstances in which women have difficulty finding employment, particularly at wages comparable to those of men, such limitations on support payments might be considered unjust. That unfairness is blunted in Cuba by the accessibility of free education, the right to a job and the general equity in pay between women and men. Yet if a man does not fulfill his obligations during the marriage and the woman shoulders all the housework and child-care, the marriage responsibilities will inevitably impede the woman's opportunities for development and advancement, and she will receive no compensation for her efforts upon divorce. Perhaps economic reality, if not higher consciousness, may push Cuban women to enforce the equal sharing provisions of Article 26.

In the event of divorce, custody can be arranged by agreement between the parents.[61] Similar to the practice in the United States, if the parents do not arrive at an agreement on custody, a court will decide on the basis of what is most beneficial to the child. In guiding that decision, the Code provides:

> Under equal conditions, the court will generally decide that the children be left under the care of the parent in whose company they have been until the disagreement arose. Preference is given to the mother in the case that the children lived with both father and mother, unless special reasons make another solution advisable.[62]

Thus, in practice, custody is granted in most instances to the mother. Some of the opinions issued by the Supreme Court indicate just how strong the presumption is in favor of the mother, particularly for children under three years old who are considered all but inseparable from their mothers even for periods as short as two weeks.[63] Visitation rights at regular periods are awarded to the parent who does not have custody.[64]

Child support remains the mutual and enforceable obligation of both parents regardless of marital status or who has custody.[65] Moreover, the obligation to provide support continues even if the parent has been legally stripped of the right of *patria potestad* as the result of criminal or grossly derelict behavior toward the child or other gross misconduct.[66] As elsewhere, Cuban women often have a difficult time collecting child support payments. This problem was especially noted by the FMC at its 1984 congress.[67] Support payments can be enforced by garnishing the father's salary.[68] Criminal sanctions may also be brought against parents who abandon their legal duty to support their children.[69]

Although the Code provides that child support will be shared by the parents proportionate to their respective incomes,[70] there is no provision apportioning child care responsibilities. Thus, although divorce does not inequitably shift the financial burden of child support to women, at least not as a matter of law, women in most instances assume the sole responsibility of child care after divorce. Access to day-care centers for a modest fee, extended family relationships and the availability of elderly women who seek to augment their pensions by caring for children help to lighten this burden. Yet the responsibility and household work that comes with care of children is an impediment to women's economic and political development. Presumably support payments contribute to the cost of child care services, but they do not compensate women for providing care for lost opportunities resulting from being the sole caretaker.

Under the Family Code, marital property is held jointly and is to be divided equally at divorce.[71] This property generally consists of the house or apartment, savings, furnishings and other personal property. If the couple does not come to an agreement on the division of property, a court will order liquidation or an appropriate division based on the needs of the party with custody of the children.[72] If no measures are taken within one year of divorce to resolve the division of property, the parties will be entitled to retain whatever property is in their possession.[73] This last provision is significant in that women must quickly decide to bring a judicial proceeding against their former husbands to claim property. Although this is a legal right, one writer on women in Cuba observed that it is still psychologically difficult for some women to take that step.[74]

Recognition of Informal Unions

The 1940 Constitution permitted courts to treat a non-formalized marriage as comparable to formal marriage for reasons of equity in appropriate circumstances. Although the legislature never enacted complimentary provisions to govern such situations, the courts did exercise their power to recognize property interests comparable to those of a formal marriage when the relationship between two people legally capable of contracting marriage was proved to be both stable and exclusive. The provision apparently was used exclusively in cases involving issues of inheritance.[75] Thus, recognition gave the surviving member of the union rights to inheritance under intestacy laws. Because the remedy was to be given only for reasons of equity, the mere existence of an informal marriage did not necessarily require recognition of rights, regardless of its stability or longevity.

Despite its limited application, this provision was unique and quite progressive for its time.[76] It transcended moral disapproval of cohabitation out of wedlock, and provided special protection for women before married women even had the right to administer property.

The 1975 Code not only codified recognition of informal marriage, but substantially expanded the scope of its legal implications. Under the new

Code, recognition is not based on requirements of equity as defined by the courts, but solely on the character of the relationship. Thus, the Code states:

> A matrimonial union between a man and a woman who are legally fit to establish it and which is in keeping with the standards of stability and singularity, will be just as binding as legally formalized marriages when recognized by a competent court.

The provision has implications not just for the division of property when one party dies, but for obligations to support and presumptions of paternity. In essence, it grants the parties the same rights and duties as those formally married.

Couples who wish to formalize their marriage may seek to have the effect of formalization be retroactive to the date their union began.[77] Where the informal union has ended one party may seek legal recognition of the past relationship, and, in such circumstances, legal recognition will be given effect only from the date of the formation of the relationship to the date of its termination as established by judicial decision. Recognition of a past informal union does not affect the current marital status of either party.

Although the law requires that both parties be "legally fit" to marry, the legal marriage of one of them to someone else will not prevent the other from seeking recognition of the informal union if he or she acted in good faith. Such equitable considerations for the party who has acted in good faith would not have been recognized in the past when the marriage of one party would vitiate the requirement of exclusivity. In one case, the Supreme Court overturned denial of recognition by the lower court where the woman found out that the man was already married but continued to remain in cohabitation with him. The Court ruled in 1975 that the stability and length of the relationship were the determining factors in deciding her right to property the couple held in common.[78] Yet, it is not at all clear what the legal effect would be respecting the conflicting claims and duties as between the various parties.

Clearly the purpose behind the statute is one of equity rather than encouragement of informal marriage. It is a significant advance and is consistent with the concept of family based on mutual affection as opposed to economic dependence. Informal marriage was not recognized in other socialist countries when the Family Code was enacted. Further, most states in the United States do not recognize common-law marriage,[79] and several still reject any recognition of rights derived from non-marital cohabitation.[80] Generally, in the United States, effect will be given to non-marital relationships only on the basis of express or implied contract or on the theory of unjust enrichment, but not when one party is legally married to another.[81] In such cases, the woman must demonstrate either evidence of an agreement or that she contributed quantifiable services for which compensation is deserved. Cuban law, on the other hand, accords rights and interests based on the "marital" quality of the relationship as defined by its stability and faithfulness of both parties, not its economic character.

Adoption

The adoption provisions are another innovation of the Cuban Family Code, and they have contributed to the incorporation of orphaned and abandoned children into stable family situations. The new section on adoption greatly reduced the barriers to adoption posed by the former law, which reflected irrational biases in favor of natural children. The pre-revolutionary law permitted adoption in very limited circumstances: when the couple had no legitimate children of their own and had reached the age of forty-five.[82] Such limitations are not atypical in Latin American countries, although Cuban law contained the highest age requirement.[83]

The primary goal of the new provisions is to promote the interest of the child to be nurtured and cared for in a family. The 1975 Code permits adoption both when the adoptive parent has other children or is childless, thus increasing both the numbers and varieties of potential families for children. Further, the age required of parents is now twenty-five,[84] but the adoptive parent must be at least fifteen years older than the adopted child.[85] This requirement is meant to assure that the parent will be sufficiently mature in comparison to the child.

All legal distinctions between adopted and natural children have been eliminated, and the relationship between the child and natural parent are severed by adoption. Although the 1975 Code established that the relationship between the adoptive parents and the child shall be the same as between natural parents and children,[86] more recent legislation has extended the equality of legal relationship to include that which exists among all family members.[87] Thus, an adopted child may inherit by intestacy from a brother or sister or other blood relative of the adoptive parents. The converse is also true. Likewise, such relatives may have the duty to provide support under certain conditions.

The law provides numerous avenues for adoption in addition to the case of a child whose parents are deceased.[88] A child may be adopted with the consent of the natural parent, which may be the situation where the parents are separated by divorce and the new spouse of one wishes to adopt the child. In addition, a child may be legally adopted if the parent has lost guardianship through a court process or has intentionally abandoned the child. The law contains no requirement that adoption only be by one or both members of a heterosexual couple, but adoption by *more than one person* can only be by a husband and wife.[89] The law seemingly allows a single person to adopt a child. Although homophobia has abated, Cuban society is not approaching acceptance of adoption by homosexual couples.

Unlike marriage, which can be formalized by a notary, adoption requires court authorization. The court must find that the legislative requirements are met both with respect to the eligibility of the adoptive parent(s) and the legality of the severance of the relationship with the natural parent.[90] Adoption proceedings are initiated by the person or persons wishing to adopt the child. An adoption may be opposed not only by the natural parent, but also by grandparents, aunts or uncles and older siblings in cases where adoption arose in situations where one or both parents had been deprived of *patria potestad*.[91] Opposition must be filed at the time of the adoption procedure, or within six months of the adoption if just cause for the delay can be established.[92]

In 1984, Cuba created a network of national institutions including orphanages and day-care centers for children who did not have benefit of family either through abandonment, death or judicial action against the parents. Through these institutions the government saw that these children received adequate care and attended school. Decree Law No. 76 which established these institutions also created a system of substitute families who would care for these children until they were either adopted or reached the age of majority.[93] According to family law specialist Raúl Gómez Treto there were 185 judicially approved adoptions in 1986, whereas during the same year the courts deprived 41 mothers and fathers of *patria potestad*.[94] Similar statistics hold for 1984 and 1985. There are no studies available from which to evaluate how well the system functions.

Support Obligations of Children and Siblings

Although the primary object of the Family Code is the regulation of marriage and the parent-child relationship, Cuban law also recognizes duties of children to parents as well as duties among siblings. For example, the Housing Law grants such relatives protection from eviction if they have lived for a requisite period of time with the homeowner.[95] Similarly, the Family Code contains provisions regarding obligations of Cubans to support their parents and siblings.[96] Thus, parents may demand support from their children and siblings may demand support from each other when they are unable to support themselves due to age or disability, but there are no statistics I am aware of that demonstrate how many, if any, do so. Yet this provision as well as others reinforces the concept of obligation running to the extended family.

Because of the possibility of competing demands and the potential that more than one person may be obligated to contribute, the law provides for priorities among recipients. Spouses have first priority, followed by parents, children and siblings. Courts may also apportion the obligation according to ability to pay in cases where the obligation falls to more than one person, as in the case where a parent seeks support from more than one child. Inheritance laws are also consistent with the obligation to provide for those family members unable to support themselves. Thus, the only class for whom there is a "forced share" is that of close family members who have depended on the deceased for support and who are unable to support themselves.[97]

Family Planning

There has never been any legislation or public policy regarding optimum numbers of children, nor incentives to have more or fewer children. One exception to this rule was the priority given to couples with children for housing or special amenities such as washing machines. Rather, Cuban policy has been to give families choices regarding family size, not to limit them in any way. Thus, contraceptives were introduced and distributed at low cost, and abortion was made available on demand. However, the policy of making contraception readily available was not accompanied by sufficient educational efforts either by institutions or parents. As a result the numbers of unwanted pregnancies began to rise, leading to increasing numbers of abortions as well as adolescent mothers.

Since 1959, Cuban youth, like their counterparts elsewhere, increasingly engage in sexual relations starting with puberty. Although sex education was introduced in schools, it was not adequate to instill in youths a sense of responsibility for both the emotional or physical consequences of sexual relations. Parents were unaccepting of the new "liberation," particularly of girls who either failed to get medical advice on contraception because of parents' disapproval or did not sufficiently understand their use. Thus, although contraceptive devices were readily available, ignorance of their proper use abounded even among adults, and in the case of birth control pills improper use increased the chances of unwanted pregnancy.

Moreover, responsibility is almost universally placed on females for preventing pregnancy either by abstention or use of birth control devices. Only recently have professionals and officials in Cuba begun to talk about the responsibility of males. Abstention or use of condoms by males is a hard sell, particularly in a country where male potency is revered with almost religious fervor. Although condoms were recommended as the preferred contraceptive more than a decade ago, there is still a social bias against their use. Nevertheless, because of the introduction of HIV, more and more Cubans are beginning to use them. However, despite continuing efforts to promote their use, current economic difficulties exacerbate the problem by making condoms and other contraceptives more difficult and expensive for Cuba to obtain.

Dramatic increases in teenage pregnancy in the early 1980s posed special strains on the family. In 1985, one-third of all births were to teenage mothers.[98] The phenomenon created not only health risks to the mother as well as the child, but the education and employment opportunities of these girls were limited by motherhood. In addition, officials became increasingly concerned for the nurturing and development of the children of such young mothers who were frequently unmarried as well. In response, the issue has been one of concern within the FMC, the Ministry of Health, the youth organizations as well as those involved with family law. These groups have concerted their efforts in educational campaigns.

Although the percentage of youths under the age of twenty who are married has declined slightly in the last decade, many perceive the problem of teenage pregnancy and family instability as linked. Some specialists look to possible modifications of the Family Code as a partial solution to the problem. One recommendation is to establish the age of legal marriage as eighteen under all circumstances as a means of better assuring the emotional preparation of the couple for marriage.[99] Although it is hoped that such a change would instill greater responsibility to avoid unplanned pregnancies by youths, the result of such a provision, however, would more likely be that either more children would be born out of wedlock or the numbers of abortions would increase.

Impact of the Family Code

In the eighteen years since its passage, the Family Code has not succeeded in creating a new "socialist" family. Since there never was a typical family, the diverse family patterns made it all that more difficult to establish a stable model for the socialist family. To a degree some of the same social and regional differences in family patterns persist. For example, white women are more than twice as likely to be formally married than to live in consensual unions, whereas the differences are not so great among black and mulatto women.[100] Moreover, in 1981 in the eastern provinces the percentage of consensual unions was three times greater than in central or western provinces reflecting pre-revolutionary patterns of wealth and class.[101] Thus, family structures in Cuba are as disparate today as before, and marriages are certainly not more stable as shown by the high rates of divorce.

Nor has the law been able to remold the Cuban marital relationship into one of absolute equality. The government could neither predict the impact of other legislation on the family nor shield the family from pressures arising from social change. Nor could it root out the remnants of patriarchal traditions and customs. Although the Family Code eliminated all the measures of the Civil Code that reinforced the double standard of sexual morality so strictly adhered to in pre-revolutionary Cuba, other legislation maintained old prejudices. For example, until quite recently, the Criminal Code provided for imprisonment of three to nine months for anyone who had sexual relations with a single woman between the ages of fourteen and sixteen if sexual relations were obtained by fraud, promise to marry or abuse of authority.[102] However, if the offender married the woman he would not be subject to prosecution. Thus, the law perpetuated patriarchal concern for injury to family honor resulting from the young woman's pre-marital sexual relations. The 1987 Criminal Code eliminated the defense.[103]

Even though pre-revolutionary law regulated a family model not generally found among the majority of Cubans, where it existed it was maintained by economic conditions which dictated dependence of women and children on the stability of marriage. Once such economic dependence disappeared, without strong religious underpinning or social custom to maintain the family structure, the only basis for marriage became the emotional bond. Yet, paradoxically, although the government strived to create optimum conditions for establishing marriages based on shared affection, some of the very provisions of the Code that were meant to nurture mutual relations put strains on emotional bonds still rooted in machismo. Stability in the emotional relationship, however, could not in fact be legislated because it is so intimately tied to psychological and social factors.

Yet some specialists continue to look to possible modifications of the Family Code as a partial response to family instability and the problems linked to dissolution. As noted previously, some have recommended raising the age of marriage as a way of curbing teenage marriages. Another concern focuses on the difficulties of inter-spousal communication and the need to instill greater commitment to marriage. It has been suggested that the government organize family counseling units to mediate family disputes with the aim of both reducing the numbers of divorces and increasing parental involvement with children during marriage and after divorce. Although submission to counseling would not be obligatory generally, it might be a prerequisite to filing a petition for divorce.

For most, however, the emphasis remains on widespread education and discussion of family issues in the schools, in the workplace, in social and mass organizations, and in the media. Yet such proposals presuppose that there is a single model of the family that is not only widely accepted but also attainable. Given the various stresses of social conditions and the persistence of conflicting sexual mores, such as the glorification of male promiscuity, the goal appears ever more illusive.

Yet the Code has had and continues to have significant impact on the lives of women both because of its influence on attitudes and because of the positive rights it grants to women. Except for the small percentage of women who were more or less made economically secure by pre-revolutionary family law, for most women the 1975 Code represents a net gain. The ideological support given to the principles of the Code by the Party, the mass organizations and the governing bodies, has translated into very real, if limited, empowerment for women.

Notes

1. Ley No. 1289 (Código de la Familia), Preamble, *Gaceta Oficial,* February 15, 1975.

2. Margaret Randall, *Women in Cuba: Twenty Years Later* (New York: Smyrna Press, 1981), pp. 87–89.

3. Olga Mesa Castillo, "El Divorcio: Otro Angulo de Análisis," *Revista Cubana de Derecho,* No. 38 (July-September 1989), p. 114.

4. Ibid.

5. Raúl Gómez Treto, *The Church and Socialism in Cuba* (New York: Orbis Books, 1988), p. 37.

6. The poignant depiction of one such experience is found in the video documentary about the life of artist Ana Mendieta who came to the United States through this program at age ten and remained separated from her parents for five years. "Ana Mendieta: Fuego de Tierra" (1987), Nereyda García Ferraz and Kate Horsfield, producers.

7. Raúl Gómez Treto, "Hacia un nuevo código de la familia?" *Revista Cubana del Derecho,* Vol. 34 (1988), pp. 32–33; see also, Lisandro Pérez, "The Family in Cuba," in *The Family in Latin America,* Man Singh Das and Clinton J. Jesser, eds. (New Delhi: Vikas Publishing, 1980), pp. 238–39.

8. Pérez, p. 238.

9. Ibid.

10. Código Civil (1889), Art. 83(3).

11. Elizabeth Stone, *Women and the Cuban Revolution* (New York: Pathfinder Press, 1981), p. 6. The reports on the percentage of women employed in the late 1950s vary from 13 to 17 percent, representing 200,000 to 260,000 women. Carmelo Mesa-Lago, *The Economy of Socialist Cuba* (Albuquerque, N.M.: University of New Mexico, 1981) (13.1 percent in 1958); Padula and Smith, "Women in Socialist Cuba," in *Cuba,* Sandor Halebsky and John Kirk, eds. (New York: Praeger, 1985), p. 80.

12. Código Civil (1889), Arts. 57–59.

13. Código Civil (1889), Art. 321 (as modified by Law of June 18, 1916, Art. 2).

14. Interview with Monika Krause, Director of the Cuban Institute of Sex Education, Havana, Cuba, December 27, 1985.

15. Ley sobre Divorcio con Disolución del Vínculo Matrimonial de 29 de julio de 1918, Art. 104.

16. Código Civil (1889), Art. 105.

17. Ley de 29 de julio de 1918, Art. 3(13). The divorce law was modified several times but maintained the list of grounds, which had to be proven in court. See, for example, Decreto-Ley No. 206 (May 10, 1934), Art. 3.

18. Ley No. 9 (December 20, 1950).

19. Ley No. 9 (December 20, 1950). Article 1 replaces Article 57 of the Civil Code and reads: "The spouses must provide mutual protection and observe the considerations owed each other." Article 11 repeals the provision which grants to the husband the right to administer the marital property. Article 12 further revokes, without specification, all existing legislation which diminishes equality between the sexes.

20. Interview with Raúl Gómez Treto, Legal Advisor to the Archbishop of Havana, Cuba, December 20, 1986. Gómez Treto was one of the authors of the Cuban Family Code and recently drafted amendments to its adoption provisions.

21. Pérez, p. 240.

22. Código de la Familia (1975), Preamble.

23. Ibid., Art. 1.

24. The preamble of the Family Code must be read together with Article 16, which states the duty of parents to educate and guide their children "according to the principles of socialist morality."

25. Ibid., Art. 1.

26. Constitución (1976), Arts. 35–38.

27. See, for example, the codes of Poland (Law No. 25, 1964), Bulgaria (Decree No. 225, 1968), Czechoslovakia (Law No. 94, 1963) and the Soviet Union (Bases of Legislation on Matrimony and the Family, 1964). See also, Peter Juviler, "Soviet Marxism and Family Law," *Columbia Journal of Transnational Law,* Vol. 23 (1985), p. 385.

28. Código de la Familia (1975), Preamble.

29. Ibid., Art. 3.

30. Ibid.

31. Código Civil (1899), Art. 83(1).

32. In the United States, state laws frequently specify lower marital age for girls than boys. Yet statutes which differentiate the age of majority based on gender have been held unconstitutional as a violation of equal protection. See, *Stanton* v. *Stanton,* 429 U.S. 501 (1977).

33. Código de la Familia (1975), Art. 16.

34. Although more than 700,000 women joined the labor force from 1969 to 1974, more than 500,000 simultaneously dropped out. *Sobre el pleno ejercicio de a igualdad de la mujer, Tesis y Resolución,* (Havana: Empresa de Medios de Propaganda, 1976), p. 16.

35. Ibid., pp. 15–16.

36. Carollee Benglesdorf, "Emerging From Underdevelopment: Women and Work," *Cuba Review,* No. 4 (1974), p. 9.

37. Interview with Rita Perrera, Federation of Cuban Women, Havana, Cuba, June 4, 1984.

38. Ibid.

39. Ibid.

40. Monika Krause, *Algunos temas fundamentales sobre educación sexuál* (Havana: Editorial Científico-Técnica, 1988), pp. 34–35.

41. Raúl Gómez Treto, "Hacia un nuevo código de la familia," p. 31; interview with Monika Krause.

42. *Draft Thesis: Cuban Women: 25 Years of Revolution,* IV Congress of the FMC (1984), p. 27.

43. Ibid., p. 28.

44. Mesa Castillo, pp. 112–114.

45. Código de la Familia (1975), Art. 51.

46. Ibid., Art. 53.

47. Ley No. 7 (Ley de Procedimiento Civil, Administrativo y Laboral), Art. 381, *Gaceta Oficial,* August 26, 1977.

48. Séfer Zárate, "El Código de la familia a la luz de su interpretación y aplicación por el Tribunal Supremo Popular," *Revista Cubana de Derecho,* Vol. 19 (1983), pp. 82–85.

49. Ibid.

50. Mesa Castillo, pp. 118–119.

51. Rigoberto Hernández León and Miguel Fernández Díaz, "Crítica de la regulación jurídica estatal del divorcio en Cuba," *Revista Jurídica,* No. 12 (July-September, 1986), pp. 174, 177.

52. Ibid., p. 174.

53. Mesa Castillo, p. 122.

54. Ibid., p. 114.

55. Ibid., p. 127, n. 4.

56. Both women and men have a constitutional right to a job: "The socialist state … guarantees that every man or woman who is able to work has the opportunity to have a job." Constitución (1992), Art. 9(b).

57. Interview with Raúl Gómez Treto.

58. Código de la Familia (1975), Art. 56(1).

59. Ibid.

60. The retirement age for women is sixty in most instances and fifty five in jobs which are particularly taxing physically. The respective ages for men are sixty-five and sixty. Ley No. 24 (Ley de Seguridad Social), Art. 81, *Gaceta Oficial,* December 25, 1979.

61. Código de la Familia (1975), Art. 88.

62. Ibid., Art. 89.

63. Zárate, pp. 98–99.

64. Código de la Familia (1975), Art. 90.

65. Ibid., Art. 59.

66. Ibid., Arts. 95–96.

67. *Draft Thesis IV,* p. 32.

68. Ley de Procedimiento Civil, Administrativo y Laboral (1977), Arts. 460–463.

69. Código Penal (1987), Art. 373, *Gaceta Oficial Ext.,* December 30, 1987.

70. Código de la Familia (1975), Art. 60.

71. Ibid., Art. 38.

72. Ibid., Art. 41.

73. Ibid., Art. 40.

74. Interview with Jean Stubbs, Havana, Cuba, December 23, 1985.

75. María Elena Cobas Cobiella, Nancy de la C. Ojeda Rodríguez and Gisela María Pérez Fuentes, "Reconocimiento judicial de matrimonio. Problema que plantea la interpretación y aplicación del articulado del Código de Familia," *Revista Cubana de Derecho,* Vol. 35 (1988), pp. 105, 110.

76. Constitución (1940), Art. 43.

77. Código de la Familia (1975), Art. 19.

78. Zárate, p. 73.

79. William J. Wagner, "The Contractual Reallocation of Procreative Resources and Parental Rights: The Natural Endowment Critique," *Case Western Reserve Law Review* (1990), Vol. 41, No. 1, p. 64.

80. Tammy L. Lewis, "Standing in the Shadows: Honoring the Contractual Obligations of Cohabitants for Support," *University of Puget Sound Law Review* (1991), Vol. 75, p. 177.

81. Ibid., pp. 181–193. See also *Marvin* v. *Marvin,* 557 P.2d 106 (Cal. 1976).

82. Raúl Gómez Treto, "La adopción de hijos en el derecho histórico, comparado, internacional y cubano y la protección a la niñez y la juventud," *Revista Jurídica,* No. 3, (April-June, 1984), p. 87.

83. Mexico has the second highest age requirement (forty), but several others including Uruguay and Peru require adoptive parents to be at least thirty years of age. Ibid.

84. Código de la Familia (1975), Art. 100.

85. Ibid., Art. 102.

86. Ibid., Art. 99.

87. Decreto-Ley 76 (January 20, 1984), Special Provisions, *Gaceta Oficial Ext.,* January 21, 1984.

88. Código de la Familia (1975, as modified by Law No. 9, August 22, 1977), Art. 103.

89. Ibid., Art. 101.

90. Ibid., Art. 104.

91. Ibid., Art. 108.

92. Ibid., Arts. 109–110.

93. Decreto-Ley 76 (January 20, 1984), Arts. 11–15.

94. Gómez Treto, "Hacia un nuevo código," p. 43.

95. Ley No. 65 (Ley General de la Vivienda), Art. 65, *Gaceta Oficial,* December 23, 1988.

96. Código de la Familia (1975), Arts. 121–136.

97. Código Civil (1889), Arts. 806–822.

98. Smith and Padula, p. 180 and n. 18.

99. Gómez Treto, "Hacia un nuevo código," p. 60.

100. Sonia Isabel Catasús Cervera, *La nupcialdad cubana en el siglo XX,* (Havana: Centro de Estudios Demográficos, Universidad de la Habana, 1991), p. 124.

101. Ibid., p. 118.

102. Código Penal (1979), Art. 361, *Gaceta Oficial,* March 1. 1979.

103. Código Penal (1987), Art. 305.

7

Criminal Justice

Perhaps no other area of Cuban law has received as much attention in the foreign media as its criminal justice system. With some exceptions, much of this commentary has centered on the sensational aspects of the Revolutionary Tribunals that tried Batista collaborators and counter-revolutionaries in the 1960s, the treatment of political prisoners and most recently the trial of General Arnaldo Ochoa and three other military officials who were convicted and executed in 1989 for involvement in drug trafficking schemes. Although these events and issues have importance, they are exceptional in post-revolutionary Cuban history. The development of criminal law and procedure in Cuba is far more complex and substantial than such a limited focus would reveal.

From the time the revolutionaries established tribunals in the Sierras to prosecute "war criminals" during the armed rebellion to the present, the leadership has shown concern for legality, and those involved in the development of legal institutions have expressed commitment to creating a criminal justice system that is efficient, fair and devoid of its former class bias. In practice, they have fallen short of this goal, but over the last three decades, criminal law and procedure have evolved toward a convergence of the societal interest in the prosecution of criminal activity and the right of the accused to a fair process. In this quest, Cuban jurists continue to address issues of both form and substance. Thus, reforms have focused not only on improving the law itself, but also on improving the quality of the personnel entrusted to effectuate the law and its objectives.

One of the first changes the new government made in the judicial process in 1959 was formally to establish special Revolutionary Tribunals under military control to prosecute the members of the Batista regime, including the hated secret police. These courts were similar to those that had been established in the guerrilla camps in the Sierras. By the end of 1959, the Revolutionary Tribunals also tried the cases of those accused of participating in counter-revolutionary activity. Among the reasons for usurping the jurisdiction of the existing courts over such crimes was that the ordinary criminal courts were not trusted by the new government. Many of the judges had been loyal to Batista and were unsympathetic to the revolution.

Because the Revolutionary Tribunals kept citizens from taking indiscriminate vengeance on former members of Batista's secret police force and army, Cuba did not experience a "bloodbath" in the aftermath of the revolution.[1] Although hundreds of people were sentenced to death during this period,[2] the Revolutionary Tribunals did not act arbitrarily; nor did they routinely impose death sentences. Many thousands were tried and sentenced to prison terms, the maximum term being twenty years except in cases where the death sentence has been commuted, in which case the term is thirty years. By 1967, the armed insurgency was quelled and relatively few cases were brought to the Revolutionary Tribunals after this period.

Detractors have disparaged the Revolutionary Tribunals for the summary procedures used and for the "public show" atmosphere that surrounded many of the trials of the more notorious Batista henchmen,[3] but the procedures have also been defended, even by those who later turned against the revolution. Twenty-five years after leaving Cuba for Miami, Raúl Chibas, who served as a judge in some of these trials at Castro's personal request, maintained that they were justifiable:

> Sincerely, I was in agreement with these trials. ... I was in agreement beforehand, and I discussed with Fidel (in the Sierra) the need for carrying out justice after Batista's fall ... on the grounds that if there is no justice, people would enforce it as in the time of Machado when mobs dragged corpses through the streets. ... When one tries to do it legally, adverse reaction sets in. Unfortunately, this is people's hypocrisy, and we talked about it with Fidel in the Sierra. ... They had been forewarned because we issued proclamations from the Sierra that justice would be applied to all those who robbed and murdered the peasants, and I thought we had to act accordingly.[4]

Even former United States Ambassador Philip Bonsal wrote afterward that the Revolutionary Tribunals were an improvement over the bloodbath following the revolution that ousted dictator Machado.[5]

In the context of disorder and revolutionary fervor, it would have been remarkable if the leadership had replaced a biased, corrupt legal system with one that functioned smoothly with enhanced procedural protections. Revolutionary zeal and disdain for those responsible for the egregious repression under Batista played heavily in shaping the judicial attitudes of the newly appointed judges who were more concerned with "moral justice" than with process. Yet neither during its most violent period of counter-revolutionary activity of the 1960s nor since has Cuba experienced the appalling extra-judicial executions common in more recent years in other countries of the region, such as El Salvador, Guatemala, Chile, Argentina and Colombia.

Criminal justice in Cuba has not only been scrutinized by outsiders but also by Cuban jurists themselves who have actively engaged in serious study and debate for more than three decades. Concern for improvement and modernization of the system is amply demonstrated by the substantial body of literature on criminal law authored by Cuban scholars.[6] While emphatically rejecting outside pressure to conform to foreign models, Cuban jurists have actively engaged in discussion with jurists from all over the world and have studied other experiences. This analysis has been translated into legislative reform with the active participation of all sectors of the criminal justice system, including defense attorneys, prosecutors, police, the judiciary and officials of the Ministry of Justice. Important modifications have been adopted in the last several years. In 1987, Cuba adopted a more flexible and less severe Criminal Code, and at the end of 1992 a commission proposed changes in the Code of Criminal Procedure that are quite advanced in comparison with other systems, particularly in Latin America. Until recently, improvement in practice had been significantly impeded by incompetence among members of the judiciary as well as the defense bar, police and prosecutors. Advances in training and professionalism are now beginning to correct this problem.

Unfortunately, however, the stress of the current economic crisis has placed a heavy burden on a system struggling to be more efficient and fair. Cuba not only faces severe shortages of material goods and services needed to maintain daily judicial and legal activities, but is also feeling the impact of increased criminal activity, particularly robberies and economic crimes. Efforts to reform the system will most certainly be hindered by these objective conditions as well as a continuing deficit in numbers of well-trained personnel.

Substantive Criminal Law

Prior to 1979, Cuba continued to enforce, with some modifications, the Social Defense Code (CDS) adopted in 1936, which was heavily influenced by Spanish tradition and contemporary Italian law.[7] Efforts to develop a new criminal code that reflected socialist values began as early as 1969, although the new code was not finally enacted until 1979. Despite desire to adapt the new code "to the new social, economic and political conditions of the country; on the road to the construction of socialism," Cubans did not leap to copy codes of other socialist countries. Rather, the 1979 code developed out of a long, laborious process.

The legislative process began with an analysis by the Commission on Juridical Studies, established by the Party in 1969, which, in 1973, presented its preliminary proposals to another commission composed of representatives of the Supreme Court, the University of Havana and the Ministry of Justice. The latter group studied the proposals and sent back a revised text in 1974.[8] This text was then reviewed by the Commission on Juridical Studies and by a third commission that was charged with revising the 1973 law on the organization of the judicial system as well as drafting new codes of both criminal and civil procedure.[9] In 1977, the draft was distributed to deputies of the National Assembly, the heads of central organs of government, the provincial committees of the Party, the courts, the procurator general, the municipal organs of the Poder Popular, and the ONBC.[10] A summary version was also submitted to the CDRs for public discussion. A final draft was elaborated by the Political Bureau of the Party that incorporated 495 recommendations resulting from the various bodies that had reviewed the proposed text.[11] In December 1978, it was approved by the National Assembly and went into effect in February 1979.

Fundamental to the new jurisprudence was the destruction of class privilege. Corruption was rampant in the pre-1959 legal system and prosecution almost always favored the middle and upper classes to the detriment of the poor and working class. A number of Cuban authors have noted that the essential difference between the 1979 Criminal Code and its predecessor is that the former represented and protected the interests of the propertied class whereas the new Code reflected the interests of the workers and the socialist state.[12] One of Cuba's most prominent jurists, Francisco Varona Duque y Estrada, has written that the revolution "restored the fundamental equality before the penal law."[13]

In its preamble, the Code explains that a new statute was necessary in order to replace "penal norms ... which no longer correspond with the reality of our economic, social and political development" and to integrate socialist principles into the penal law. The purposes of the law were enumerated in Article 1: (1) to protect society, individuals and the social, economic and political order; (2) to protect socialist, collective and personal property; (3) to promote the observance of both the rights and duties of citizens; and (4) to contribute to the respect for socialist legality.[14] Although maintaining much of the structure of the previous law, the 1979 Code introduced many new substantive concepts and provisions.

The 1979 Code, like its predecessor, treated criminal conduct severely, but it also contained major jurisprudential advances. First, it provided a definition of a punishable crime as "every socially dangerous action or omission, prohibited by law resulting in penal sanction."[15] The CDS contained no definition and simply provided that no act that was not found in the Code could be considered a crime. Cuban jurists considered the new provision important because it established as a legal principle that only conduct that was socially harmful could be punished.[16] Second, the new Code introduced for the first time a range of alternatives to incarceration for lesser offenses and first-time offenders. Thus, instead of being put in prison, a person convicted of a crime could remain in the community but with certain restrictions on personal liberties for a designated period of time. For example, a person could be required to stay within a described area or denied entrance to taverns or bars.

The new Code, which also recognized defenses of necessity and impossibility of compliance, strengthened provisions that exempted from criminal responsibility those who suffered from mental incapacity. In addition, the age of criminal responsibility was raised from twelve to sixteen,[17] and the 1979 Code gave judges some flexibility in applying sanctions to those who were under the age of twenty.[18] Thus, a judge could reduce a sentence by half for a defendant who was between sixteen and eighteen years of age and by one third for those between eighteen and twenty.

Socialist legality also required lawmakers to promote compliance with the new economic norms and to protect socialist and collective property. Among the crimes added in the new Code were those acts that harmed the national economy.[19] New provisions punished malfeasance by those in charge of economic activities,[20] as well as abuse and misuse of social property by officials and functionaries. The Code also included provisions related to the destruction and illegal exploitation of natural resources and the environment[21] and crimes against cultural patrimony of the nation.[22] Collective forms of property received special protection. Penalties for robbery were substantially enhanced under aggravating circumstances, among which was listed the theft of socialist, state or cooperative property.[23]

In addition to protecting the socialist economy, the 1979 Code contained provisions dealing with crimes that threatened the security of the state. Included in this category were actions such as espionage, sabotage, treason and armed rebellion. Sanctions for such crimes could be imprisonment for periods of four to twenty years or death in cases where violence is used or the threat to security is particularly serious.[24] Also included was the crime of "Enemy Propaganda" which criminalized conduct that incited opposition to the social order, international solidarity and the socialist state. Sentences for violation of this section were lighter, ranging from one to eight years.[25] The Code continued the criminalization of unauthorized entry or departure from the country, which had become part of Cuban criminal law in the 1960s, when such activity was linked to counter-revolutionary attacks.[26]

With the exception of "illegal departure," these provisions were not a dramatic departure from previous Cuban law, which traditionally prohibited both acts and expression in opposition to the state as well as those that threatened the existing order. What was different was the severity of the penalties imposed after 1959. For example, the 1936 Code provided penalties of up to ten years for those who promoted violence against the state or who impeded the functioning of organs of government, even for brief periods of time.[27] Further, it also penalized shouts, demonstrations, posters, writings or similar conduct that "provoked an alteration in the public order."[28] The sanction was up to six months in prison and/or a fine. Another provision made it a crime to incite "hatred among the social classes putting public tranquility in danger."[29]

The 1987 Criminal Code

Although providing significant improvements over the law inherited from the previous regime, the 1979 Criminal Code left much to be desired. It maintained a regime of severe sentencing that gave judges insufficient flexibility to treat individually first time offenders who committed major offenses.[30] Although the 1979 Code was ten years in the making, its imperfections were recognized even as it was enacted, but according to one jurist, it was enacted anyway because Cuba needed a new code that gave coherent definition to its criminal law, and the 1979 Code was perceived to be far better than the former code.[31] The new Code was not in effect long, however, before Cuban jurists embarked on an extensive analysis of its effectiveness and consistency with principles of justice.

Some insight into the evolution of thinking with respect to criminal justice in Cuba is found in a statement by then Vice Minister of Justice Carlos Amat in June 1987:

> In the first period, we operated under the idealistic criteria which governed law-making in the country. One of the basic principles governing our philosophy was that if delinquency and criminal behavior is a product of the social system of exploitation and oppression, then if we change that situation and do away with exploitation and oppression, then crime and criminals would be eliminated. That was the "bobo" [stupidity] at the beginning. So we began to deal with crime very severely, imposing very heavy penalties to suppress crime, because we thought that any manifestations of crime had to be carry-overs of the prior system. And this same approach was adopted in the Criminal Code of 1979, which was very severe.
>
> But experience has shown us that severe treatment has neither prevented crime nor eliminated criminals. New forms of crime developed, and harsh sanctions did not serve as the slightest deterrent to crime.[32]

Thus, the philosophical framework within which the 1987 Code was drafted was different. Whereas there had been a tendency in the early years to treat delinquents as enemies who were unable to conform to the values of the new society,[33] contemporary jurists were cognizant of the dialectical relationship between social development and criminal behavior and the impact of criminal law on both. Cubans acknowledged that severe sentences had not only failed to deter crime, but that they carried social costs as well—the human and material price of incarceration.

Efforts to revise the four-year-old code were facilitated by important changes among the top officials of the legal institutions. In 1983, Juan Escalona Reguera was appointed Minister of Justice, filling the vacancy left by the death of former minister Osvaldo Dórticos Torrado. Escalona's appointment was followed by changes at the top of the Ministry of Interior, which is responsible for running the prison system, and the appointment of Ramón de la Cruz as Procurator General. Both Escalona and de la Cruz energetically pursued continued modernization of Cuban criminal law, and they organized a commission to analyze the 1979 Code and to propose reforms.

In the course of its work, the commission studied the contemporary criminal codes of both socialist and capitalist countries, including some state codes from the United States. Moreover, several international conferences were held in Cuba to discuss approaches to criminal justice. Cuban legal literature suggests that the work of the United Nations in this area was also important in shaping the Cuban approach.[34] As a result of the commission's work, a proposal for a new criminal code was presented to the National Assembly and adopted in December 1987.

One of the objectives of the commission was to substantially reduce the prison population, which had grown to about 30–40,000. The size of the prison population was perceived as partly the result of unduly long sentences meted out by the courts. Moreover, even though the 1979 Code permitted alternatives to incarceration, many judges did not apply such alternatives when possible.[35] The proposed reforms would reduce the prison population by lowering sentences, by permitting alternative sentences for more offenses and by allowing greater flexibility in sentencing for first-time offenders. Further, the proposal would decriminalize a number of minor offenses, such as traffic violations and some misdemeanors that had been included in the 1979 Code.

Even before the National Assembly considered the proposed reforms, however, justice officials began reviewing the sentences in individual cases pursuant to a decree-law passed in 1985[36] which gave the Supreme Court authority to review cases to determine whether the sentences imposed were too severe. Under this process of *revisión,* review could be requested by the person convicted, a relative or a state official. A commission comprising persons from the Ministry of Justice, the president of the Supreme Court and judges of the Provincial Tribunals studied more than 4,000 cases in 1986 and 1987. By June 1987, 1,000 cases had been submitted to the Supreme Court for *revisión,* and many of the prisoners were released or received reduction of their sentences.[37] For example, under the 1979 Code, theft of state property (such as goods from a factory) could be punished by a sentence of up to ten years.[38] After review, the sentence could be reduced to three years in cases where no force or violence was used (unless the economic loss was substantial).

In addition, a broad effort was made to review all cases of prisoners eligible for conditional release, a process similar to parole. According to Escalona Reguera, this process was available under the 1979 Code but had not been implemented consistently.[39] As a result of the review process, approximately 15,000 prisoners were given conditional release between August 1985 and April 1988.[40]

Although following the basic structure of the 1979 Code, the 1987 Code eliminated some crimes, substantially revised other provisions, and reduced sentences for many crimes. For example, the penalty for theft of property was reduced from six months to three years to a penalty of six months to two years and/or a fine.[41] In cases of robbery with the use of force, the difference is even more marked: The 1979 Code provided for a sentence range of ten to twenty years or death when certain aggravating circumstances were present; the 1987 Code eliminated the death penalty and reduced the prison term to four to ten years.[42] Whereas the theft of socialist property had been considered an aggravating circumstance under the 1979 Code, the 1987 Code draws no distinction between theft of state or socialist property and theft of private property.

Among the crimes transferred from criminal prosecution to administrative proceedings were certain forms of misfeasance, violations of regulations and traffic violations. Acts of misfeasance that were decriminalized included conduct of managers of state enterprises, such as failure to fulfill legal obligations, which resulted in harm to the enterprise or in the production or sale of below-standard goods.

The adoption of the 1987 Criminal Code was not without controversy, however. Some members of the Party leadership, including Fidel Castro, initially opposed the revisions, arguing that it was too soon after the enactment of the 1979 Code. In fact, in a statement made to the Third Congress of the Party at the end of 1986, Castro had called for stiffer penalties for those who committed robberies.[43] Moreover, a substantial segment of the population protested the new law as being too lenient on criminals and delinquents. Some jurists and Party members reported that their neighbors were alarmed by what they perceived to be the weakening of the criminal code and felt that the leadership was wrongly bowing to international pressure to moderate its penal law. They predicted that Havana would soon resemble crime-ridden New York.[44] The commitment of the new leadership, however, held firm. The Minister of Justice, the Procurator General and the President of the Supreme Court all participated in televised addresses and newspaper interviews in an attempt to convince the population that the new Code was not only just but would not result in an increase in crime.

A contemporaneous report indicated that recidivism rates were quite low.[45] Some lawyers questioned the significance of these figures since the report was based on statistics gathered only a short time after the release of the many prisoners. The statistics of cases handled by the *bufetes colectivos* from 1987 to 1989 does show a substantial increase in the number of criminal cases handled. Contracts for criminal defense rose from 42,482 in 1987 to 49,480 in 1989. These statistics may not, however, indicate high rates of recidivism as more criminal cases were handled by the *bufetes colectivos* in 1982 and 1983 (55,710 and 59,446 respectively) than in 1989.[46]

The 1987 Code maintains similar provisions regarding crimes against the security of the state as the previous codes. The article on "enemy propaganda" is identical to the 1979 Code,[47] and in the last few years, a number of people have been prosecuted for violation of this provision for having given false reports to the international press, for distributing leaflets against the Party, and for making an illegal film. Despite the international sentiment against these prosecutions, the Cuban government is unlikely to moderate its stance. Long the object of destabilization efforts by the United States, the stability of the Cuban government has been threatened by the growing economic crisis. In 1992, there were also a number of armed raids and attempts at sabotage by groups based in Miami. With tensions running high, the government made it clear that it would not tolerate either the organization or incitement of unrest or opposition. Cuban officials perceive all attempts to organize illegal dissident activities as being tied to or fueled by outside forces, most notably elements of the exile communities in Miami and Spain. Much of it clearly is.[48] Yet no one has been arrested or sentenced simply for voicing criticism of the government, its leaders or its policies.

Death Penalty

Current Cuban law does permit imposition of the death penalty, but only in exceptional cases and in the gravest circumstances in which it is permitted.[49] It cannot be applied to a defendant who was under twenty years of age at the time the crime was committed. Nor can it be applied to a woman who was pregnant either at the time the crime was committed or at the time of sentencing.[50] The 1936 Code exempted pregnant women from execution because it would kill the fetus as well. Cuban jurist Juan Vega Vega asserts that the current provision is more humanitarian, showing concern for the infant's need for its mother.[51]

A mandatory review is designed to assure that the death penalty is not applied arbitrarily. Thus, in every instance in which the trial court imposes the death penalty, it is automatically reviewed by the Supreme Court.[52] The appeal involves complete review of the evidence tantamount to a new trial. It is not unusual for the Supreme Court to commute the death sentence to the maximum prison term of thirty years.[53] If the Supreme Court ratifies the death sentence, it must be reviewed again by the Council of State (the highest executive body of the state) before it can be carried out. Once the final decision has been made, the sentence is carried out within twenty-four hours. Execution is by firing squad.

According to José Raúl Amaro Salup, President of the Supreme Court, the death sentence is applied very infrequently. With respect to common crimes, it is imposed in the most heinous cases involving homicide. Amaro Salup reported that there were no executions in 1985 or 1986 and two cases had arisen as of June 1987.[54] Even though there are no firm statistics, the rates appear to be lower than states of comparable population in the United States. For example, in 1992, there were 145–150 persons on death row in Illinois who had been sentenced to death since 1977 when the Supreme Court reaffirmed the death penalty's constitutionality. The state of Virginia has sentenced to death an average of five persons a year since 1982. Although the death penalty is reportedly applied with much less frequency in Cuba, there is no proposal to eliminate it.

Because of the spotlight which U.S. hostility keeps focused on Cuba, the application of the death penalty in Cuba has attracted disproportional international attention. Since the 1960s, there has been no occasion where the death penalty has been imposed on any civilian for what might be considered a political offense that did not involve acts of violence.[55] In one case decided in early 1992, the defendant had murdered a police officer in cold blood during an attempt to steal a boat, a crime punishable by death in virtually every state in the United States that has the death penalty.[56] Yet the case received a great deal of attention in the international press. In an earlier case, the Cuban courts condemned an exile, Eduardo Díaz Betancourt, who had illegally entered Cuban territory with arms and explosives, which he admitted were to be used for sabotage. The death sentences of two co-conspirators were commuted by the Cuban Supreme Court to thirty years imprisonment. Betancourt acknowledged he was in charge of the operation and was part of a terrorist group based in Miami. Numerous heads of state as well as the Pope sought clemency for Betancourt from the Cuban government, but they showed no concern for the fourteen people executed in the United States in the same year.[57]

Amnesty International sent a protest to the Cuban government concerning these executions and expressed alarm that Cuba would use the death penalty against those convicted of "political" crimes. Although Cuba continues to deal harshly with those who oppose the regime, it has not sentenced to death or executed anyone who did not engage in or conspire to commit serious acts of violence against the population. The only exceptions were the 1989 executions of General Ochoa and three other military officials, but they were not executed for political opposition either.

The imposition of the death penalty in the case of military officers Arnaldo Ochoa, Jorge Martínez, Amado Padrón and Tony de la Guardia sparked controversy inside Cuba as well as outside, although for different reasons. The court's rationale for the death penalty was derived from the Law of Military Crimes[58] and the civilian Criminal Code. Article 13 of the Law of Military Crimes provides for a penalty of two to ten years' imprisonment for abuse of office when such abuse results in serious consequences for the activities or interests of the military. If such abuse occurs during time of war, as in the case of these defendants, the penalty may be increased to ten to twenty years or death.[59] Article 110.2 of the Criminal Code provides for the death penalty in cases in which a person commits an act hostile to a foreign state which results in retaliatory measures against Cuba or its citizens, humiliation or the alteration of diplomatic relations with Cuba. The prosecutor sought the death penalty for seven of the fourteen defendants; the Court imposed the penalty on four.

In the case of General Ochoa and Captain Martínez, they made contact with the Medellín drug cartel in Colombia for the purpose of negotiating a deal on drug trafficking during the time that Cuba was in active military engagement in southern Africa. Thus, these acts and other acts of corruption admitted to and demonstrated at trial were arguably the kind of abuse covered by the Law on Military Crimes. Given the gravity of the offense, even though no drug deal was actually consummated, the court imposed the death sentence.

In the case of Amado Padrón and Tony de la Guardia, who were not involved in the Angolan defense, the drug trafficking could not be considered an "abuse of office in time of war." Rather, the prosecutor looked to the article in the Criminal Code related to hostile acts against a foreign country. It is indeed ironic that Cuban officers would be sentenced to death for hostile acts against the United States which has pursued a course of extreme hostility toward Cuba for more than thirty years in its attempt to topple the Cuban government. At the time of trial, however, no acts of reprisal or alteration in diplomatic relations had occurred unless intensification of the U.S. anti-Cuban campaign was to be considered an act of "reprisal." Certainly, the relentless campaign against Cuba by the United States with respect to alleged drug trafficking placed the country in some danger of reprisal, which was demonstrated by the U.S. invasion of Panama a few months later. The statute also speaks, however, of resulting "humiliation" to the Cuban nation and people, and unquestionably the scandal seriously damaged the prestige of the nation. Since the drug dealing also threatened the security of the nation by compromising Cuba's territorial integrity as well as the loyalty of its military officials, it was considered within the realm of treason, and the prosecutor called for the severest of penalties.

Had the defendants been involved in almost any other type of crime, theft for example, the penalty would most certainly have been imprisonment, not death. The gravity of having engaged in drug trafficking when the Cuban government had consistently denied long-standing U.S. allegations was profoundly felt in Cuba. Even so, there were questions concerning the legal foundation for the application of the death penalty.[60] Rumors circulated at the time that several members of the Central Committee dissented from the majority vote approving the decision to impose the death penalty. A number of lawyers also engaged in debate over the legality of the sentence and the quality of defense counsel.[61] Nevertheless, even among those who did not like the decision, many believed that the country had no choice under the circumstances but to execute the officers. The collective needs won out over individual protection.

In the United States, on the other hand, commentators in the media set aside discussion of legal questions and focused primarily on speculation that General Ochoa had been tried because he represented a political challenge to the leadership of Fidel Castro and/or that Castro himself had approved or been involved in the drug schemes. No credible evidence has yet been offered to support either speculation.[62] There was, however, ample evidence that the drug dealing did take place and that the persons charged were in fact key figures in the scandal. Much of this evidence is corroborated by testimony given at trials in the United States of drug traffickers who had dealt with the Cuban officials.[63]

Although the death penalty in Cuba has been politicized internationally, it has not become a political issue in Cuba. First, it is likely that the majority of the Cuban population, like those in the United States, support the death penalty in exceptional cases, and there is not a popular perception that it has been used arbitrarily. Second, the continued effort by the United States to crush the Cuban government and the socialist revolution has heightened tensions and concern for national security. Perhaps encouraged by the sharp rhetoric and interventionist policies of Reagan/Bush administrations, some exiles began to launch sporadic armed attacks in 1991.[64] This is not a climate conducive to relaxation of the death penalty, or other security measures for that matter.

Social Dangerousness

Perhaps one of the more controversial substantive provisions in Cuban criminal law is that entitled "Social Dangerousness," which gives the state authority to take preventive measures with respect to persons who have certain indicia of anti-social behavior. This provision, which existed in the 1936 Social Defense Code, also appears in the laws of other countries.[65] Although the 1936 provision was influenced by the contemporaneous Italian Criminal Code, post-1959 jurists who favored its retention, albeit with modification, found support in the codes of the former socialist countries of Europe. Its retention was viewed as consistent with the function of law as the instrument of social change. Nevertheless, the provision has been modified substantially since the revolution, and its character and validity remain the subject of internal debate.

The Social Defense Code of 1936 provided that an individual could be detained if found to have "a certain unhealthy, congenital or acquired predisposition ... which favors the inclination to commit a crime,"[66] whether or not the individual had actually committed a crime.[67] The 1936 Code listed twelve categories of behavior considered to be indicia of a dangerous state that predisposed one to criminal behavior. Among the categories were mental illness as well as mental retardation, drug addiction, habitual drunkenness, gambling and vagrancy, habitual use of physical threats, habitual lying, infection with contagious venereal diseases, practice of prostitution among minors, infraction of regulations legally imposed by authorities, and the practice or exploitation of morally repugnant vices.[68]

In 1942, a thirteenth category was added: suspicious behavior during a State of Emergency or at any time the Constitutional Guarantees were suspended because of disruption of the public order.[69] Persons subject to this provision included both nationals and foreigners who were suspected of cooperating in whatever form with the enemy or with those creating public disturbances.[70] Those found to be "suspicious" were tried by the Tribunal de Urgencia, a special court which conducted summary proceedings based on accusations made by the military or police authority.[71] After the triumph of the revolution, the section on "suspicious behavior" was repealed in 1959 when the Tribunals de Urgencia were abolished, but in all other respects the provision remained identical to the pre-revolutionary law until 1979, with one notable exception. As an expression of the policy to eliminate prostitution altogether, the provision was broadened to specifically include all forms of prostitution, not just prostitution involving minors.

The 1979 Code narrowed the definition of "dangerous state" to signify habitual behavior that showed a "special proclivity ... to commit criminal acts, as demonstrated by observed conduct which is manifestly against the norms of socialist morality."[72] The list of indicia of such pre-delinquent behavior was reduced from twelve to seven categories: habitual drunkenness, drug addiction, pandering, prostitution, vagrancy, the exploitation or exercise of socially repugnant vices, and a catch-all category designated as antisocial conduct that is defined in the statute as habitually engaging in acts of violence or use of provocative or menacing gestures or phrases that threaten the rights of others or frequently disturb the order of the community.[73] It is perhaps significant that the phrase "morally repugnant vices" was replaced by the phrase "socially repugnant vices" indicating that socialist values have a different meaning than the religious moral values of the past era. Under the new law, mental illness or retardation was considered a dangerous state only when the person was not able to comprehend or control his actions and posed a threat to the safety of others.[74] The measures to be applied to those adjudicated to be "socially dangerous" included therapeutic treatment, re-education programs and supervision, but not imprisonment.[75]

The 1987 reforms further reduced the categories of conduct to include only three: habitual drunkenness, drug addiction and antisocial behavior.[76] Today, a person may be considered to be in a "dangerous state" when his or her antisocial conduct

> habitually breaks the rules of social coexistence by acts of violence, or whose other provocative acts violate the rights of others or whose general comportment

harms the rules of social coexistence or disturbs the community order, or who lives as a social parasite ... or who exploits or practices socially repugnant vices.[77]

According to one lengthy analysis, the provision with respect to "socially repugnant vices" was rarely, if ever, applied since conduct that fell under the term was treated separately under the Code in sections entitled "public scandal," and "corruption of minors."[78]

Despite this effort to more narrowly restrict the reach of "social dangerousness," some lawyers in Cuba argue that security measures, whether punitive or therapeutic, should only be legally imposed in cases of criminal conduct and that drug addiction, alcoholism and dangerous conduct of the mentally ill should be treated outside of the criminal process altogether.[79] A commission of the ONBC, charged with making proposals for the modification of the Code of Criminal Procedure, concluded that detention and imprisonment of one presumed to be dangerous should be clearly prohibited, and that the process by which therapeutic measures could be imposed be based on more precise legislation with the same guarantees of defense for those who have been accused of committing a crime. Some have taken note of criticism that the doctrine imposes sanctions on those who have not yet committed a crime and thus risks violating fundamental rights of individuals to due process. Others, like Antonio Cejas Sánchez, chair of the department of criminal law at the University of Havana, defend the doctrine on the grounds that it is important to the prevention of crime and that the statute establishes a sufficiently narrow definition that is capable of proof.[80]

The subject remains the object of debate in Cuba.

Homosexuality

In the 1960s, homosexuality was considered not just deviant behavior but against socialist morality and linked with counter-revolutionary activities. Repressive measures were taken, and many homosexuals were denounced as counter-revolutionaries and sent to the infamous UMAP work camps (Military Units to Aid Production). These camps, where inmates were required to do mostly agricultural labor, were opened in 1965. Castro ordered their closure in 1967 after receiving protests about the brutal treatment of UMAP draftees.[81] A number of military officers responsible for mistreating inmates were court-martialed.[82]

Antagonism toward homosexuals in Cuba was the product of several aspects of Cuban society. First, Cuban society is traditionally and pervasively homophobic, stemming from the influence of both the Roman Catholic church as well as the Afro-Cuban religions. Second, the revolutionary forces initially considered homosexuality a remnant of bourgeois, capitalist decadence that the "new society" would eliminate. Homosexuality was, thus, considered an affront to socialist morality. Over time, official attitudes have changed, and today an atmosphere of tolerance, if not acceptance, prevails in Cuba.

Homosexual conduct was not expressly mentioned in the criminal code of Cuba before 1979. To the extent that it might have been, it would have had to be considered as "socially dangerous" conduct under an interpretation of morally repugnant or socially repugnant behavior or implicitly included in other provisions that sanctioned behavior that corrupts the morals of minors or that creates a public scandal. None of these sections, however, specifically referred to homosexual behavior.

In contrast, the 1979 Code explicitly listed homosexual conduct among the misconduct defined in Article 359 as constituting a "public scandal" and in Article 367 on the corruption of minors. It was never, however, included in Article 76 on "social dangerousness." With respect to homosexual conduct, the article on "public scandal" provided for a sanction of three to nine months, a fine, or both in cases where (1) a person made a public display of his homosexuality or solicited another to engage in homosexual conduct; and (2) a person engaged in homosexual acts in a public place or in a private place exposed to the involuntary view of others. Article 367, dealing with the corruption of minors, stated in subsection 1: "He who induces a minor of less than 16 years, of either sex, to engage in homosexuality ... incurs a sanction of one to eight years in prison."

Reflective of changing attitudes, the provisions penalizing public display of homosexuality or even engaging in homosexual acts in public view were eliminated from the Criminal Code in 1987. Bothering or pestering another with solicitations to engage in homosexual acts, however, is included as conduct creating a public scandal, and may be punished by three months to one year imprisonment, or a fine.[83] The provision regarding corruption of minors under the age of 16 remains unchanged.[84]

Thus, consensual homosexual relations in Cuba have been freed from the reach of criminal law. Although the criminal code still defines some conduct with specific reference to homosexuals, it is limited to conduct in which either unwelcome advances are made or which involves a minor under the age of 16. In addition, homosexuals are no longer subject to official harassment for simply being identified as homosexuals, and there are a growing number of public places where gay men and lesbian women openly meet and socialize.

A clear indication of changing official attitudes, sex education books no longer teach that homosexuality is a disease or a manifestation of psychological abnormality. Instead, they now describe homosexuality as a normal expression of human sexuality. Restrictions on employment have also been virtually eliminated. Although Party membership purportedly remains closed to those who profess their homosexuality, there are many members of the Party who are either gay or lesbian and, who, while not entirely closeted, are not "out" publicly. Further, the subject is no longer taboo for public discussion.

In an interview with Tomás Borge, Fidel Castro expressed opposition to policies that discriminated against gays and lesbians.[85] The subject also arose at the April 1992 congress of the Union of Young Communists (UJC) at which Vilma Espín, president of the Federation of Cuban Women and member of the Council of State, called for an end to discrimination and said that gay and lesbian youth should be respected and accepted.

Today, the situation for gays in Cuba is in many ways better than that of gays in the United States and other Latin American countries. In 1986, more than twenty states in the United States still had statutes criminalizing private, adult, consensual homosexual relationships.[86] Although Cuban society remains largely homophobic, as does most of the rest of the hemisphere, Cuban gays are not subject to the kind of violent attacks that have become increasingly prevalent in the United States, Colombia and Mexico. Nor has the advent of AIDS resulted in a backlash against gay men in Cuba where AIDS is not publicly viewed as a gay disease. The majority of HIV cases in Cuba have been found among heterosexuals, and educational programs are primarily targeted at heterosexual conduct. Although failure to direct educational efforts at gay men may itself be a form of discrimination, the Cuban policy of limited quarantine of those found to be HIV-positive, whatever criticism it may provoke, cannot be seen as a measure to repress gay men.[87]

Criminal Procedure

Soon after the new Criminal Code was adopted in 1987, Cuban lawyers and officials also began a review of the Code of Criminal Procedure, long the object of criticism for its lack of precision and for being inefficient and out of date. At a forum organized in 1990 by the Cuban Society of Penal Sciences to discuss reforms of the procedural law, Procurator General Ramón de la Cruz stated that the problems in the current procedural law are profound: "We cannot simply reform the law," he said. "We have to revolutionize it." For de la Cruz the fundamental issue was "how to construct the proper balance between individual guarantees and the guarantee of the security of society and between the need for swiftness and the need for quality." A proposal for reform was submitted to the government at the end of 1992 that would not only correct some of the deficiencies of the previous procedures but would introduce significant advances.

Cuban criminal procedure is derived from the investigatorial or inquisitorial system of Spain rooted in the civil law tradition of most European countries. The inquisitorial proceeding is based on public prosecution and investigation in which the prosecutor is obligated to investigate all circumstances and evidence, that which inculpates as well as that which exonerates the accused. The fundamental objective is to determine the truth. To that end the relationship between prosecution and defense is not adversarial, but cooperative in seeking evidence of the truth. The role of defense counsel is to protect the interests of the accused, but not in opposition to those of society. The investigative process up to the time of formal charge remains secret even if the accused is in custody, but the defense has access to the files once the charge is filed and may propose proofs and evidence that the instructor is obligated to explore.

Nevertheless, most inquisitorial systems also incorporate elements of the accusatorial or adversarial system that guarantee rights of the accused. Cuba is no exception, and the presence of U.S. influence in the first half of the century left an imprint on its criminal procedure. Thus, although Cuba maintains the features of instruction and investigation characteristic of the inquisitorial system, it also guarantees rights of the defendant typical of the accusatorial system.

Many procedural guarantees are established in the Cuban Constitution such as the right to defense[88] and the right not to testify;[89] confessions must be voluntary and those that are not are considered void.[90] In addition, no one can be prosecuted or sentenced except by a competent court "by virtue of laws which existed prior to the crime,"[91] and criminal laws shall be retroactively applied only when they "benefit the accused or person who has been sentenced."[92] The Constitution also provides protections against unauthorized searches and seizures.[93]

Moreover, unlike some systems, such as the French and the Argentine, Cuba expressly maintains the presumption of innocence until convicted.[94] Further, the accused may not be forced to make any declaration,[95] but if he should voluntarily do so, he cannot be convicted based on a confession alone or on the statements of his spouse or close relatives.[96] Thus, the burden of proving guilt remains on the prosecution. In contrast to the traditional inquisitorial process where the court directs the examination at trial, Cuban procedure allows both the prosecutor and the defense to question witnesses as well as the court.

In Cuba, as in other inquisitorial systems, there is no such thing as a plea of guilty or plea bargaining that would vitiate the need for a trial. Thus, an oral hearing of the evidence before the court is mandatory even when the defendant has confessed his guilt. In all cases, the prosecution must prove guilt by submitting evidence independent of any statement made by the defendant in order to obtain a conviction.[97] The rule is taken seriously, and in cases where the trial court failed to observe it, the Supreme Court has overturned convictions based solely on the confession of the defendant.

Further, like most civil law countries, Cuba does not provide for a jury trial in either civil or criminal matters. Cuba does, however, have a system of lay judges who have equal footing in judicial determinations as professional judges. These lay judges are selected from workplaces to serve for periods of one month at a time. They are selected presumably for their moral qualities and exemplary work performance. Party membership is not a prerequisite, and although the majority have been members of the Party, a substantial percentage are not.[98] At the municipal court level, there are two lay judges and one professional judge presiding over each trial.[99] At the Provincial Court and Supreme Court, there are three lay judges and two professional judges presiding.[100]

Prior to the revolution, Cuban law provided that the investigation and instruction of the charges be done by a judge called the *juez instructor.* The pretrial process was divided into two phases: the *sumario* in which it was determined whether to bring charges, and the *fase preparatoria* in which the case was prepared for trial. Since 1977, the tasks of instruction and investigation were delegated to special personnel in the police department under the supervision of the prosecutor.[101] The two phases have been combined into one, the preparatory phase, which includes all procedures preliminary to trial.

When the instructor determines there is sufficient evidence of a crime and the probable identity of the author, he makes a ruling to that effect which is to be communicated immediately to the prosecutor along with the files in the case.[102] Then the instructor continues to develop the case through investigation to gather the evidence needed. By law, this phase should be completed in not more than sixty days at which time the case is to be submitted to a court for a determination whether there is sufficient evidence to proceed to trial. At any time the prosecutor believes that there is insufficient evidence to demonstrate guilt, he may also dismiss charges. Statistics from one recent study suggest a fairly high rate of dismissals. According to this study, defense lawyers at Havana's largest *bufete* obtained acquittals in criminal cases in approximately 22 to 31 percent of cases, depending on the type of crime, in 1991.[103]

One of the most debated provisions has been the point of time in the process when the accused has a right to defense counsel. The pre-revolutionary procedure provided for a right to defense from the time of formal indictment, but there was no time limit set for the issuance of the indictment. Thus, although a person detained had to be brought before a judge within 24 hours of arrest for a determination whether or not to ratify a decision to detain the accused provisionally, a decision that the court had up to three days to make, the person could be held for long periods without a right to defense until the indictment issued. Further, in cases where the defendant had not appointed counsel at the time of indictment, the court would only appoint one at the time the case was opened for oral trial at the end of the preparatory phase.

The current law provides that the right to defense counsel arises at one of two points depending on the situation of the accused: (1) when the prosecutor issues an order for provisional detention or some other precautionary measure to assure the presence of the accused at trial; or (2) when the court ratifies the indictment and opens the case for trial. If the accused has been arrested and detained, the police must turn the accused over to the instructor within twenty-four hours. The instructor must then prepare a case for prosecution and deliver it to the prosecutor within seventy-two hours. The prosecutor has an additional seventy-two hours to determine whether to impose provisional detention or some other precautionary measure authorized by law. This decision is in turn submitted to a court for approval. Estimates of the numbers of accused held in pre-trial detention in 1987 ranged from 25 to 35 percent. Alternative provisional measures for those who have been arrested include release on signature; release with special conditions; release on money bail. As in other civil law systems, there is no requirement that a defendant be arrested in order to be charged with a crime. He or she may be simply cited to appear to answer the charges.

From the moment that the court makes a determination approving provisional measures against the accused, the accused "becomes a part of the process and may, by himself or through his defense attorney, propose proofs or evidence in his favor."[104] Thus, the right to counsel may not attach until seven to ten days after arrest in cases where the prosecutor decides to seek provisional measures against the accused. In other cases, where no provisional measures are taken, the right to counsel does not attach until the case is certified for trial at the end of the preparatory phase.

The unfairness of this procedure has been pointed out by Cuban lawyers who note that the accused who is arrested and provisionally detained has greater rights than one who is not because the role of the defense counsel during the preparatory phase is important, if not critical, to obtaining a dismissal before the trial since it is during the preparatory phase that the prosecution develops its case.[105] Moreover, in either case, the defense counsel does not formally participate until after the prosecutor has determined whether or not to proceed. In cases where the accused had not appointed defense counsel prior to the opening of the oral trial, the court will appoint counsel for him in advance of trial. The defense must respond to the written charges and propose evidence for the court's consideration.

In practice, a family member frequently contracts for the services of a defense lawyer from the time the accused has been arrested. Although there is no formal right to defense at this point, the lawyer may begin on his or her own to gather evidence. The lawyer might also begin to prepare arguments to oppose provisional detention in the event the prosecutor should seek detention. However, the lawyer may not have access to the case files or propose lines of inquiry or witness testimony until the accused becomes "part of the process."

Today, there is virtual consensus among Cuban officials and jurists that the right to defense must enter earlier in the process; the debate has been over just how early. The perspective of the Cuban defense bar was formulated by a national commission of the ONBC formed in 1989 to analyze the deficiencies in the criminal procedure.[106] The ONBC commission proposed that the prosecutor be required to seek indictment within seventy-two hours of arrest, and that, once the prosecutor makes this decision, he or she must interview and inform the accused of the charges and permit the accused to make a formal declaration. The ONBC argued that the accused must have the right to have counsel present at this interview. In some cases, the ONBC suggested that the accused be permitted to represent himself *pro se*. This is the same process followed in most Latin American countries, although the period between detention and instruction of the charges varies from one to three days,[107] and in some systems court-appointed defense is guaranteed only during the interview with the accused and at trial, but not during the intervening preparatory phase.[108]

With respect to the definition of participants in the preparatory phase, the ONBC submitted that the accused and the defense attorney as well as the victim and his or her representative should be full participants in the process, which would include the possibility of questioning and being questioned during the oral trial. Accordingly, the defense attorney would have the ability to intervene at any point in the process and have the right to propose evidence in favor of the accused. In light of the unsatisfactory experience many defense attorneys have reported with the police instructors, the ONBC proposed that the preparatory phase be entrusted to the prosecutor who should be authorized to determine the provisional measures to be taken. They also proposed that the accused have greater rights with respect to provisional detention.[109]

It took approximately two years to develop a consensus among the various sectors on the general content of the reforms. A proposal was submitted to the Council of State for approval in the fall of 1992. Similar to the analysis that led to the 1987 Criminal Code, Cuban jurists studied the experience of other countries. All sectors of the penal system took part in shaping a legislative proposal. In addition to the work of the ONBC, the Cuban Society of Penal Sciences held several forums where proposals were discussed, as did the Ministry of Interior, the Supreme Court, the Office of the Attorney General and the Ministry of Justice. The *Revista Cubana del Derecho* published articles by several experts on procedural reform. At an April 1992 meeting of the Society of Penal Sciences, some of Cuba's top experts and officials met to debate draft legislation that was being prepared for submission to the Council of State. The draft contained important modifications, but it was not viewed as the last word. Felix Pérez Milián, head of the juridical department of the Central Committee, who presented the draft, suggested that in two years' time, after thorough review, a new integrated code should be adopted.

With respect to the right to defense, the proposed law is indeed revolutionary and introduces significant advances not found in other investigatory systems. Under the new law the accused becomes part of the process from the moment he is instructed of the charges. This is similar to most other systems, but it has special significance in the Cuban procedure because it signals not only the right to name a defense lawyer, but also confers on the defense the right to participate in the process, to have access to all the files and inquiries carried on by the investigator and to communicate with the accused in private. Moreover, if the accused has not appointed a lawyer within forty-eight hours, the court will appoint one to defend him.

In contrast to the usual investigatory procedure in which the prosecutor/investigator alone is empowered to carry on the investigation, although obligated to incorporate evidence suggested by the accused, the proposed law sets up a procedure for parallel investigation by the defense attorney. Thus, the defense has not only the right to participate in the process but is obligated to make independent inquiries and search for evidence that favors the accused. The defense then creates its own record, which is later incorporated with the record of the instructor at the conclusion of the preparatory phase. It is hoped that this will improve the quality of investigation and better assure that the accused is able to get all exonerating evidence into the record. The law will also give the defense the right to appeal, first to the prosecutor and then to the court, in any instance where access to evidence is impeded. A number of other reforms are included in the proposal that would give the prosecutor greater responsibility to supervise the work of the instructor, streamline procedures with respect to lesser offenses, and improve the appeal process.

Another change involved in the right to defense is the elimination of the special *bufete* that provides free legal defense (de oficio) to those accused who did not name their own defense lawyer. Under the new system, the Ministry of Justice will create a team of lawyers attached to the courts. When an accused has failed to name a lawyer, one of these lawyers will be appointed. The accused will be obligated to pay for the defense services at the end of the trial at a rate equivalent to that received by lawyers working at the *bufetes colectivos*. Only in cases where the defendant is without resources to pay will the service be provided free.

Despite enthusiasm for the reforms, Cuban jurists are aware of the subjective hurdles in making such substantial changes in the procedures. More than one Cuban jurist has noted that the reforms will require a high level of professionalism in the work of the defense bar and new provisions would make the role of the defense significantly more active in the process. All personnel involved in the process will have to change the way they do things, and this will not be easy. Such significant changes will require retraining of the police, instructors, the prosecutors, defense lawyers and the judiciary. These reforms come, however, at a time when Cuba has already embarked on a campaign to improve the training of this personnel. "Maybe, the youngest will adapt the best," the President of the Supreme Court remarked at the April 1992 forum, putting his confidence in the new generation of lawyers.

The enactment of these reforms will undoubtedly alter and invigorate the dynamic of criminal procedure. If the principle of cooperation can be preserved while expanding the procedural guarantees of the accused, Cuba will have obtained a major achievement in the perfection of the inquisitorial system.

Prisons

Consistent with the reforms in criminal justice, considerable attention is being paid to the rehabilitative function of incarceration. Having recognized that long sentences do not serve the goal of rehabilitation, sentences for most crimes, particularly those committed by first-time offenders, have been substantially reduced. As a consequence, the prison population has decreased and prison conditions have improved.

Cuba has both maximum and minimum security facilities. At Combinado del Este, one of the newer maximum security prisons located outside Havana, prisoners are housed in units of 600–800 each. Each unit contains dormitories with approximately fourteen to twenty inmates to a cell, sleeping in double bunk beds. Prisoners have space for personal belongings such as books, pictures, etc. Although the space is quite small allowing little room to move about, inmates spend little time in these quarters. They spend the entire day either at work, recreation, classes or meals. Each unit has a dining room, classrooms, a library, and a common lounge area where there is a television set.

Some prisons are known to be rougher because of the prison population, for example, Kilo 7 in Camagüey province. Others are extremely supportive such as Melena del Sur in Havana Province, where a local chapter of the National Union of Writers and Artists takes an interest in prisoners interested in the arts. In Combinado del Este, prisoners have related that the relationship between inmates and guards is not tense, although there are occasional blows from guards, but not beatings.[110] Guards do not carry firearms. Inmates also report occasional fights between inmates over personal differences.

The Cuban prison system also includes work farms (*granjas*) where prisoners live in open barracks with minimum security. The prison has no walls or gates. Those sent to the *granjas* are prisoners convicted of minor offenses. In addition, a prisoner eligible for early release may be sent to the open farm several months prior to release. The prisoners do agricultural work, much of which provides food for the prison system. Some are engaged in experimental hydroponic agriculture. Prisoners in these facilities often have furlough privileges and go home on weekends to visit their families. In addition, there are two women's prisons.

Innovative programs for counseling, education and training are employed in the prison system which takes an individualized approach to rehabilitation. After an initial orientation program, each new prisoner is assigned to a group—called a detachment—of approximately eighty inmates supervised by a rehabilitation counselor. Civilians and prison officials also work directly with the prisoners. The prisoner is provided educational programs in basic learning skills, if needed, and courses in history and the sciences. Prisoners who have the requisite education may work as teachers within the prison. There are also a variety of cultural and sports activities.

With the exception of prisoners considered violent or dangerous, each prisoner is expected to work, although it is not obligatory, and everyone is expected to learn a trade if he or she does not already have one. At Aguica, a maximum security prison for men in Matanzas Province, the major enterprise is the construction of prefabricated parts for housing. There is also work in carpentry and crafts. Combinado del Este also has several enterprises including one in leathercraft. About 10 percent of the prisoners work outside the prison in areas such as maintenance, carpentry or electrical work.

Cuban inmates not only engage in productive work, but they are paid the same wage as workers on the outside doing comparable work whether it be construction work, repair work or handcrafts. In this way, inmates can continue to support their families or save money for themselves for use later on. The prisoners pay one-third of their salary for their maintenance; therefore, the major portion of their income is available for their own use or to support their families. This is a significant improvement over the pre-revolutionary system, which made work obligatory and gave none of the income to the prisoner.

Moreover, the system encourages family contact. When a prisoner first enters the prison, his or her family is interviewed by the head of the prison. The prisoner's counselor also convenes regular meetings with the family and inmate to discuss the inmate's progress. Visits are encouraged and are normally scheduled monthly. Families and friends can be seen visiting every day of the week. At Aguica, they meet inmates in a large open pavilion with long tables. Combinado del Este and the Women's Prison have similar arrangements. Guards are present, but do not stand close by.

Another striking feature, which is unheard of in most U.S. prisons, is the general right to conjugal visits. Prisoners (both men and women) are generally permitted three-hour conjugal visits every three to four months and some more frequently. Special quarters—pavilions—are provided for these visits. The rooms are separate and private and look much like normal bedrooms— each brightly decorated with a double bed, private bathroom and a small kitchen. Combinado del Este has twenty-six such rooms. Officials suggest that with the reduction of the prison population the frequency of such visits may be increased to every two months. Denial of conjugal visits is frequently used as punishment when an inmate violates prison rules.

Prisons also provide comprehensive medical care to all inmates, including dental care. Every prison of significant size, such as Aguica and Combinado del Este, has a hospital that is clean and well equipped. The hospital at Combinado del Este has 200 beds and three operating rooms for general surgery. The prison also has its own pharmacy, an area for out-patient services and an area for physical therapy. The prison also has dental care facilities with a full complement of equipment. Smaller prisons have infirmary facilities, and prisoners are transferred to hospitals when necessary.

Until fairly recently, physical conditions at some of Cuba's maximum security prisons were below international standards in some aspects. But as a result of improvements and the decrease in prison population, which has permitted the closure of some of the older prisons, physical conditions have improved markedly. In the late 1980s, Cuba's prisons were operated well below capacity and some were being phased out. For example, Aguica, built in the mid-1960s to accommodate 1000 inmates, housed approximately 700–800 male prisoners in 1987. Combinado del Este, which has three times the capacity of Aguica, was also operating below capacity in 1987 with a population of approximately 2500. Officials report that the prison population in Cuba in the first half of 1987 numbered approximately 40,000. After implementation of sentence reduction and conditional release policies, it was reduced to about 25,000 to 30,000.

In the mid-1980s, Cuba's prisons became a focal point of accusations of human rights abuses. Some anti-Castro exile groups made exaggerated allegations about the number of prisoners in Cuba. Some of these estimates ranged as high as 100,000 to 200,000 prisoners supposedly being kept in more than 200 identified installations. In 1988, a team of British journalists working on a film documentary attempted to find the alleged prisons and found that many did not exist, calling into question the exaggerated claims of these exile critics.

In 1987, Cuban authorities began to let outsiders visit the prisons. A number of delegations of U.S. lawyers and researchers did visit as did a delegation from Amnesty International. These delegations found no widespread complaints from common prisoners about their treatment in the prisons.[111] A similar tour of U.S. prisons by Cuban authorities was barred by the State Department, which refused to grant visas to a delegation invited by the Institute for Policy Studies in Washington, D.C., as reciprocation for permission granted by Cuban authorities to visit the island's prisons.

As a result of Amnesty's review of the Cuban prisons, the Cuban authorities have taken measures to bring all prisons up to international standards. For example, Combinado del Este had isolation or punishment cells located in a building separate from the other dormitories. These cells are used almost exclusively for non-political prisoners who have committed acts of violence in prison. The attachment contained 140 single cells that were small, rectangular rooms. In May 1988, the cells were closed for renovation to bring them up to international norms. Additional ventilation was added as well as increased artificial light to augment the natural light that reaches each cell. Officials were also contemplating putting in beds that would fold up when not in use to provide the prisoner more room to move about.

The prison system is under the authority of the Ministry of Interior. The Attorney General, however, has oversight authority to assure that the prisons follow the law and respect prisoner rights. A representative of the Attorney General's office, whose responsibility it is to inspect prison conditions and to hear and investigate prisoner complaints, is attached to each prison. In addition, inmates have their own governing bodies. Each detachment elects a council that expresses the concerns of the detachment to the prison management. Prisoners who commit crimes while in prison are charged and tried in the same manner and in the same courts as those who commit crimes outside of prison. They also have the same entitlement to a defense attorney.

Reports of mistreatment have come primarily from prisoners who were convicted for crimes against the security of the state, particularly those who fought against the regime in the 1960s and who refused to work or accept other prison programs. The major group of such prisoners is known as the *plantados,* the planted ones, because of their resistance. They were convicted in the 1960s and continued to reject the authority of the Cuban government. The *plantados* called a number of hunger strikes and refused to wear normal prison garments.

Until the mid-1980s, most *plantados* were kept at the century-old Boniato prison on the east coast of the country. There have been several written accounts of mistreatment of these prisoners, especially at Boniato. Even among these prisoners, however, the complaints date primarily to the 1960s and 1970s. When it visited Cuba in 1987, Amnesty International reported on information it received from "plantados." Although Amnesty cited reported incidents of ill-treatment, it found no evidence to substantiate charges of torture.[112]

As another indication of change, by the end of 1987 the *plantados* were no longer held in separate facilities and were moved to the more modern facility at Combinado del Este. According to prison officials, all prisoners convicted of crimes against the security of the state are now housed at Combinado del Este. In the mid-1980s, partly as a result of the personal intervention of French author Regis Debray, Jesse Jackson and others, Cuba began releasing political prisoners, including the "plantados." Officials reported that there were approximately 1,000 political prisoners in June 1987, including about fifty to sixty *plantados;* by 1990 all *plantados* as well as other long-term political prisoners had been released.

Current estimates on the numbers of political prisoners vary. Cuba contends that there are about 200 prisoners who have committed crimes against state security, including acts of sabotage. Generally, those convicted of acts of violence are not considered political prisoners under international conventions.

Political prisoners who do not resist prison regulations, work and educational programs are integrated with the regular prison population during daily activities. One former political prisoner who was released in January 1987 and who chose to stay in Cuba agreed to a private interview that was arranged through a neighbor.[113] Having left Cuba during the 1980 Mariel boat lift, he settled in Miami for a short while before becoming a member of a conspiracy to infiltrate Cuba for purposes of sabotage. The conspiracy was sponsored by Alpha 66, an anti-Castro exile group based in Miami. The former prisoner had been the driver of the boat that carried four saboteurs to Cuba. He was caught, convicted and sentenced to 20 years in prison but released after seven years for good behavior. He reported that he was well treated and was unaware of any mistreatment or abuse of any other political prisoner. Upon release he was given a job and now resides with his family in Cuba.

As with every other sphere of Cuban life, the prisons are affected by the current economic crisis. Shortages of materials and fuel affect prison industries and services, as well as the quality of food. Moreover, if criminal activity continues to increase, the prisons may be once again filled to capacity putting further strain on the system. Given the other pressing priorities of the government, it is unlikely that scarce resources will be allocated to continue to improve prison conditions.

Conclusion

With respect to criminal justice, Cuba has come a long way since 1959 and the turbulent 1960s. Now in its fourth decade, the Cuban revolution has shown progressive reform and modernization of its criminal law and procedure. Modernization of the written law, however, will not correct deficiencies without substantial efforts to raise the level of competency and commitment of not only the criminal defense bar, but of the judiciary, the prosecutors and the police. Although there is still room for improvement, there are few examples in Latin America where the criminal justice system is as fair and efficient as it is today in Cuba.

Notes

1. In his biography of Fidel Castro, Tad Szulc quotes several people connected with these tribunals who have since left Cuba who felt the tribunals were justified since they prevented mobs from taking justice into their own hands. Tad Szulc, *Fidel: A Critical Portrait* (New York: William Morrow and Company, 1986), pp. 482–485.

2. According to Szulc, Fidel Castro has acknowledged approximately 550 such executions. Ibid., p. 483.

3. International Commission of Jurists, *Cuba and the Rule of Law* (Geneva: International Commission of Jurists, 1962).

4. Quoted in Szulc, p. 484.

5. Ibid., p. 483.

6. In addition to numerous books, articles on the subject are published frequently in the *Revista Cubana de Derecho,* published by the National Union of Cuban Jurists, and the *Revista Jurídica,* published by the Ministry of Justice.

7. In fact, the CDS incorporated the vast majority of provisions from the Penal Code of 1870 imposed during the Spanish colonial rule.

8. Antonio Rodríguez Gavira, "El Sistema Jurídico Penal y el Sistema Judicial Cubano," *Revista Jurídica,* No. 16 (July-September 1987), pp. 53–54.

9. Ibid.

10. Ibid.

11. Ibid. See also the preamble to the 1979 Criminal Code which discusses the process by which it was developed.

12. See, for example, Francisco Varona Duque de Estrada, "La Transformación de la Justicia Penal en Cuba," *Revista Jurídica,* No. 1 (1983), p. 134.

13. Ibid., p. 157.

14. Código Penal (1979), Art. 1, *Gaceta Oficial,* March 1, 1979.

15. Ibid., Art. 8.

16. Juan Vega Vega, "Comentarios a la Parte General del Código Penal Cubano de 1979," *Revista Cubana del Derecho,* No. 17 (1981), p. 159.

17. Código Penal (1979), Art. 16. This change had already occurred in 1973 by an amendment to the Code of Social Defense. In 1983, legislation created a separate process for dealing with juveniles which does not involve the court system.

18. Ibid., Art. 17.

19. Ibid., Arts. 262–294.

20. Ibid., Arts. 262–269.

21. Ibid., Arts. 287–294.

22. Ibid., Arts. 295–299.

23. In the case of robbery with the use of force or intimidation the penalty was increased from a maximum of six years to a maximum of twenty years with the possibility of the death penalty in egregious circumstances. Ibid., Arts. 386.3(g) and 387.2(d). These provisions were later eliminated in the 1987 Code.

24. Ibid., Arts. 95–136. Included in this section also are crimes which violate international law such as the crime of genocide (Art. 124) and of racial violence and persecution (Art. 128).

25. Ibid., Art. 108. The sentence for the distribution of false information or malicious information for the purpose of stirring public alarm or discontent under this section is one to four years unless the convicted has used mass media to distribute the information in which case the sentence is seven to fifteen years. Ibid.

26. Ibid., Arts. 246 and 247. Failure to comply with legal formalities for entry into the country may be punished by one to four years; illegal departure could be punished by six months to three years unless aggravating circumstances such as the use of violence were present in which case the sanction was three to eight years. Ibid.

27. Código de Defensa Social (1936), Arts. 148 and 149. Curiously, the sentence for temporarily impeding the functions of the congress, the president or the supreme court, were harsher than those for interfering in the process of elections.

28. Ibid., Art. 246.

29. Ibid., Art. 218. The sentence was one to six months.

30. See Rodríguez Gavira, p. 67. For example, theft without the use of force carried a sentence of three to eight years. Theft with the use of any kind of force, such as breaking a car window to steal something inside, carried mandatory sentencing of ten to twenty years. Theft of state property regardless of value also carried a sentence of ten to twenty years.

31. Interview with Carlos Amat Fores, Vice Minister of Justice, Havana, Cuba, June 12, 1987. In 1990, Amat was promoted to Minister of Justice to replace Juan Escalona Reguera who was elected president of the National Assembly.

32. Ibid.

33. See Francisco Varona, p. 167.

34. Antonio Cejas Sánchez, "El Régimen de Peligrosidad Social y las Medidas de Seguridad en la Legislación Vigente," *Revista Jurídica,* No. 14 (January–March, 1987), p. 69.

35. Interview with Juan Escalona Reguera, June 16, 1988, Havana, Cuba.

36. Decreto-Ley 87, July 22, 1985 (Council of State), *Gaceta Oficial Ext.,* July 22, 1985. A decree-law is a law adopted by the Council of State or the Council of Ministers while the National Assembly is in recess. The statute is then presented to the Assembly at its next session for rejection or approval. It takes effect, however, upon adoption by the Council.

37. Interview with Juan Escalona Reguera.

38. Código Penal (1979), Art. 380.5. A higher sentence could be imposed if the thief recruited the participation of a minor.

39. Interview with Juan Escalona Reguera.

40. Ibid.

41. Compare Article 380 of the 1979 Code with Article 322 of the 1987 Code.

42. Compare Article 386.3 of the 1979 Code with Article 327.3 of the 1987 Code.

43. Fidel Castro, "La Educación Jurídica y el Cumplimiento de la Legalidad Socialista," in *La Educación Jurídica de la Población* (Havana: Ministry of Justice, 1988), p. 15.

44. I heard numerous such complaints from people I encountered in Havana, and a number of lawyers and officials related to me that they had also encountered such reactions among their neighbors and the members of their CDRs.

45. "Menos de uno por ciento de los exreclusos de la capital han reincidido," *Granma,* June 26, 1988, p. 3.

46. "Principales Indicadores de la Prestación de Servicios Jurídicos," mimeograph report (ONBC, 1989).

47. Código Penal (1987), Art. 103.

48. In 1992, Jorge Más Canosa, president of the Cuban American National Foundation, even used U.S. funded broadcasts over Radio Martí, a project of Voice of America which broadcasts to Cuba, to call for a revolt. In July, when Fidel Castro was attending the Earth Summit in Rio, Más gave a speech in which he called on the Cuban military to block Castro's return to Cuba. He arranged to have the speech broadcast over Radio Martí. There has also been an increase in armed raids and sabotage by groups based in Miami.

49. Código Penal (1987), Art. 29.1.

50. Ibid., Art. 29.2.

51. Vega Vega, p. 159. In another provision Cuban law also shows leniency for pregnant as well as menopausal and menstruating women. The 1936 Code as well as the current Code establish that when such conditions cause emotional disturbance they should be considered as attenuating circumstances by the court.

52. Ley de Procedimiento Penal (1977), Art. 60, *Gaceta Oficial,* August 15, 1977.

53. The maximum prison sentence under Cuban law is twenty years with the exception of those who have been sentenced to death. If the death sentence is commuted, the prison term imposed is thirty years.

54. Interview with José Raúl Amaro Salup, President of the Cuban Supreme Court, Havana, Cuba, June 14, 1987.

55. Interview with Amaro Salup, Havana, Cuba, October 10, 1992.

56. Newspaper reports of the incident stated that several Cubans had tried to steal a boat in order to leave the island. They were discovered in the act by a police officer. The group first tied up the officer on shore and then tried to start the boat. When they could not get the boat started, they shot the officer and fled.

57. According to a report published by the Bureau of Justice Statistics, eight states executed 14 prisoners in 1991, increasing to 157 the total number of executions in the United States between 1977, when the Supreme Court reaffirmed the death penalty's constitutionality, and Dec. 31, 1991. U.S. Newswire, October 22, 1992.

58. Ley de los Delitos Militares (1979), Art. 37(d), *Gaceta Oficial,* March 1, 1979.

59. Ibid., Art. 37(d).

60. I was in Cuba during the trials, and this observation is based on notes of informal discussions I had with Cuban jurists at the time.

61. None of the fourteen defendants exercised their right to appoint their own defense counsel, and all were appointed military lawyers to defend them. This decision was controversial among some in the legal community because some of the defense counsel had little experience in criminal trials, and their efforts at trial were not adept. For a discussion of the impact of the trial on Cuban lawyers, see Chapter three.

62. Several U.S. journalists have attempted to educe such evidence, but their versions rely on conjecture and not evidence. See, for example, Julia Preston, "The Trial that Shook Cuba," *New York Review of Books,* December 7, 1989, p. 24; Andres Oppenheimer, *Castro's Final Hour* (New York: Simon and Schuster, 1992).

63. For a description of the connections, see Debra Evenson, "Dealing With Drugs in Cuba," *Covert Action Information Bulletin,* No. 33 (Winter 1990), p. 59.

64. "Cuba says U.S. Turns blind eye on Terrorists in Florida," United Press International, October 14, 1992.

65. See, for example, the Italian Criminal Code (1977), Arts. 202 and 203.

66. Código de Defensa Social (1936), Art. 48(a).

67. Ibid., Art. 48(b).

68. Ibid.

69. Acuerdo-Ley No. 3, Art. 8, *Gaceta Oficial,* January 7, 1942.

70. Ibid.

71. Ibid., Art. 9.

72. Código Penal (1979), Art. 76.

73. Ibid., Art. 77.

74. Ibid., Art. 78.

75. Ibid., Art. 82.

76. Código Penal (1987), Art. 72.

77. Ibid., Art. 73.2.

78. Cejas Sánchez, p. 60.

79. For example, see Mario Alberto Taglo y Babé, "Contribución para el Perfeccionamiento del Vigente Código Penal Cubano," in *Enfoques Jurídicos de Abogados Cubanos* (Havana: Organización Nacional de Bufetes Colectivos, 1989), pp. 202–264; Carmen López González, et al., "Algunas Consideraciones Sobre el Estado Peligroso en Cuba," in *Ponencias Derecho Penal,* a compilation of papers presented at the National Juridical Conference of the National Organization of *Bufetes Colectivos,* November 30 to December 2, 1989, pp. 153–178.

80. Cejas Sánchez, pp. 46–48.

81. Domínguez, p. 357.

82. Ibid.

83. Código Penal (1987), Art. 303(a).

84. Ibid., Art. 310. The provision which also includes soliciting a minor under 16 years to engage in acts of prostitution provides for a punishment of two to five years' imprisonment.

85. Tomás Borge, *Un Grano de Maíz* (Mexico: Fondo de Cultura Económica, 1992), pp. 235–237.

86. *Bowers* v. *Hardwick,* 478 U.S. 186 (1986). In *Bowers,* the Supreme Court ruled that the criminalization of private, consensual homosexual conduct does not violate the constitutional rights of gays and lesbians.

87. When AIDS first began to appear in Cuba in the mid-1980s, Cuba adopted a policy of quarantine for all those who tested HIV positive. Over time, the policy has relaxed so that those who are living in quarantine may go home for weekly visits and even return to their normal work. Those who have tested positive live in sanitoria in extremely good conditions where they receive comprehensive health care and a diet superior to that of the general population. For a description of the program, see Chapter two.

88. Constitución (1992), Art. 59.

89. Ibid.

90. Ibid.

91. Ibid.

92. Ibid., Art. 61.

93. Ibid., Arts. 56–57.

94. Ley de Procedimiento Penal (1977), Art. 3.

95. Ibid., Art. 161.

96. Ibid., Art. 3.

97. Ibid.

98. Marjorie Zatz, *Socializing Law, Localizing Justice: The Production of Socialist Legality in Cuba,* unpublished manuscript, p. 274. This book is scheduled to be published by Routledge Press in 1994.

99. Ley de la Organización del Sistema Judicial (1977), Art. 46.

100. Ibid., Arts. 19 and 35.

101. Código de Procedimiento Penal (1977), Art. 105.

102. Ibid., Art. 106.

103. Raymond Michalowski, "Socialist Legality and the Practice of Law in Cuba," paper delivered at conference on "Cuba: Thirty Years of Revolution," November 23–24, 1989, Halifax, Nova Scotia.

104. Código de Procedimiento Penal (1977), Art. 249.

105. Mariano Mieres Martí, "El Abogado en la Fase Preparatoria," *Ponencias Derecho Penal,* a collection of papers presented at the National Legal Conference of the ONBC (1989), pp. 55–77.

106. The ONBC commission comprised eighteen members, one from each province and four others.

107. The Argentine code is particularly unclear on this point. The law says that a judge must interview the "presumed guilty" person within a maximum of 48 hours after being put at the judge's disposition by the police. There is no precise time period in which the police are obligated to do so. Código de Procedimientos en Materia Penal (Argentina, 1988), Art. 237. Although Article 4 of the code says they should do so immediately, Argentine lawyers say there are frequent delays.

108. In Venezuela, for example, the accused has a right to defense at the time of the first investigatory interview where an unsworn statement is taken (declaración indagatoria). This must take place within forty-eight hours of detention. The code then speaks of the necessity of naming a lawyer again (either ratifying the provisional lawyer named previously or naming a new lawyer) at the end of the preparatory phase when the process passes to the trial stage. But the code says nothing about the rights of the defense counsel. See, Código de Enjuiciamiento Criminal de Venezuela (1962), Arts. 195 and 209.

109. The ONBC also argued for other changes including that special procedures should be eliminated because they violate the principle of equality of persons before the law. The 1977 law provided for special procedures to be implemented in three specific instances: (1) the prosecution of members of the Political Bureau of the Party, high officials of the government and judges of the Supreme Court (Arts. 385–393); (2) presidents of the lower courts, professional and lay judges, and prosecutors (Arts. 394–397); and (3) crimes against the security of the state in exceptional cases (Arts. 398–403). Additional arguments for their elimination were that, in practice, they have not been used in Cuba and they never appeared in the laws of other socialist countries.

110. National Lawyers Guild, *Criminal Justice in Cuba* (New York: National Lawyers Guild, 1987), p. 14.

111. See, for example, Amnesty International, *Cuba: Recent Developments Affecting the Situation of Political Prisoners and the Use of the Death Penalty* (New York: Amnesty International, 1988); Institute for Policy Studies, *Preliminary Report: Cuban Prisons* (Washington, D.C.: Institute for Policy Studies, 1988); National Lawyers Guild, *Criminal Justice in Cuba.*

112. Amnesty International, *Cuba: Political Imprisonment* (1988), pp. 150–154. In 1986, treatment of prisoners in Cuba had become a major focus of anti-Cuban political movements. In February 1987, the United States used the issue to attempt to obtain censure of Cuba by the United Nations Human Rights Commission for outrageous violations. At the same time, the United States delegation maneuvered to keep the commission from considering the case of Chile. This clear attempt to politicize the issue of human rights was rejected by a narrow vote of the commission.

113. Interview with Luís González, Jaimanitzas, Cuba, June 10, 1988.

8

Private Property

Fundamental change in property relations was a goal of the revolution well before it was openly declared to be socialist. In his 1953 courtroom defense of himself and others who took part in the attack on the Moncada Barracks, Castro described five revolutionary laws which would have been declared had the assault succeeded. The first would have reinstated the 1940 Constitution. The other four had profound implications for specific property rights: The second would have given land to "tenant and sub-tenant farmers, lessees, sharecroppers and squatters;" the third would have granted "workers the right to share in thirty percent of the profits" of all large commercial enterprises; the fourth would have granted "sugar planters the right to share fifty-five percent of the sugar production;" and the fifth would have confiscated "all the holdings and ill-gotten gains of those who had committed frauds during previous regimes."[1] This was not all. Castro declared that these measures would be followed by further agrarian reform as well as the nationalization of utilities, reductions in rent and massive construction of public housing.[2]

Once in power, the revolutionaries moved quickly to implement some of these objectives. Fulfilling promises of agrarian reform made in the 1940 Constitution,[3] the agrarian reform acts of 1959 and 1963 targeted large agricultural landholdings for expropriation and redistribution. Further, in the early months of 1959, landlords were prevented from evicting delinquent tenants,[4] and in 1960 all commercialization of housing was prohibited.[5] At the same time, whether the result of conflict or design, all major industries and oil refineries were nationalized. In early 1961, Castro declared the socialist character of the revolution, and by the end of the decade all the means of production, with the exception of small farms, were in state hands.

Yet not all private property was socialized by the Cuban revolution. Unlike the Soviet Union, which eventually eliminated all private farm holdings,[6] Cuba specifically recognized rights of small private farmers to own and work their land within the socialist system.[7] Moreover, individual ownership of primary and vacation homes has been promoted,[8] and individual rights to other forms of personal property protected.[9] Further, while most commercial enterprises were nationalized, individual service businesses were tolerated as long as no one other than immediate family members was employed.[10] The socialist regime has also created property rights in the agricultural cooperatives.

Imposition of a Cuban-styled socialist economy was highly experimental at first, and only in the mid-1970s did the Cubans adopt models and formulas from the Soviet Union. Even then, Cuba continued its own innovations in housing, agricultural and other private property rights. Thus, the development of property law has not always followed a smooth progression and has undergone continuous, sometimes abrupt, modification.

If there is a unifying principle guiding the experimentation, it is that private property should always be used in ways which serve social goals and not private enrichment. For example, rights to agricultural property depend on its productive use, and housing law is based primarily on recognition of its important social function as opposed to its commercial or investment value. Further, inheritance and property transfer laws take into account the needs of those dependant on the testator or owner whether closely related or not, and the division of marital property is also influenced by social concerns.[11] Thus, rights to private property in Cuba continue to exist but within a sphere of use and enjoyment that is bounded by social, economic and political considerations. The dimensions and shape of that sphere have contracted and expanded since 1959 and continue to evolve, but the outer edges have always been defined by the prohibition of individual exploitation of resources for private gain.

Although personal property law is the object of analysis and adjustment, the post-1989 economic crisis has compelled dramatic changes in commercial property law in order for Cuba to integrate into the international market and obtain needed capital investment. The law governing commercial enterprises, including joint ventures with foreign companies, is discussed in Chapter nine. The present chapter focuses on individual property relations and interests, specifically housing, personal property, and agricultural property. Inevitably, however, changes in the law affecting socialized property will have consequences for private property as well.

Housing

Housing law in Cuba has been guided by the social objective of providing shelter to all citizens. Individual rights to housing and to home ownership, although protected and promoted, are limited by this goal as well as a policy that eschews the enhancement of personal property interests through investment or speculation. The principle is expressed in the introduction to the new General Law on Housing adopted in 1988:

Personal property in housing must be understood … essentially as a right to enjoyment of the house by the owner and his/her family, without having to pay anything after paying its price, but in no case can this right of personal property in the house become a mechanism of enrichment or exploitation.[12]

Cuban citizens may own both a primary resident and a vacation home, but no more. In sum, "housing is to live in, not to make a living from."[13]

Housing disparities in pre-revolutionary Cuba dramatically illustrated the contrast between the haves and the have-nots. The worst conditions were in the rural areas where more than four-fifths lived in thatched-roof shacks with dirt floors, and less than 10 percent had electricity or plumbing.[14] Although better than rural housing, more than half of urban dwellings were considered substandard and lacked complete sanitary facilities.[15] Despite pre-revolutionary laws providing for rent control, landlords found ways to circumvent restrictions, and new housing development in the 1950s centered on condominiums for which mortgage holders charged usurious rates.[16]

The eradication of profiteering and speculation in housing was one of the first items on the revolutionary government's agenda in 1959. Within the first months, the government prohibited evictions and ordered the reduction of rents by 30 to 50 percent, depending on the income of the lessee.[17] Other measures encouraged individual home construction such as tax exemptions for newly constructed owner-occupied homes.[18] Finally, the Urban Reform Law of October 14, 1960, prohibited all private rental housing, converting housing into a public service and making the state the primary landlord. Tenants continued to pay reduced rents to the state for a period of time ranging from five to twenty years depending on the age of the building, after which time they became the owners of their dwellings. Most landlords were permitted to retain their own homes and received monthly payments from the state in compensation for the loss of their investment property.[19]

The government, however, did not nationalize private housing, nor did it embark on any program of housing redistribution. Rather, those who remained in Cuba were entitled to maintain ownership of their homes regardless of size. The homes of those who left Cuba, however, were considered abandoned and were confiscated and either given to legal occupants, sold or rented to other families or converted to social or government uses.[20] The housing policy set forth in the Urban Reform Law projected a second stage of implementation during which the government would begin to build housing and to lease it to citizens who would pay no more than 10 percent of family income.[21] The idealism of the time was reflected in the expressed goal of a third projected stage whereby the state would provide free housing to all.[22]

Despite efforts that have been made, the government has not been able to keep up with the demand for housing, particularly in urban areas, a point of considerable frustration for the population. Virtually all of the substandard rural housing has been replaced, but shortages and deteriorating housing stock in the cities remain a serious problem. Thus, although the constitutional guarantees of economic and social rights such as employment, health and education have been substantially realized,[23] the state has not yet been able to guarantee the right to housing. Recognizing the inability of the government to fulfill such a pledge, the Constitution states that the "socialist state ... strives to provide each family a comfortable place to live."[24]

In the 1980s, the government embarked on a new housing policy, one that was intended to stimulate individual initiative in both rehabilitation and new housing construction. Thus, the General Housing Law adopted in 1984 paved the way for a private housing market in which individual owners could freely sell primary and vacation homes. In addition, the law permitted individuals to borrow funds and obtain materials for new construction and remodeling.[25] Further, the law simplified procedures to encourage those who continued to rent their homes or apartments to convert their tenancy into ownership.

The 1984 law reflected the contemporary liberalization of some market mechanisms in Cuba, including the introduction of farmers' markets where small farmers could sell surplus produce at unregulated prices.[26] In operation, the measures that were meant to stimulate home improvement and construction almost immediately led to speculation and black marketeering in housing.[27] Unregulated, housing prices soared. Within two years, officials in the National Housing Institute began to propose revisions to the 1984 law to deal with the distortions taking place in the housing market. A commission was formed composed of representatives of the National Housing Institute, the Ministry of Justice, the Courts, the Procuracy, the National Assembly and the Council of Ministers.[28] As a result, in 1988, the National Assembly adopted a new law that eliminated private speculation without reducing private ownership. Similarly, the farmers' market was also eliminated around the same time because it had produced distortions in food production and a cadre of middlemen who were profiting at the expense of consumers.[29]

The new housing law did not simply modify but reorganized the entire structure of the previous statute. In contrast to the 1984 law, which emphasized sale and transfer of ownership, the new statute gave primary consideration to legal issues surrounding construction. Thus, after setting forth general principles, the law begins with sections devoted to regulation of the microbrigades that had become the chief force in housing construction.[30] The microbrigades were made up of workers assigned from different work centers. Employees of the centers that contributed workers to the microbrigades had a say in decisions regarding the distribution of the housing built.

Second, the law deals with the rights and regulations governing individual construction and rehabilitation.[31] Cubans who construct their own homes gain title to and may retain them as long as they do not have another primary residence. The significance of individual initiative is seen in the fact that more than two-thirds of housing built since 1959 has been built by individual efforts as opposed to public projects.[32] Such private building, however, is regulated. The builder must obtain a building permit for all construction projects, and materials and equipment can be legally obtained only from authorized state agencies.[33] The builder may contract for labor with state agencies or hire workers after hours.[34] Construction is financed by the Popular Savings Bank, and the loan is considered a personal debt, unsecured by the home.[35] The bank may require, however, that other adult inhabitants co-sign the loan or that the debtor have someone else guarantee the loan.[36]

State constructed housing is transferred through sale to individuals by the Popular Savings Bank.[37] Prices of newly constructed homes are based on square footage, location and amenities such as gardens.[38] The price is amortized over a period ranging from fifteen to twenty years, and buyers make monthly payments to the bank. Other adults who live with the buyer at the time of purchase are considered to be co-debtors.[39] Title passes upon full payment, which can be accelerated if the buyer so chooses.[40]

Because the main purpose of the policy is to assure that individuals and families have adequate housing, the state is not interested in dispossessing a home owner who has defaulted on payments either for construction or purchase loans. Since the loan is considered unsecured personal debt, failure to repay does not result in foreclosure but rather attachment of the salary of the purchaser-debtor or of the co-debtors.[41] Alternatively, the bank can renegotiate the loan to reduce the monthly payments and stretch out the amortization period.[42] Even in the event that no suitable arrangement can be made for payment, the bank will not foreclose, but will seek attachment of other property of the debtor. Only, in the rare case that there is no other recourse and the debtor fails to make payments for three months, will he or she lose the right to purchase the house and be converted into a lessee of the state.[43] Failure to pay rent, however, can result in the occupancy being declared illegal,[44] but even in that case, the remedy would generally be removal to other, perhaps less desirable, housing.[45] Policy considerations reject a result that would leave a debtor or any illegal occupant living on the street except in cases of flagrant violation of the law.[46]

An interesting question unanswered both by the statute and commentators is whether the co-debtors living in the home who are called upon to pay the debt thereby acquire any ownership interest in the property. Since these persons are generally related to the owner and have lived in the dwelling, they may have already acquired some tangible interest in occupancy as discussed below, but it is not clear whether they gain any equity interest in the home. Thus, if the co-debtor is not an occupant or heir, he or she may have no legal property interest in the dwelling and may be left with an uncollectible debt against the purchaser in default.

Another initiative that looks to private arrangements as a way of alleviating the housing shortage is found in the provisions that permit those who have title or the lease to their homes to rent rooms.[47] Although it does not regulate the rents charged, the law specifies that only two rooms can be rented at a time.[48] Renters have no rights arising from their tenancy other than what is part of their contract with the lessor. However, once giving someone permission to occupy a room in the house, the owner may have difficulty removing the tenant because the law does not make it easy to evict tenants. If the tenant does not leave within thirty days of notice to do so, the owner may apply to the courts for an attachment of salary of up to 30 percent.[49] If the tenant has not left after three months the attachment may be increased to 50 percent of income.[50] Only in the case of clear anti-social conduct will the authorities intervene to forcibly remove the unwanted tenant,[51] who will be relocated to another dwelling.[52]

Although most tenants generally occupy the property at the will of the owner and have little protection, certain kinds of tenants receive special legal protection. Thus, the owner cannot evict close relatives, a mother with one or more children fathered by the owner or who has lived in the house for three or more years, elderly persons who have lived in the house for three or more years or anyone else whose eviction might be considered inhumane.[53]

Cuba is a nation of homeowners. By 1984, more than half of the 2.5 million Cuban homes and apartments were owner occupied. Between 1984 and the passage of the new law, more than 750,000 additional homes had been converted from rental to individual ownership.[54] Thus, the vast majority of Cubans now have equity in their homes and may exchange, sell and bequeath them. In order to eliminate the speculation that resulted from the 1984 law, the new statute provides that all sales must be authorized by the Provincial Housing Office, which has the right to purchase the house at the legally established price.[55] Parties to an illegal transfer of housing are punishable under the criminal law by three months to one year in prison and/or a fine.[56]

Because the transfer of ownership through sale may be cumbersome and restricted by regulations, most owners transfer homes through a popular process known as *permutas* (exchanges), which may be bilateral or multilateral. People wanting to move try to find someone else who wants to swap their apartment or home. For example, a single, elderly person may wish to exchange a large third-floor apartment for a smaller ground floor apartment in a certain neighborhood. Sometimes, the transaction may require multiple, simultaneous transactions in which owner A moves to B's apartment who moves to C's apartment who moves to A's. A popular Cuban movie made in the mid-1980s, entitled "Se Permuta," treats the subject with biting wit and satire. With the closure of the classified advertising section of the popular monthly publication *Opina*, advertisement is done through word of mouth and by posting a sign outside the front door. In 1988 there were approximately 20,000 such exchanges.[57]

Exchanges must be formalized in writing by a notary. Those who exchange their homes do not automatically exchange their debt liability and generally remain responsible for continuing to make any outstanding payments to the bank.[58] They may, however, apply to the bank to have the obligation transferred partially or in full to the new owner where the swap was unequal in value. Further, an exchange may be prohibited if it is done for financial gain or if it might cause injury to the same classes of inhabitants protected from eviction—mothers, children, the elderly, etc.[59] In exceptional cases, depending on the size and structure, houses also may be divided or joined.[60]

Although dwellings may be bequeathed by will, the law sets out complicated rules of inheritance designed primarily to protect the rights of heirs or others who have occupied the house for a substantial period of time prior to the testator's death to continue living there.[61] Thus, an heir who has not lived in the house at the time of the testator's death may not claim a right to occupy the house unless it is unoccupied. Heirs who were not living in the house, however, have a right to compensation from the occupants for the value of their inheritance. If someone who inherits a house already owns another house, he or she must sell one of them since no one can have more than one primary dwelling. If the owner dies intestate, title to the house will go first to those heirs who occupy the house or, if unoccupied, to heirs according to succession provided in the law.[62] In addition to the duty to compensate the other heirs, those who receive title acquire any debt outstanding to the bank related to the purchase or construction of the house.[63]

The complexity of the law and the unsatisfied demand for housing produced tens of thousands of claims and disputes that are resolved by administrative procedures. The process of bringing a complaint is fairly informal and may take the form of a simple letter setting forth the facts.[64] Complaints are processed by Municipal Housing Institutes, of which there are 168 in the country. One of the approximately 400 lawyers working in these institutes will review the complaint and seek clarification or further information as deemed necessary. The lawyer then submits the file to the director of the institute who makes the final decision. If any of the parties is not satisfied with the decision, he or she can appeal to the provincial court. The court does not simply review the decision of the institute, it also reviews the entire case *de novo* and makes an independent decision.

According to Rodolfo Dávalos Fernández, legal director of the National Housing Institute (INV), there were more than 100,000 claims filed in the first year.[65] Only about 10 percent of the cases are appealed, but that represents a significant number of cases appealed to the courts.[66] There is no fee for filing a complaint with the housing institute, but anyone seeking an appeal must contract a lawyer from one of the *bufetes* and pay the required fees.

In the case of someone who has been declared an illegal occupant, however, there is no right of appeal to the courts.[67] The determination is made in the first instance by the municipal housing office, and the defendant in the proceeding may seek review of that decision by the president of the National Housing Institute whose decision is final. The review process represents an improvement. Prior to 1986, there was no review of the municipal decision at all.[68] As noted previously, however, anyone declared an illegal occupant for any of the reasons set forth in the statute will not be put out on the street. Rather, he or she will be relocated, and, further, will be entitled to acquire title to the new dwelling if he or she so chooses. Even given the generosity of the law, a lawyer at the *bufete colectivo* in Sagua la Grande argues forcefully that administrative review is insufficient in many cases involving housing matters.[69]

Because the law has created some confusion and uncertainty with regard to rights, the newspaper *Trabajadores* began publishing a regular column explaining various provisions of the law in response to letters from readers. In addition, the National Union of Cuban Jurists began a program of free consultations for citizens, two nights a month. Dozens of people show up to have questions answered.

Neither changes in the law, nor construction efforts have solved the housing shortage in Cuba, and the housing situation will undoubtedly get worse in the coming period. The economic crisis has virtually halted new construction in urban areas as well as impeded needed repairs, leading to further deterioration of existing housing stock. Fortunately for Cuba, its rural and urban policies have saved the country from the problems related to large-scale migration to the cities that afflict almost every other Latin American country. Between 1970 and 1981, Cuba experienced only 12 percent internal migration to the capital, Havana.[70] Authorities have never regulated internal movement, but rural development programs and the dispersal of industrial development to areas outside Havana have kept the population more evenly distributed. At a time when food is more plentiful in the countryside, Cuba will probably be spared migration to cities where services and food distribution are severely hampered by energy shortages. Under the circumstances, rural life is far more attractive.

Cuba's housing policy has converted the majority of Cuban adults into homeowners. In contrast to the often repeated axiom about property rights in the United States, occupancy, rather than possession, is "nine tenths of the law" in Cuba. Ownership, while providing some real benefits, does not give the owner complete control over the property. Social considerations override many decisions regarding use and disposition. Thus, occupants have substantial legal protection, are difficult to dislodge, and are rarely, if ever, left out on the street. Further, inheritance rights depend on whether an heir already resides in the testator's house or not. As a result of these policies as well as shortages, one apartment may house two and sometimes three generations. Although people complain bitterly about crowded conditions and the inability to find privacy, they still take a certain pride in the fact that, despite the difficulties, there are virtually no homeless people in Cuba.

Abandoned Property

One issue that has received considerable attention in the Cuban community in Miami since the fall of the socialist governments in eastern Europe is the status of property formerly owned by expatriates. Tens of thousands who left Cuba in the last thirty-three years left homes and other personal property behind, title to most of which has passed to Cuban citizens who now live there. In anticipation of political change, some lawyers in Miami have begun suckering exiles into paying $150 in order to have their property claim listed in a book they planned to publish.[71]

Even assuming that changes will occur in Cuba that would permit the introduction of property claims by exiles, many factors would impede their success. Under contemporary Cuban law, no such claims to personal property or personal realty would be valid. As a practical and legal matter, it is difficult to imagine any Cuban court dispossessing Cuban citizens of their homes or requiring them to make payments to those who abandoned them to take up residence in another country. Moreover, any such measures would seriously affect the political stability of any government overseeing such restitution. If there is to be any restitution at all, it will likely come as the result of a political accommodation, not judicial decision. In addition to practical and political concerns, pre-revolutionary law regarding acquisition of property by *prescripción* weighs against claims to the personal property that was left behind by expatriates.

Since 1889, the Cuban Civil Code has recognized the legal doctrine of *prescripción* or *usucapión*, the term now used, by which a person who is in uninterrupted possession of property for a specified period of time may acquire legal title to the property in his or her possession. The Civil Code that was in force from before the revolution and which was not repealed until 1987 provided for two forms of acquisition by prescription: ordinary and extraordinary.[72] For ordinary acquisition the possessor was required to demonstrate a legitimate basis for the claim of ownership as well as possession in good faith.[73] In the case of personal property other than real estate, the term of required possession was three years.[74] In the case of real property the term was ten years if the actual owner was present in the country and twenty years if absent.[75] However, with respect to extraordinary prescription, the law provided that even if there was no legitimate basis for the claim or good faith on the part of the possessor, title was perfected after six years for goods and after thirty years for real property.[76]

It seems apparent that even under long-standing pre-revolutionary law, few valid claims could be made with respect to title to personal property such as automobiles, furniture, jewelry, etc. The same law would clearly defeat claims to real property left more than thirty years ago, at least to the extent that the possessor could show uninterrupted possession. The new Civil Code of 1987 recognizes acquisition by prescription (although it uses the more modern term *usucapión*), but has abolished the concept of extraordinary prescription.[77] Thus, there can be no such acquisition of title in the absence of just claim and good faith.[78] However, the 1987 Civil Code considerably shortens the period of required possession to perfect title: three years for goods and five years for real property.[79]

Cuban courts today, however, would not apply either the former or the 1987 Code provisions on *usucapión* of real property that has been left by those leaving the country. According to the General Law on Housing, title to the home of someone who "abandons the country definitively" passes to the state except in cases where there is co-ownership and one party remains.[80] Thus, title to housing that has been abandoned can only be acquired from the state. As with other aspects of housing law, preference is given to certain persons who have lived in the house for a period of five years or more (three years under the 1984 housing law).[81] Included in this class is the spouse or ex-spouse, ascendants and descendants, siblings, nieces and nephews, and first cousins. The 1988 housing law gives the local legislative assembly authority to make exceptions to the period of required occupancy in cases where it would be just to do so.[82] If there is no person entitled to acquire the property, the state may sell the property to any purchaser. Occupancy by anyone not within the recognized classes is considered illegal, making it impossible for anyone not granted title by the state to satisfy the just claim or good faith requirement for *usucapión*. Thus, title to abandoned homes can only be acquired pursuant to the housing law and, generally, only by purchase from the state.

Consequently, in order to challenge the title of anyone who has acquired title under Cuban law and who has occupied a home for five years, one would have to declare both the housing law and the Civil Code void and unenforceable and, in addition, demonstrate that the possessor did not acquire just claim to the property in good faith. Yet even under the pre-revolutionary law, persons in possession as a result of grant by legal authority would likely have been considered entitled to retain ownership of the property because they had obtained colorable title in good faith. Further, those in possession for thirty or more years would have rights recognized by both pre- and post-revolutionary law.

Experience in the former socialist countries of Europe shows that restitution of property is a particularly complex and thorny problem. The approaches are varied, and none satisfactory to prior owners. Czechoslovakia, for example does not recognize claims by those who do not reside in Czechoslovakia or who have taken up citizenship in another country.[83] East Germany will not return property that has been acquired by others in good faith, but will provide some form of compensation.[84] Hungary has decided against outright return of property, favoring the issuing of bonds as compensation.[85] In every instance compensation is not for the full value since none of the fragile economies could absorb such enormous costs.

Restitution of or compensation for commercial property that was confiscated by prior governments in eastern Europe has raised other issues related to the needs of the national economy. Typically, the time for bringing a claim is exceptionally short because of the importance of resolving title in order to attract investment in commercial property. Further, to pay off fully such claims would bankrupt the country and prevent it from reorganization.

Given the severe economic crisis and the magnitude of Cuba's outstanding debt, it is very doubtful that any future Cuban government could offer full compensation. Nor is it likely that Cuba would offer to restore property to former owners. Such a decision would meet such public opposition as to make it politically unfeasible.

Inheritance of Personal Property

The Constitution specifically protects the rights of citizens to personal property, which consists of one's income and savings, one's principle house and vacation house, means or instruments of personal or family work and other forms of goods that satisfy the material and spiritual necessities of the individual.[86] Further, the right of inheritance of personal property, either by a written will or by intestacy, is recognized in Article 24 of the Constitution, and it is regulated by Articles 466 to 547 of the Cuban Civil Code.

The particularity of Cuban law governing inheritance is found in various restrictions imposed on testamentary disposition. As noted previously, although the intent of the testator will generally be respected, the disposition of a house or farmland is subject to legal limitations intended to protect social and economic interests. In addition, specific categories of persons are prohibited from receiving inheritance: those who have attempted to kill the testator or a beneficiary under the will;[87] those who have used fraud, deceit or violence to obtain a disposition or a change in a will;[88] and those who having an obligation to provide care of the testator have denied food or necessary attention to the testator.[89] Such incapacities can be overcome if the testator has expressly or tacitly forgiven the actions of the heir or beneficiary.[90]

Moreover, Cubans who "abandon" the country to establish residence or citizenship abroad lose their right to inherit property from Cuban nationals.[91] They will also not be able to make testamentary disposition of any property left in Cuba since it will have been acquired by remaining family members or confiscated by the state. On the other hand, pursuant to legislation enforcing the U.S. embargo against Cuba, Cuban nationals are blocked from receiving the proceeds of any inheritance situated in the United States whether the testator resides in Cuba or elsewhere.[92]

Unlike prior law derived from the Spanish Civil Code, Cuban law no longer gives special deference to either the spouse or children of the testator in opposition to a valid written will unless they qualify as "specially protected heirs."[93] Such protected heirs are persons who are incapable of working and who have been dependent on the testator and include the following: children or their descendants in the case the children predecease the testator; a surviving spouse; and parents.[94] If there is more than one protected heir, each will share equally in the estate.

The legal requirements for a valid will and the process of distribution in Cuba are governed by the Civil Code[95] and the law of civil procedure.[96] The procedures for validation of a will and distribution of the estate are very similar to those followed in other civil law systems, particularly those derived from Spanish law. Thus, there is no process analogous to probate. A will is generally validated and filed with a notary who is also empowered to distribute the property upon the death of the testator.[97] Only where there is a dispute as to the validity of the will or its contents will the matter be taken before a court.[98]

Agricultural Property

Farm workers in the 1950s earned little and lived in deplorable conditions. Most of the peasant population either labored as tenant farmers, sharecroppers or squatters or eked out a living as seasonal workers on large private sugar and tobacco farms. The average farm worker earned one-quarter the average national income. It was among this population that the guerrilla forces gained its greatest support, and on the eve of the revolution, about three-quarters of the revolutionary soldiers were peasants.[99] It is not surprising, therefore, that government policies in the early years focused on improving conditions for the peasantry. Government efforts included not only measures that gave more than one hundred thousand peasants title to the land they worked[100] but also organized a massive literacy campaign, replaced shacks with new housing equipped with electricity and running water and provided farming equipment and supplies.

No one in Cuba in 1959 could have seriously doubted that the new government was going to make good on its promise of agrarian reform. Yet implementation fired a great deal of hostility among landowners. The first measure confiscated large landholdings of more than thirty *caballerías* (approximately one thousand acres), but left more than a quarter of the land in the hands of a small group of farmers, many of whom began to support resistance directly or by sabotaging or reducing production. The Agrarian Reform Act of 1963 eliminated this group of farmers and left all agricultural land either in the hands of small farmers or under the control of state-run farms in a proportion of roughly 30 to 60 percent respectively.

From the start, the plan was to maintain most of the land under state control, either as state farms or state-supported cooperatives, as the best way to increase food production and equitable distribution. The remaining land was to be farmed by small landowners who were assured by Castro that they would be able "to cultivate their land as they see fit."[101] Although there was a plan to also develop agricultural cooperatives, the cooperative movement did not take hold until the mid-1970s.

Agricultural production and the maintenance of sufficient food for the population have been major concerns of the government since 1959. It was never entirely successful, but in the last few years the loss of foreign food and other imports necessary to agricultural production have placed agricultural policy at the center of government activity. Throughout, laws governing the property rights of private farmers have undergone analysis and revision in an attempt to assure that all agricultural land is used productively and primarily for social, rather than private, benefit.

Today, about 75 percent of agricultural land is owned by the state, and the 25 percent that is privately owned is roughly equally divided between individual farmers and the agricultural cooperatives.[102] The proportion of state-owned to privately owned land varies both by crop and region. For example, state ownership of tobacco land is only about 25 percent of the total.[103] Today the state owns only about half of the agricultural land in Havana Province; the remainder is split almost evenly between cooperatives and individual farmers.[104]

From the beginning, state policy has favored the concentration of food production on state farms and agricultural cooperatives. While protecting certain rights of land ownership, the law does not encourage expansion of private ownership other than by incorporation into agricultural cooperatives. The cooperative movement got its first big boost at the Party Congress in 1975, and legislation since has favored the integration of small farms into the cooperatives. In addition, life at the cooperatives was made increasingly attractive by new housing construction, day-care centers and other amenities. Between 1976 and 1983 there was a surge in the formation of cooperatives, and the number grew from forty-four in 1977 to 1,480 by 1983 when it peaked.[105] Agricultural production also rose significantly, tripling output in some sectors.[106]

After 1984, membership in the cooperatives declined partly due to the aging of members who for the first time had rights to pension at retirement.[107] The opening of farmers' markets in 1980 also had a negative impact on cooperative movement. In addition to other problems facing cooperatives, such as difficulties in organization, the farmers' markets created pressures for "illicit" extra-agricultural activities, which lowered morale as well as production at the cooperatives.[108] In recent years, membership in cooperatives has increased slightly as have their land holdings, but the number of cooperatives has not.[109]

The law does not permit state-owned land to be sold to private persons, but in 1991 the Council of State approved a new law governing agricultural property that permits the state to both exchange property with individual farmers or cooperatives as well as grant them use of state land.[110] In consultation with the National Association of Farmers (ANAP), the Ministry of Agriculture continues to explore ways of improving production and coordination between the cooperatives and state farms. There are signs that the government may also be looking for efficiency in smaller state farming operations. In early 1993, some large state-owned sugar estates were reportedly broken up into smaller units.[111] While land was not transferred to individual farmers or to cooperatives, the work force has been given material incentives to produce cane as well as individual plots to grow produce for their own consumption.[112]

The loss of assured shipments of wheat, grains, feed and other produce has caused critical shortages in Cuba's food supply. The halving of oil imports and breakdowns in machinery for lack of spare parts has jeopardized the country's ability to sustain its own agricultural production. Faced with this threat to national survival, the government has intensified national coordination of production and use of limited resources. It has expanded the agricultural labor force by recruiting idled factory workers and organizing volunteer brigades from the cities. Oxen have replaced tractors. Several new agricultural projects, which have taken a community based and ecological approach, such as the "Turquino Project" in the Escambray Mountains (started several years ago), are considered promising as a way to stabilize rural communities and increase productivity as Cuba continues to look to self-sufficiency in agriculture as a way out of the current crisis. So far, by stringent rationing, the government has been able to supply each citizen with basic staples and an adequate, though very reduced, diet.

Independent Farmers

Article 19 of the 1992 Constitution maintains provisions of the previous charter that recognize the rights of independent farmers to own their lands as well as structures and other property necessary to agricultural production.[113] Despite the recognition given to the rights of small farmers, however, government policy has favored incorporation of small farmers into agricultural cooperatives, and the number of independent, small farmers has steadily declined since 1963 although they continue to own about 12.5 percent of the land. Ownership rights of farmers, like those of homeowners, are circumscribed by social policies. Because agricultural land is such an important resource, the government exercises considerable control over its use and transfer, even when privately owned.

In the case of independent farmers, continued enjoyment of property rights depends on continued productive use of agricultural land that contributes to social consumption and the national economy.[114] Thus, a farmer cannot simply live on his or her land and leave the fields unplanted. Nor can he or she engage in subsistence agriculture. Moreover, a farmer who becomes permanently incapable of farming due to age or illness may lose the right to retain the land unless a close relative continues to keep it productive.[115] Further, a farmer must produce crops in accordance with state production plans and may only employ others to work the land in accordance with Ministry of Agriculture rules.[116] Violation of these restrictions or illegal commercialization of products may result in the confiscation of the farm.[117] If confiscated, the farmer will receive payment for its appraised value.[118]

The transfer of land of a small farmer is also highly restricted. All sales must be authorized by the Ministry of Agriculture,[119] and transfer may only be made to the state, to a cooperative or to another farmer. The state cannot expropriate the land of an independent farmer except for violations mentioned above. Sales to the state are strictly voluntary, but at prices established by appraisal in accordance with Ministry of Agriculture schedules.[120] Nor can farmland be rented, except to or from the state.[121]

Further, a farmer cannot dispose of his farm by a testamentary instrument.[122] Rights to inherit land by intestacy are also limited and have been further restricted by the 1991 statute pursuant to which land can only be inherited from the deceased by children, parents, siblings or spouses who have been actively working the land for five years, and in some cases grandchildren or nieces and nephews.[123] Exceptions are made for those heirs who have been away in military service or attending educational institutions or who were minors at the time of the testator's death if they demonstrate that they can personally work the land.[124] Decisions over the claims of heirs to the land are made in the first instance by the Ministry of Agriculture, which reportedly had been fairly flexible in applying the time requirements in the mid-1980s.[125]

Because rights to land are derived only from their use, only farmers and their dependents have legal right to compensation for their value. Certain heirs who have not worked the land for the requisite period have the right to receive the value of the land, but only if they do not have another source of income and have been dependent on the testator for five years.[126] Otherwise, the land escheats to the state with no compensation. Goods or property that are not connected with farm production can be sold or transferred by inheritance according to the Civil Code.[127]

The previous statute governing inheritance of farms, enacted in 1982, established one year as the requirement for having worked the land or demonstrated economic dependency. The increase in the required period to five years is not explained and has been criticized as excessive by at least one Cuban lawyer who is employed by the Legal Department of the Ministry of Agriculture.[128] Moreover, the 1982 law did not limit inheritance to close relatives but permitted the testator to grant the land to anyone who had worked it for the requisite year.[129] The new restrictions may reflect impatience with the slowness of the integration of individual farms into the agricultural cooperatives and/or the intent to keep agricultural land only in the hands of experienced and dedicated farmers.

Special provisions are made with respect to persons who occupy the farmer's house at the time of his or her death if they do not have the right to inherit the property. According to the statute, they may continue to live in the house until they either find another place to live on their own or are relocated by the National Housing Institute or the Ministry of Agriculture.[130]

Small farms cannot be divided. Even in the case of divorce or inheritance,[131] one party will get the land if he or she has been working it, the other(s) will get the value of the portion due in cash. By law, heirs who are eligible to inherit the land itself receive equal shares but cannot divide the land except to cede their portion to the state or to join a cooperative.[132] They can, however, decide to own the land in common as a condominium as long as they continue to work the land.

Decisions regarding transfer and expropriation are made by the territorial entities of the Ministry of Agriculture and are appealable only to the Ministry and not to the courts.[133] Exception is allowed for appeals to the provincial courts concerning the amount of compensation in cases of confiscation. In a 1981 opinion, the Cuban Supreme Court ruled that administrative decisions that affect legal rights may be appealed to the provincial courts.[134] Thus, the 1991 statute abrogates that decision. Lawyers at the *bufetes colectivos* provide legal assistance to farmers. The subject of agrarian law and the role of lawyers in protecting the rights of farmers featured prominently in a recent conference of the *bufetes colectivos*.[135]

According to one author, Cuban officials had hoped to integrate 90 percent of all privately held farms into cooperatives by 1990.[136] Despite policy and restrictions, the share of independent ownership remains fairly stable at about one half of private holdings. Although encouraging integration into agricultural cooperatives, the state has nevertheless provided support to independent farmers. Most independent farmers are members of credit and service cooperatives that offer credit, technical assistance and shared use of farm equipment and other resources. Farmers earned high profits during the brief existence of the free agricultural markets, but even sales to the government at government prices have allowed farmers to enjoy a high standard of living compared to other Cubans.[137] Some blame the recent growth in the black market of food products on illicit marketing by the independent farmers, but other officials deny this is the source of the problem, pointing the finger at thefts from state farms and warehouses.[138] Nevertheless, the thrust of legislation since 1991 has been to encourage further the disappearance of the independent farm and its integration into the state farm or cooperative system.

Agricultural Cooperatives

It was not until 1982 that the government integrated regulations pertaining to the agricultural cooperatives into a single statute, the Law on Agricultural Cooperatives.[139] The statute establishes two main forms of cooperatives: (1) agricultural production cooperatives and (2) service and credit cooperatives.[140] The integration of individual farmers into cooperatives is voluntary,[141] and the cooperatives enjoy a fair degree of autonomy over internal governance,[142] although production must be in line with national social and economic needs.[143] Cooperatives are governed democratically by a General Assembly of Members to which all members belong and which elects a board of directors.[144] One way in which the state encourages the growth of cooperatives is by providing special economic and technical assistance.

Any land or other property that an individual brings to the cooperative when becoming a member becomes the property of the cooperative. The individual is entitled to compensation for the contribution, which is paid out over time from the cooperative's earnings.[145] If a member should separate from the cooperative, he or she will receive both any unpaid portion of this contribution plus any accumulated share of profits.[146] Participation in the earnings of the cooperative, however, is not at all related to the value of property invested by the individual member, but rather on the basis of the member's work.[147]

Production and commercialization of produce are governed by the plan established by the national government in consultation with ANAP, but the cooperative may also set aside a portion of land for its own consumption. While the 1982 statute generally permitted the sale of cooperative land for reasons of public utility or the exchange of property to benefit the cooperative, the 1991 statute restricts such transfer to sales or exchanges between cooperatives or to the state.[148]

Consistent with the policy promoting the growth of cooperatives, the law protects the integrity of cooperative property. Thus, cooperative property cannot be subject to lien.[149] Nor can a member separate his or her land from the cooperative once joined. Further, cooperative property cannot be inherited as the land, most dwellings and structures belong to the cooperative, not the individual.[150] In the case of a house that was owned by the farmer before joining the cooperative, it can be inherited according to the housing laws, but it cannot be either sold or exchanged without approval by the cooperative.[151] In addition, the earnings as well as any unpaid portion of the value of the member's contribution will be transferred first to those heirs who are linked to the cooperative or to the deceased's dependents.

Credit and service cooperatives are formed by voluntary association of individual farmers who maintain ownership of their farms.[152] Membership in such cooperatives gives the farmers access to state resources, credit and technical assistance. To join, a farmer makes a contribution to a common fund, which is used to provide both credit and payment of services, including use of heavy equipment and materials. Membership in these cooperatives in no way encumbers the farmer's land.

Property of Mass, Social and Religious Organizations

Property may also be owned by a wide variety of social, political and religious organizations. Certain political, mass and social organizations are given special recognition in the Constitution. These include the Communist Party and the mass organizations, such as the Central Organization of Cuban Workers, the Federation of Cuban Women, the National Association of Farmers, the Union of Communist Youth and the Federation of University Students. Many professional organizations also function, such as the National Union of Writers and Artists, the National Union of Jurists, the Union of Journalists and so forth. In addition, communities may form social clubs, and religious institutions may own property as well. The property belonging to such organizations is that which is used in the furtherance of their work or activities. It includes buildings, installations, vehicles and other goods as well as funds that come from the contributions of its members or affiliates.

Depending on their charters, these organizations can create enterprises that serve the work of the organization, and this property cannot be seized or burdened by liens. For example, the National Union of Cuban Jurists owns a small book shop and cafe for the benefit of its members and other visitors. Profits from sales are also used to support the activities of the Union. Similarly, religious organizations may own buildings where members worship as well as congregate for other institutional purposes. Recently, the Baptist church of pastor Raúl Suárez, who was also elected as a delegate to the National Assembly in February, began to initiate independent economic development projects including a bicycle repair shop, an agricultural cooperative and arts and crafts workshops.[153] The alienation of the property is controlled both by legislation as well as by the by-laws that govern the organization.

Because of shortages of goods and capital, institutions that formerly were able to pay in Cuban pesos for imported goods obtained from the state now have to purchase such goods in "hard currency" meaning U.S. dollars. They have been encouraged to find ways of becoming economically self-sufficient, and in order to earn this currency many have begun to organize seminars for foreigners or to sell products to visitors. In some cases, they may even offer cultural activities like musical or dance performances for tourists. These activities are increasingly necessary for the survival of the sponsoring institution, but they also introduce experience with entrepreneurship and autonomous control of property.

Notes

1. Fidel Castro, *History Will Absolve Me* (New York: Center for Cuban Studies, undated), pp. 25–26.
2. Ibid., pp. 127, 131.
3. Constitución (1940), Art. 90. The article reads:

Latifundio is prohibited, and in order to dissolve them, the Law will establish the maximum size of property which each person or entity may possess for each kind of use to which land can be put.

The Law will strictly limit the acquisition and possession of land by foreign persons or companies and will take measures which will tend to revert foreign land holding to Cubans.

4. Jill Hamburg, "Cuban Housing Policy," in Sandor Halebsky and John Kirk, eds., *Transformation and Struggle* (New York: Praeger, 1990), p. 235.
5. Ley de Reforma Urbana de 14 octubre de 1960, *Gaceta Oficial,* October 14, 1960.
6. George M. Armstrong, Jr., *The Soviet Law of Property* (The Hague: Martinus Nijhoff, 1983), pp. 51–52.
7. Both the 1976 and 1992 Constitutions contain provisions recognizing the right of small farmers to own their lands and other means and implements of production. See Articles 20 and 19 respectively.
8. Ley No. 65 (Ley General de la Vivienda), December 23, 1988, Art. 2.
9. Constitución (1992), Art. 21. This is virtually identical to Article 22 of the 1976 Constitution.
10. Ibid.
11. See Chapter six, "Family Law."
12. Ley General de la Vivienda (1988), Preamble.
13. Rodolfo Dávalos Fernández, *La Nueva Ley General de la Vivienda* (Havana: Editorial de Ciencias Sociales, 1989), p. 2.
14. Jill Hamburg, *Under Construction* (New York: Center for Cuban Studies, undated), p. 2.
15. Ibid.
16. Ibid.
17. Hamburg, "Cuban Housing Policy," p. 235.
18. Hamburg, *Under Construction,* p. 3.
19. Ibid.
20. Ley No. 989 (December 5, 1961). Dávalos Fernández, pp. 216–223.
21. Ley de Reforma Urbana (1960), Art. 1.
22. Ibid.
23. Constitución (1992), Art. 8(b). The same provision appeared in the 1976 Constitution.

24. Ibid., Art. 8(c).

25. Ley No. 48 (Ley general de la Vivienda), December 27, 1984, Arts. 38, 60–63, *Gaceta Oficial Ext.,* December 31, 1984.

26. Medea Benjamin, Joseph Collins and Michael Scott, *No Free Lunch* (San Francisco: Institute for Food and Development Policy, 1984), pp. 66–80.

27. Dávalos Fernández, p. 27.

28. Interview with Rodolfo Dávalos Fernández, Legal Director of the National Housing Institute of Cuba, Havana, March 24, 1989.

29. The reasons for elimination of the farmers markets vary. The government claimed it was closed down because of price gouging as well as development of a corrupt merchant class of brokers. Castro also contended that some small farmers were using state resources, particularly fertilizer, to produce crops for the private market instead of for the crops contracted to the state. See debate at the Fourth Congress of the Cuban Communist Party, October 10–14, 1991, published in *Este es el Congreso Más Democrático* (Havana: Editora Política, 1991), pp. 111–117. Still another reason may lie in its negative impact on the cooperatives whose members argued for its elimination at the May 1986 meeting of ANAP. Jean Stubbs, "Gender Issues in Contemporary Cuban Tobacco Farming," *World Development,* Vol. 15, No. 1 (1987), p. 52.

30. Ley General de la Vivienda (1988), Art. 8, *et seq.*

31. Ibid., Art. 13, *et seq.*

32. Hamburg, "Cuban Housing Policy," p. 238.

33. Ley General de la Vivienda (1988), Art. 13.

34. Ibid.

35. Ibid., Art. 33.

36. Ibid., Art. 35.

37. Ibid., Art. 41.

38. Ibid., Art. 42.

39. Ibid., Art. 41.

40. Ibid., Art. 45.

41. Ibid., Art. 35.

42. Ibid., Art. 43.

43. Ibid., Art. 44.

44. Ibid.

45. Ibid., Art. 112.

46. Ibid., Art. 115.

47. Ibid., Art. 64.

48. Ibid., Art. 74.

49. Ibid., Art. 64.

50. Ibid.

51. Ibid.

52. Ibid., Art. 112.

53. Ibid., Art. 65.

54. Interview with Dávalos Fernández.

55. Ley General de la Vivienda (1988), Art. 70.

56. Código Penal (1987), Art. 231.

57. A. Shelton, "Acerca del Proyecto de Ley General de la Vivienda (I)," *Granma*, December 17, 1988, p. 2.

58. Ley General de la Vivienda (1988), Art. 68.

59. Ibid., Art. 69.

60. Ibid., Art. 73.

61. Ibid., Art. 78.

62. Ibid., Art. 77.

63. Ibid., Art. 79.

64. Interview with Dávalos Fernández.

65. Ibid.

66. Ibid.

67. Ley General de la Vivienda (1988), Art. 111.

68. Orestes Rodríguez Reves, "La Ocupación Ilícita de Viviendas. Medios de Impugnación," *Ponencias Derecho Económico, Agrario y Administrativo* (Havana: Organización Nacional de Bufetes Colectivos, 1989), p. 149.

69. Ibid.

70. Hamburg, "Cuban Housing Policy," pp. 243–44.

71. Howard Kleinberg, "Don't Look for Castro's Fall Soon," *St. Petersburg Times*, August 15, 1990, p. 18A.

72. Código Civil (Annotated Edition, Ministry of Justice, 1975), Arts. 1940, *et seq.* These articles were in force in 1959 and were not modified significantly prior to 1989.

73. Ibid., Art. 1940.

74. Ibid., Art. 1955.

75. Ibid., Art. 1957.

76. Ibid., Arts. 1955, 1959.

77. Ley No. 59 (Código Civil), July 16, 1987, Arts. 184–190, *Gaceta Oficial Ext.*, October 15, 1987.

78. Ibid., Arts. 186.1 and 187.

79. Ibid.

80. Ley General de la Vivienda (1988), Art. 81. A person is considered to have abandoned the country when he or she has left the country without authorization or has violated the terms of the authorization to leave the country or one who has requested to leave the country permanently after 1959 giving up his or her property and who may only return upon receiving special authorization of the Cuban government. Ley No. 989 (1961).

81. Ley General de la Vivienda (1988), Art. 81.

82. Ibid.

83. "Eastern Europe's Policy of Restitution of Property in the 1990s," *Dickinson Journal of International Law*, Vol. 10, No. 2 (1992), p. 368.

84. Ibid., p. 367.

85. Ibid., pp. 373–374.

86. Constitución (1992), Art. 21. The article is virtually identical to that contained in Article 22 of the 1976 Constitution.

87. Código Civil (1987), Art. 469.1(a).

88. Ibid., Art. 469.1(b).

89. Ibid., Art. 469.1(c).

90. Ibid., Art. 469.2.

91. Ibid., Art. 470.

92. Cuban Assets Control Regulations, 31 C.F.R. Part 515.

93. Código Civil (1989), Art. 492.1.

94. Ibid., Art. 493.1(a), (b) and (c).

95. Ibid., Art. 476.

96. Ley No. 7 (Ley de Procedimiento Civil, Administrativo y Laboral) (1977), Arts. 567–577.

97. Ley No. 50 (Ley de las Notaria Estatales), Art. 10(c), *Gaceta Oficial,* March 3, 1985.

98. Ley de Procedimiento Civil, Administrativo y Laboral (1977), Art. 567.

99. Benjamin, et al., p. 150; Leo Huberman and Paul M. Sweezy, *Socialism in Cuba* (New York: Monthly Review Press, 1969), p. 78.

100. Benjamin, et al., p. 154.

101. Huberman and Sweezy, p. 116.

102. "Aspects of the Food Program and the Status of Its Execution," speech by Adolfo Díaz, Vice President of the Council of Ministers at the opening sessions of the National Assembly, December 26, 1991 (Source: British Broadcasting Corporation transcript, January 8, 1991).

103. Ibid.

104. "Fidel Castro Addresses Party's Fourth Congress on Agricultural Policy," transcript in English by British Broadcasting Corporation, October 28, 1991 (Source: Cuba Vision Television).

105. Benjamin, et al., p. 167; see also, Stubbs, p. 52.

106. Stubbs, p. 52

107. Ley No. 36 (Ley de Cooperativas Agropecuarias), Art. 20, *Gaceta Oficial,* August 24, 1982.

108. Stubbs, p. 52.

109. René G. Montes de Oca Ruíz, "Las Formas de Propiedad en Cuba," *Revista Cubana de Derecho,* Vol. 2, 1991, p. 26.

110. Decreto-Ley No. 125 (Régimen de Posesión, Propriedad y Herencia de la Tierra y Bienes Agropecuarios), Art. 3, *Gaceta Oficial Ext.,* January 30, 1991.

111. *Latin America Weekly Report,* February 18, 1993, p. 75. According to the report, 156 state-owned sugar estates were broken into medium-sized farms of 1,700 to 2,000 hectares with a work force of about two hundred workers each.

112. Ibid. The work force on each unit numbers up to two hundred workers.

113. Constitución (1992), Art. 19.

114. Decreto-Ley No. 125 (1991), Arts. 8–10.

115. Ibid., Arts. 22–24.

116. Ibid., Arts. 8 and 9.

117. Ibid., Art. 10. If the owner has left the farm for other work, he or she may return within sixty days and reclaim rights to the land by reincorporating him or herself into the working of the farm. The farmer at risk of losing the land may also seek incorporation into a cooperative.

118. Ibid.

119. Ibid., Art. 12.

120. Resolución No. 171/84 (Ministry of Agriculture), September 20, 1984.

121. Decreto-Ley No. 125 (1991), Art. 26.

122. Ibid., Art. 28.

123. Ibid., Art. 18. Grandchildren and nieces or nephews can only inherit land if they have worked the land and their parent is either deceased or otherwise ineligible to inherit the land because he or she has not worked the land for the requisite period of time.

124. Ibid., Arts. 21–23.

125. Benjamin, et al., p. 160.

126. Decreto-Ley No. 125 (1991), Art. 20. There is an exception to the five-year requirement for minors under five years of age.

127. Ibid., Art. 24.

128. Orlando Rey Santos, "Régimen de sucesión de tierras," *Revista Cubana de Derecho,* Vol. 4 (1991), pp. 54, 60.

129. Decreto-Ley No. 63 (December 30, 1982), Art. 1.

130. Decreto-Ley No. 125 (1991), Disposiciones Especiales, Sexta.

131. Rigoberto Hernández León, "El Servicio Jurídico al Pequeño Agricultor en la Jurisdicción del Derecho Agrario," *Ponencias: Derecho Económico, Agrario y Administrativo* (Havana: Organización Nacional de Bufetes Colectivos, 1989), p. 9.

132. Decreto-Ley No. 125 (1991), Art. 6.

133. Ibid., Art. 41.

134. Hernández León, p. 7.

135. See collection of papers presented at a 1989 regional conference entitled *Ponencias: Derecho Económico, Agrario y Administrativo* (Havana: Organización Nacional de Bufetes Colectivos, 1989).

136. Benjamin, et al., p. 167.

137. Benjamin, et al., p. 160.

138. *Este es el Congreso más Democrático,* pp. 137–141.

139. Ley sobre Las Cooperativas Agriculturas (1982).

140. Ibid., Art. 2.

141. Ibid., Art. 4.

142. Ibid., Art. 5

143. Ibid., Art. 7.

144. Ibid., Arts. 53–54.

145. Ibid., Art. 25.

146. Ibid.

147. Ibid., Art. 36.

148. Decreto-Ley No. 125 (1991), Art. 5.

149. Ibid., Art. 33.

150. Ley de Cooperativas Agropecuarias (1982), Arts. 45–48.

151. Ibid., Arts. 45, 48 and 52.

152. Ibid., Art. 69.

153. Mimi Whitefield, "Protestant Pastor Carves His Place in Cuba," *Chicago Tribune,* March 7, 1993, p. 21.

9

Economic Regulation

The transformation of the economy was perhaps the most essential task of the socialist revolution because the collectivization of the means of production was to provide the material basis and essential conditions for the evolution of the socialist state and society. Certainly the revolution did radically alter economic policy and the control of wealth by centralizing the ownership and management of productive property in the national government. Yet the development of efficient institutions and measures to administer a centralized, planned economy proved to be extremely difficult, exacting a constant process of experimentation and evaluation. Further, the resulting uncertainty, compounded by general inexperience in socialist economic practice and adoption of ineffective and inefficient models, frustrated attempts to implement a legal framework through which economic relationships could be stabilized and regulated.

The dilemma is exacerbated by the current crisis in which reform and experimentation must be accelerated out of necessity, and the ability to project even a one-year national plan is impossible. In many ways, the government now finds itself operating under conditions similar to those of the 1960s. The situation requires swift, pragmatic decisions, with little time to reflect on consequences. The objectives guiding decisions are survival and maintenance of basic egalitarian principles of distribution. Thus, to date, there is no comprehensive, coherent plan for the restructuring of the economic system. Moreover, the changed circumstances have all but nullified legal measures previously adopted to regulate state enterprises. The informal economy, which mostly operates in the black market of stolen state goods, is growing rapidly, sapping needed resources and creating imbalances in distribution.[1]

It is not yet known how and if Cuba will solve the daunting challenge of recreating a socialist economy in an increasingly difficult and hostile economic environment. In such circumstances, as in the first decade of the revolution, legal reform per force must follow rather than lead the process of adjustment.

After providing a brief overview of the progression of economic regulation during the last thirty-five years, this chapter describes the model that was attempted as a result of the institutionalization process of the 1970s and the ways in which it has already been altered since 1989. In addition, it will also describe the laws and regulations governing joint-ventures, or "mixed" enterprises as they are called in Cuba, which provide a vehicle for foreign investment in Cuba that may enhance international trade as well as the development of the internal economy.

Overview

Legal regulation of the commercial relationships among state-owned enterprises is a relatively recent phenomenon in the Cuban revolution. During the first fifteen years of the revolution, Cuba had instituted a system of central budgetary accounting under which market mechanisms were rejected,[2] economic planning and management were centralized and all production units were financed out of a central budget.[3] The system was dedicated to radical egalitarianism, relying on moral incentives to promote discipline and productivity.[4] Thus, the management personnel of individual enterprises were not accountable for balancing costs and revenues or for profitability,[5] and material incentives were eschewed.[6] The failure of the system of central budgetary accounting to achieve economic progress was painfully apparent in the early 1970s.[7] The errors in the budgetary accounting system were expressly pointed out in the Main Report of the First Congress of the Communist Party of Cuba. Specifically cited as problems were the over-centralization of management and the lack of adequate market mechanisms, norms of commercial transactions and material incentives.[8]

The sweeping reorganization of economic planning and management in Cuba, announced at the First Congress of the Cuban Communist Party in 1975, signalled a new direction in Cuba's approach to the transformation from capitalism to socialism. Key to the new approach was the decentralization of production management from central state institutions to state enterprises,[9] and the development of a system of contracts to enforce accountability among the enterprises. International trade remained centralized in the national ministries. As part of the institutionalization process, the Congress introduced the new "System of Economic Management and Planning" (SDPE) and adopted Cuba's first five-year economic plan. SDPE was modelled in large part, at least in form, after the systems adopted in the Soviet Union and numerous eastern European socialist countries.[10] The fundamental features of the SDPE included both the strengthening of centralized planning and the decentralization of production management through semi-autonomous state enterprises which were to be self-managing, self-financing and profit maximizing. Cuba adopted a system of state arbitration in 1977 to assure compliance with the national economic plan and to resolve contract and commercial conflicts between enterprises.[11]

Implementation of reforms of the magnitude embodied in SDPE would challenge even developed economies. In the case of Cuba, the task was particularly difficult because many basic economic structures and systems essential to implementation of SDPE either did not exist or were insufficiently developed for rational economic planning.[12] For example, Cuba had not developed an adequate system for collecting, organizing and analyzing statistics and data essential to central economic decision-making.[13] Thus, from 1976 to 1980 numerous new institutions were created to manage information essential to the new system, including the State Committee for Statistics, a national accounting system, state committees to regulate prices and standards, and a restructuring of the banking system.[14]

It was not until the early 1980s, however, that economic regulation and regulatory agencies actually started to function. By 1985, the errors and deficiencies of these models began to surface, and the government embarked on a measured path of reform known as "rectification," which brought about some modifications. The Main Report to the Third Party Congress pointed to the "absence of comprehensive national planning for economic development" as one of the most serious problems along with mismanagement and the lack of a coherent and disciplined approach to investment.[15] Moreover, distribution of goods was inefficient and, at times, irrational due to lack of flexibility in marketing mechanisms.[16] The debate over the direction of reform centered on whether SDPE and the economic institutions spawned by it were themselves conceptually inadequate or whether they simply had not been implemented effectively.[17] Resolution of this debate, however, would be of little help in the face of the economic crisis precipitated by the collapse of the former socialist trading bloc in 1989, which necessitated radical new alterations in Cuba's economy.

The disintegration of the socialist bloc sent shock waves through the Cuban economy, which was already stagnating because of internal inefficiencies and the general depression in the international markets. In 1989, more than 85 percent of Cuba's foreign trade was with the socialist bloc of Europe. The disruption of this relationship forced Cuba to find new international markets for its goods as well as new sources of supplies. Moreover, many factories built to supply the socialist bloc nations were idled by lack of orders as well as spare parts. In addition, even where trade continued, the terms were no longer based on socialist prices, but on world market prices. Because of a severe shortage of currency reserves, energy imports plummeted from thirteen million tons of oil in 1989 to a little over six million in 1992. Further, the functions of centralized economic planning and management institutions had to be completely reoriented toward a diverse international market as opposed to the former stable relationship established by the Council for Mutual Economic Assistance (CMEA). Cuba's tie to CMEA had previously facilitated its long-range planning. Adjustment to this new situation has posed a herculean challenge that has been made all the more difficult by persistent U.S. attempts to prevent Cuba from entering international markets.[18]

In the early 1990s, Cuba began to dismantle the former economic planning and management apparatus and to substantially decentralize international trade. In addition, Cuba began to apply different policies to international trade and foreign investments than it applied to domestic economic organization. Cuba has actively pursued foreign investment in the form of joint ventures with Cuban entities, a phenomenon that has introduced the use of market mechanisms in sectors of the economy serving these enterprises. On the other hand, domestic production and distribution of essential goods have become more tightly controlled in order to be able to shift resources from one sector to another quickly to satisfy basic societal needs, particularly food. Under such circumstances, however, planning is virtually impossible, and economic management has become a matter of administering the scarce available resources rather than planning for future production and development.

Yet some Cuban economists suggest that greater decentralization is needed in the internal economy as well and even some amount of privatization in order to stimulate production and increase efficiency.[19] In seeking potential models for transformation, Cuba has looked farther east than the Soviet Union. A number of Cuban economists have visited China and Vietnam, including Carlos Lage, Secretary of the Council of Ministers, who has been in charge of coordinating Cuba's economic management during this difficult period. Both China and Vietnam have embarked on an economic reform process that permits substantial decentralization as well as some privatization, while the national government maintains control over vital resources and industries. China and Vietnam are not identical, however, particularly in their political reforms. It remains to be seen how far Cuba will go in this direction, but already a measure of flexibility has been introduced in specific areas where goods and products are produced for local consumption.

Modifications to the Cuban Constitution approved in July 1992 are an indication of a more open attitude toward new forms of property and economic organization. The amendments introduced a potentially profound change in the definition of socialist property. Article 14 states:

> The Republic of Cuba is governed by an economic system based on socialist property of the people over the *fundamental* means of production and the suppression of the exploitation of man by man. (emphasis added)

The 1976 version did not include the highlighted qualifier. Thus, the Constitution permits forms of private ownership of property in sectors and activities that are not considered a fundamental part of the state economy. Further, Article 15 specifically permits state property to be "transformed into private property" in exceptional cases if its "economic objective is destined for ends of development of the country and which do not affect the fundamental political, social or economic policy of the State." Such transfer must have the prior approval of the Council of Ministers or its Executive Committee. The willingness to relinquish complete state control over productive property reflects the need to instill greater flexibility in the economy and to uncover new ways of sustaining the society.

Already Cuba has eliminated some of the economic planning and regulatory institutions developed in the late 1970s and early 1980s. For example, the State Arbitration System has been abolished and a new Economic Chamber of the Provincial Courts and Supreme Court established to handle inter-enterprise economic disputes. The move suggests that the groundwork may be being laid for reducing national coordination of local enterprises. Until the outlines of economic policy become clearer, however, it is difficult to predict what direction the development of law and legal process might take to implement reforms. To the extent that market-based options are incorporated in the reform measures, the modernizing and strengthening of contract law, the development of new regulations governing commercial organization and practices will become increasingly important.

The introduction of forms of private ownership will also have implications for economic legal theory. With the adoption of socialist legality, Cuba also altered the civil law systems division of public and private law. Under capitalist systems, economic law, which primarily comprises the law of business organization, contracts and commercial transactions, falls under the area of private law. In Cuba, as in other socialist countries, economic law is a purely public, autonomous branch of law because virtually everything economic is managed by the state.[20]

Thus, Cuba must begin to develop the area of private economic law. Although the Commercial Code of 1956 has never been repealed and is, thus, still in force, it is woefully out of date and must be revised substantially if it is to serve a modern economy. The new Civil Code adopted in 1987 must also be updated, since its provisions on the law of private obligations were written to govern basically non-commercial transactions such as the sale of personal property. Other areas of law must also be modernized, including banking and monetary law. The task is daunting, particularly since there is little expertise in any of these areas in Cuba at the moment. Moreover, any modifications in economic and commercial law, even small ones, will have consequences for the future direction of Cuban socialism. The line between public and private will no longer be as clear.

Socialist Contract Law and State Arbitration

It was only in the mid- to late 1970s that Cuba began to look to legal process as a tool to help build and direct a socialist economic system. As previously noted, the 1970s marked the institutionalization of the revolution when Cuba not only articulated its governmental, judicial, party and economic structure but also adopted several other important laws that governed social relations. Central to the process was the institution of a national economic plan to be implemented by self-managing enterprises. If enterprises were to become self-managing and self-financing, however, a system of regulating inter-enterprise transactions and assuring accountability had to be developed.

At the time the SDPE was introduced, however, Cuba had developed neither a system of contracts applicable to the enterprises charged with implementation of the central plan[21] nor a legal system to govern the execution, validation and enforcement of such contracts. In fact, Cuba did not draft a new civil code reflective of the changes brought about by the revolution until 1987. Although the prior civil code had undergone piecemeal change from 1959 to 1975, the law of contract had not been revised to correspond to the new economic system introduced in 1975. The first law establishing basic principles for economic contracts between state enterprises was passed in 1978.[22]

In 1977, the Council of State empowered the Council of Ministers to organize an arbitration system to investigate and resolve conflicts of an economic character, pre-contractual and contractual, resulting from monetary-mercantile relationships involving state enterprises and other various national economic entities.[23] The *Organo de Arbitraje Estatal* (OAE), as the state arbitration system of Cuba is called, was formally established by the Council of Ministers in 1978.[24] Simultaneously, the Council of State established a system of economic contracts.[25] In general concept, the OAE was based on models found in the Soviet Union and other eastern European socialist countries.[26] Like many Cuban economic institutions that took their form from European socialist models, however, the OAE was shaped by decrees and regulations that reflected the specific circumstances and experiences of Cuba.[27]

Since the economic system it was created to regulate was itself in the initial stages of development, the task of the OAE was not simply to resolve inter-enterprise contractual disputes, but also to elaborate and regulate a system of economic accountability in its entirety. Among the objectives of the arbitration system was to "contribute to the perfection of the SDPE and the strengthening of the method of economic accountability on which the system rests."[28] Thus, from commencement of its operations in 1980, the OAE served multiple functions: adjudicating disputes, promulgating regulations, providing consultation and advice to enterprises and economic institutions, investigating specific economic problems, and supplying information and making recommendations to national economic planning units.

State arbitration in socialist economies is as fundamentally different from arbitration in capitalist systems in its purpose and function as is the economic system it supports. Private contract law is the fundamental regulatory device that enables competitive markets to function.[29] In a market economy, the contract is the medium through which buyers and sellers document their bargain and make it enforceable in a court of law. In the making and accepting of offers, the parties act voluntarily and out of self-interest and seek the most profitable bargain. Prices and allocation of resources are determined for the market as a whole through this private bargaining process. It is assumed that this process, left free of manipulation by either the government or private parties, will satisfy consumer and societal needs and yield the highest quality production at the most efficient price. Accordingly, the public interest is served indirectly by this private bargaining.

Under the Anglo-American system of contract law there is a legal obligation to make good on one's bargain. If a corporation makes a contract that it cannot fulfill, it will be legally bound to pay damages for breach. Breach of contract may be the result of inefficiency, bad fortune or the calculation that it is more economically efficient to pay damages occasioned by the breach than to perform the contract. Deliberate, calculated breach is not only permitted by the law, but some argue it should be encouraged on grounds of efficiency.[30] The breaching party is not bound to perform a contract except in very limited circumstances where specific enforcement is awarded.[31]

Commercial arbitration is not compulsory. The parties either agree in the original contract to submit disputes to arbitration or do so at the time that the dispute arises. Thus, arbitrators become involved in the private contract process only if one of the parties independently brings a complaint that the contract itself is not legally binding or that it has been breached, and the parties have agreed to submit the dispute to arbitration.[32] In resolving the dispute, the arbitrator acts in a quasi-judicial capacity as an impartial fact finder, and has the authority to impose a binding decision. The arbitrator rarely is concerned with the public impact of a particular dispute. Where important societal considerations are concerned, as in resolution of antitrust issues, public policy dictates that such disputes be adjudicated by a court of law and not by arbitration.[33]

In contrast, in the Cuban socialist economy of the 1980s, a contract was not the expression of an independent bargain reflecting private interests, but an instrument in the implementation of a national economic plan that attempted to allocate resources to provide the greatest and most equitable societal benefit. The institution of SDPE and the granting of management autonomy to enterprises made the contract the primary mechanism for the internal ordering of economic activities in accordance with the national plan. The plan outlined the annual production and service goals to be achieved by state enterprises. In broad terms, the quantities and prices of goods to be produced were determined by the plan. The plan was then elaborated and made more specific and implemented through the negotiation of "planned" contracts between state enterprises.[34]

While the enterprises were self-financing and self-managing, they were nevertheless obligated to negotiate "planned" contracts with other enterprises in order to fulfill the plan. The fact that state enterprises were supposedly accountable for their profitability provided, at least theoretically, the incentive to negotiate terms that served efficiency and profit-maximizing objectives. Such terms would include specifications as to quality, quantities, date of delivery, terms of payment, responsibility for transport, storage, etc.

The state enterprises not only had a legal duty both to enter into "planned" contracts but also to demand execution as well as performance of such contracts.[35] Thus, state arbitration proceedings were brought not only to resolve disputes over performance of contracts, but also to resolve disputes that arose in the formation and execution of the contract. Where such expertise was lacking, the parties were unable to agree or one party refused to sign a proposed contract, one or both could request OAE intervention to resolve the dispute and to assure that a contract was executed and that it contained the necessary legal clauses.[36] In the event a planned contract was not executed and neither party sought intervention by the OAE, the OAE could initiate a proceeding on its own, *de oficio,* to require execution of the contract.[37] The function of the OAE was not to impose terms on the parties, but to get the enterprises to agree on fundamental provisions necessary to fulfill their obligations under the national plan.[38] The arbitrator did, however, have authority to nullify provisions if they were not lawful.

Similarly, since fulfillment of the national plan required the performance of all "planned" contracts, enterprises were legally obligated to bring claims for breach. Moreover, since funds for bonus rewards for workers depended on profitability, enterprises had a self-interest in making claims for damages resulting from breach. Damages alone, however, were not a sufficient remedy since the contracted performance was not generally available from another source, causing harm to society as well as to the enterprise. Thus, to enable the injured enterprise to fulfill its obligations under the plan, the breaching enterprise was obligated whenever possible to perform the contract in addition to paying damages. Moreover, in addition to profit incentives, administrative personnel could be disciplined for intentional or negligent failure to carry out contractual obligations, including execution of a contract.[39]

In theory, the interests of enterprises and the national interest in completion of the economic plan were mutually supportive. The system was designed to reinforce the fusion of the self-interest of the enterprises to maximize profitability with the societal interest in fulfillment of the plan with maximum efficiency. As the juridical body charged with defending the social interest in the completion of the national economic plan, the OAE played an essential role in balancing these interests. Further, the state arbitration system was given jurisdiction to resolve disputes over economic impact of environmental harms.

Moreover, the OAE's mandate went well beyond dispute resolution and included functions related to development and planning. For example, the OAE was charged with organizing a system of research and analysis concerning economic contracts[40] and with investigating the causes of litigation for the purpose of proposing measures to prevent such disputes.[41] Thus, based on its experience with various industries, particular disputes, and its own research, the OAE made recommendations to the economic planning agencies such as the National Bank, the State Committee for Finance and others directly involved in state economic planning as well as to the management of particular enterprises.[42] Thus, the OAE served an important function in the process of developing the socialist economic system.

In its first decade of operation, the OAE also worked to educate enterprise administrators concerning the nature and importance of contract in commercial relations. Decree-Law 15 governing the general nature of contractual obligations between enterprises was issued in 1978, but its implementation was impeded by the lack of experience and understanding among enterprise management. Since no system of economic contracts existed to regulate commercial transactions between enterprises prior to 1975, few management personnel understood the requirements of economic contracts or had experience in the drafting and negotiation of contracts.[43] In fact, enterprise managers did not fully appreciate the new economic system.[44] The Main Report to the Second Congress of the Communist Party noted this in 1980:

> The system of economic contracting is being established and developed even though difficulties have arisen due to lack of full understanding of the importance of such contracts in carrying out the plan.[45]

Because inexperienced management posed a significant impediment to implementation of the new system, the OAE, when it began functioning in 1980, provided technical assistance to management of the state enterprises, especially in the drafting of contracts. Regional seminars were organized by the OAE staff to teach management personnel and their legal advisors the importance of contracts in the new economic system, as well as how to draft and negotiate contracts. Seminars were also conducted to explain new regulations and to discuss problems which had been identified by arbitrators and management.

Some specialists contend that by the late 1980s the system was beginning to take root.[46] The number of *de oficio* proceedings had dropped dramatically suggesting that enterprises were complying with the system.[47] According to one Cuban jurist, in 1990 the work of the OAE was not yet finished but was beginning to show fruit with respect to instilling an understanding about the importance of contract. Yet it was precisely at this point that the government decided to eliminate the OAE.

The New Economic Courts

The decision to eliminate the OAE was made by the National Commission on the System of Economic Management in the fall of 1990. In August 1991, the Council of State established new economic chambers in the Supreme Court and the Provincial Courts with jurisdiction over contract disputes previously handled by the OAE.[48] The reason for this apparently abrupt decision is not entirely clear. It appears that it was a product of the general disruption in the economy. Since economic plans based on the former socialist market were useless and the availability of resources and imports extremely uncertain, factories and enterprises could not predict what was going to be produced and when. Contracts no longer had any meaning in the state sector and the efficacy of continuing the OAE was questioned. The OAE may have also been a casualty of a more general policy of overhauling models adopted from the former Soviet Union. In addition, while some experts contend that the system was just beginning to operate as planned, others argue that it simply never functioned effectively.

Another reason for its elimination stems from the increasing number of "mixed" enterprises resulting from foreign investment. In 1983, the OAE had been given jurisdiction over disputes arising from contracts between "mixed" enterprises and state enterprises. When the Cuban government began to promote foreign capital investment in Cuba after 1989, there was some concern that disputes arising from their operations in Cuba be resolved within the ordinary court system.[49] To some extent this was logical because the legal principles to be applied to such disputes would necessarily be different than those applied to cases arising from "planned" contracts between state enterprises.

At this time, however, it is not clear how the new economic chambers will function, and there has been little written about them. Instructions issued by the Supreme Court in September 1991 stated that the instructions that had been issued by and that had governed the OAE would continue to apply with some exceptions.[50] Notably, there would no longer be a process of conciliation by which the parties could negotiate an officially supervised settlement.[51] In addition, the procedure of *de oficio* was eliminated. According to the legislation eliminating the OAE, conflicts arising in the pre-contractual phase will be handled administratively by the relevant ministries.[52]

There has been little time to think through the complexities presented by the new forms of economic entities and how to regulate their legal structure and relationships. The Civil Code adopted in 1989 does contain provisions pertaining to contractual obligations, but the drafters did not perceive their application beyond agreements between individual citizens. Moreover, the Cuban Commercial Code is shockingly out-of-date. The Spanish Commercial Code of 1885 was imposed in Cuba in 1886 and has never been repealed, although it was subjected to modification prior to 1959. It has not been up-dated since and is woefully inadequate with respect to modern commercial dealings.

The elimination of the OAE may presage the total revamping of the former system and greater decentralization and autonomy even among state enter-prises. However, the general nature of the rules governing the legal relation-ships between "mixed" enterprises, semi-autonomous enterprises, and state enterprises is far from settled. Once again, Cuba finds itself without a suffi-ciently developed legal framework, including the law of contracts, to cover the new forms of economic organization and relationships.

"Mixed" Enterprises

Like a number of other socialist countries, Cuba adopted legislation which permitted foreign investment in joint ventures with state enterprises. Cuba did this in February of 1982,[53] several years before the Soviets took similar steps. However, it was not until 1990, when the shortage of capital for invest-ment became acute, that Cuba actively began to court foreign investment through joint ventures.[54] At the beginning, Cuba promoted such investments primarily to expand facilities for international tourism, but it has increasingly sought investment in manufacturing, mining and marketing enterprises.[55] As an indication of the importance of these investments, Cuba has given them constitutional recognition which is intended to provide a measure of security to investors.[56]

The State Committee for Economic Cooperation (CECE) has been given the task of developing and negotiating potential joint ventures. Since first en-acting the legislation governing joint ventures with foreign companies, Cuba has applied the provisions of the statute in an increasingly flexible manner in order to accommodate prospective investors. Since 1990, Cuba has signed more than seventy agreements with foreign enterprises.[57]

Major Provisions

As a sign of continuing decentralization, joint ventures have their own legal status, independent of the government.[58] To attract investors, the law gives these entities considerable flexibility and autonomy which is not enjoyed by state enterprises. Thus, a joint venture is governed by the Articles of Incorpo-ration to which the parties agree to subscribe which set forth the rules of gov-ernance,[59] permitting the partners to the venture to appoint its own board of directors to manage the enterprise. The enterprise is also free of government regulation pertaining to production plans, prices, staffing patterns, and other aspects of management.[60] It may also contract with foreign personnel for ex-ecutive, administrative and technical positions,[61] and these employees may be paid in convertible foreign currency which they may take out of the country in specified amounts.[62]

The enterprises can be organized as corporations, partnerships or other forms of commercial association. In the case of corporations, the law states that they will have "nominal shares" and will "be subject to the provisions of the Commercial Code in force." Today, it is the 1956 Commercial Code. At the beginning, the foreign participation was limited to 49 percent of the shares, but the Cubans have permitted foreign ownership up to 55 percent in some cases.[63] The parties' contribution may take many forms, including cash and other assets. Cuba, however, does not turn over ownership of land; rather it contributes the use of land as an asset. Other forms of assets which Cuba may provide include structures, materials for construction and labor.

The tax provisions of the law are fairly generous to foreign investors. No taxes are levied on the gross income, shareholders' dividends or the personal income of managers and officers.[64] The tax on net profit is 30 percent which must be paid in convertible currency.[65] Further, the enterprise must pay a 25 percent payroll tax on the salary of Cuban personnel which includes a contribution to their social security fund.[66]

Other provisions give the enterprises first option on sales to the domestic market.[67] Conversely, although the enterprise may import and export directly, Cuban enterprises are to have first option on supplying fuel, raw materials and other materials and equipment to the joint venture.[68] These provisions are intended to support and stimulate the internal economy.

The legislation gives foreign investors access to Cuba's large skilled and well educated work force. Although managerial and administrative personnel may be foreign, all other workers must be Cuban. The joint venture, however, cannot contract directly with Cuban workers but must contract for labor through a Cuban entity, either the Cuban entity which is partner to the joint venture or another especially established to supply labor to these ventures.[69] Cuban workers are paid by the contracting entity in Cuban pesos and at wages set by state agencies. Recently, however, the Cuban government has permitted some workers, particularly those in tourism, to retain tips in foreign currency which they can spend in special dollar stores.

Impact of the "Joint Ventures"

In addition to providing needed capital investment which has enabled Cuba to boost income from tourism significantly since 1990, the introduction of joint ventures also provides opportunities for Cubans to gain management and entrepreneurial skills and experience. Moreover, their operation necessitates the infusion of market analysis and the employment of market mechanisms. Perhaps the experience will provide models for the development of private or quasi-private enterprises which are wholly Cuban.

Most Cuban lawyers have no training or experience in the field of commercial law. Those that do are primarily lawyers who practiced before the revolution. Thus, there is a lot of catch up required. Cuba still does not permit foreign lawyers to operate in Cuba, and it has set up special law offices to do the necessary legal work for the formation of these ventures. This is an area of practice that will have to expand if Cuba is to profit from increased foreign investment. Moreover, disputes which arise from the formation or operation of these joint ventures are to be adjudicated by the recently established Economic Courts. Like Cuban lawyers, however, the judges of these courts have little or no experience with modern business organization or commercial practice.

Whatever benefits the joint ventures provide to the Cuban economy, their presence has introduced a new dynamic. Not only do they operate differently and more efficiently than state enterprises, thereby providing new experience for the Cuban personnel, they also generate an entrepreneurial spirit fueled by the quest for dollars. They provide opportunities which talented Cubans may find more attractive than those offered by state enterprises. In a situation where most Cubans do not have access to consumer goods, or even supplements to food rations, employment at a joint venture is very attractive. Even lower level employees are not only generally paid well, but they may also have access to goods not available to other workers. Thus, the joint ventures may establish a new class of workers and compete with Cuban enterprises for the best and brightest.

An important inquiry that emerges from the development of joint ventures is what will be its impact on labor rights and labor relations in Cuba. The legislation provides that joint ventures must comply with Cuban labor law and respect the rights of Cuban workers. Yet joint ventures have considerably more flexibility in hiring and firing decisions. Workers who are fired by the joint venture, however, apparently still work for the state agency that contracted for the labor. It is not at all clear what rights of appeal Cuban workers have in such situations. Moreover, what will become of worker participation in management decisions? Although such participation is not mandated by law, there is anecdotal evidence that foreign managers have found Cuba's experience with worker assemblies useful.

With the exception of Cuban managerial staff, whose salaries are to be comparable to foreign managerial personnel, Cuban workers will be paid salaries set by Cuban law.[70] If joint ventures follow the pattern of private enterprise elsewhere—paying managerial staff considerably higher salaries which are paid out of profits earned from the contribution of lower paid workers—deep divisions between workers and management will develop. To blunt friction, and to provide incentives to Cuban workers, the law also provides that the joint venture "must establish an economic incentive fund for Cuban workers."[71]

Nevertheless, conflicts are bound to arise. The introduction of such capitalist ventures in the midst of a socialist system raises the potential for the reemergence of class differences. Whether and how Cuba will be able to mediate this contradiction will be of great interest both to Cubans and to outside observers. There seems little doubt, however, that these joint ventures are essential to the country's economic survival and provide an important source of income that the government needs to continue to supply food, medicine and other necessities to the population, as well as to develop Cuba's economic base for the future.

Notes

1. In a recent article, Julio Carranza Valdés reports that the informal market as measured in pesos in circulation, grew from two billion pesos to ten billion pesos between 1990 and 1992. Julio Carranza Valdés, "Cuba: los retos de la economía," *Cuadernos de Nuestras Americas,* No. 1 (1993), pp. 131, 153.

2. Economists have noted that Cuba in the mid-1960s relied less on market mechanisms than any other socialist country. Leo Huberman and Paul Sweezy, *Socialism in Cuba* (New York: Monthly Review Press, 1969), p. 164.

3. Ibid., pp. 163–68.

4. Ibid.

5. Ibid., p. 164.

6. Ibid., pp. 164–66.

7. See, Joel C. Edelstein, "Economic Policy and Development Models," in *Cuba: Twenty-Five Years of Revolution,* Sandor Halebsky and John Kirk eds., (New York: Praeger, 1985), pp. 187–189; and Elaine Fuller, "Production Quotas and Profits," *Cuba Times,* No. 3 (1982), pp. 5–7. For a general discussion of the changes in economic policy in Cuba, see Edelstein, pp. 180–92; Edward Boorstein, *The Economic Transformation of Cuba* (New York: Monthly Review Press, 1968); Huberman and Sweezy; Carmelo Mesa-Lago, *The Economy of Socialist Cuba* (Albuquerque, N.M.: University of New Mexico Press, 1981); Arthur MacEwan, *Revolution and Economic Development in Cuba* (New York: St. Martin's Press, 1981); Andrew Zimbalist, *Cuba's Socialist Economy: Toward the 1990s* (Boulder, Colo.: Westview Press, 1987).

8. "Informe Central," *Primer Congreso del Partido Comunista de Cuba* (Havana, 1976), pp. 102–05.

9. Until recently, all production enterprises were owned by the state and regulated by Decree Law No. 42 (1979)(Reglamento General de la Empresa Estatal). Private enterprise in Cuba was limited to proprietary service units, such as repair services, hair cutting, street vendors, photographers, gardeners, plumbers, etc. Such people who "work for themselves" must obtain a license from the state for which they pay a monthly fee ranging from ten to sixty pesos depending on the type of service performed. Joint Resolution No. 15 of the State Committees of Finance and Work and Social Security (1984).

10. Zimbalist suggests that while the form of SDPE may have been adopted from the Soviets, the new system was in practice distinctly Cuban, particularly with respect to broad popular participation in the planning process. Andrew Zimbalist, "Cuban Eco-

nomic Planning: Organization and Performance," in *Cuba: Twenty-Five Years of Revolution,* Sandor Halebsky and John Kirk, eds. (New York: Praeger, 1985), pp. 214–217.

11. Decreto-Ley No. 10 (1977)(Competences de los Organos), Disposición autorizante.

12. Zimbalist, "Cuban Economic Planning," p. 223.

13. Ibid.

14. In 1981, the Cuban government conferred new authority and responsibilities on the National Bank of Cuba. The Bank assumed financial control of the national production and became the exclusive organ which guaranteed and adjusted payments between enterprises and economic organs. For a report on changes in banking policy in the mid-1980s and the development of a consumer savings bank in Cuba, see Elaine Fuller, "New Developments in Cuban Banking," *CubaTimes,* No. 5 (1985), p. 3.

15. *Main Report Third Congress of the Communist Party of Cuba* (Havana: Editora Política, 1985).

16. Ibid.

17. Carranza Valdés, p. 156.

18. Andrew Zimbalist, "U.S. Blockade Policy: Mission Impossible?" *Cuba Update* (February-March, 1993), pp. 3, 6.

19. Carranza Valdés, p. 158.

20. *Derecho Económico* (Havana: Editorial de Ciencias Sociales, 1988), V. Láptev, ed., p. 26 (quoting Lenin).

21. Under the system of budgetary accounting, state enterprises did not contract with each other for supplies and services but fulfilled directives from central agencies. Thus, no system of inter-enterprise commercial contracts existed until 1978. Emilio Marill, "Sobre los Contratos Económicos y el Arbitraje Estatal," *Boletín Informativo,* No. 2 (1983).

22. Decreto-Ley No. 15 (1978)(Normas Básicas para los Contratos Económicos).

23. Decreto-Ley No. 10 (1977)(Competences de los Organos), Art. 1. In 1962, the government had created Arbitration Commissions to resolve disputes between state enterprises, government entities and the private sector which existed at that time. The law, however, had substantial deficiencies which made it ineffectual; arbitration was not compulsory and had no mechanism to assure compliance with decisions. Also there was no legislation dealing with contractual relations between enterprises. The commissions were disbanded in 1967. Miguel Reyes Salia, "El Sistema de Arbitraje Estatal en Cuba," *Revista Cubana de Derecho,* No. 20 (1982), pp. 73, 78.

24. Decreto No. 23 (1978)(Del Sistema de Arbitraje Orgánico), *Gaceta Oficial,* August 17, 1978.

25. Decreto-Ley No. 15 (1978).

26. For a discussion of the Soviet state arbitration system see John Hazard, "Production Discipline: The Role of State Arbitration in the USSR," *Review of Socialist Law,* No. 4 (1982), p. 297.

27. For a discussion of the differences between the functioning of economic institutions in Cuba and the Soviet Union see Zimbalist, *Cuba's Socialist Economy.*

28. Decreto No. 23 (1978), Art. 2(d).

29. While market exchanges could take place in the absence of contract law, Richard Posner suggests that private contract law serves three primary functions in the market-

place: It provides an efficient system for holding parties to their bargain; it reduces the complexity of market transactions; and it provides information which assists rational decision-making with respect to the bargain. Richard Posner, *Economic Analysis of Law* (Boston: Little Brown, 1972), pp. 67–69.

30. Posner argues that the law should not discourage such "economic" breaches. Ibid., pp. 88–90.

31. Under the Anglo-American legal system, specific enforcement is an equitable remedy which is granted in the absence of the availability of adequate legal remedies. Generally, the plaintiff can be made whole by receipt of monetary damages in which case specific performance will be denied. The common exception has been in contracts for the sale of land because land is thought to be unique, making compensatory damages an inadequate substitute.

32. An exception to the general rule of voluntary arbitration occurred with the functioning of the National War Labor Boards under the War Labor Disputes Act passed in 1943. The institution of mandatory arbitration within the guidelines of the war wage stabilization program was based on the requirement for resolution of disputes consistent with the war emergency. In operation, they were analogous to state arbitration systems in the character of resolution dependent on the perception of public interest and not wholly dependent on the interests and legal claims of parties before the board. F. Witney, *Government and Collective Bargaining* (Philadelphia: Lippincott, 1951), pp. 547–580.

33. Arbitration awards may also be set aside when the award or the arbitration agreement itself is against public policy.

34. "Planned" contracts are those which implement the national economic plan. There were also unplanned, or *nonplanificado,* contracts. These were contracts which an enterprise can enter into on its own initiative with surplus supplies or services not necessary to fulfill the national plan. Decreto-Ley No. 15 (1978), Arts. 4 and 5.

35. Ibid., Arts. 4 and 33.

36. Decreto-Ley 15 (1978), Art. 33. Interview with Dr. Benito Besada, Vice President of the OAEN, Havana, Cuba, May 23, 1984.

37. The OAE learned of failures of enterprises to execute required contracts by means of a third party who was affected by the situation, through other state reporting mechanisms, or by means of the OAE's own inspection procedures. In the initial years of its existence, the OAE frequently sent arbitrators to visit enterprises to discuss the system and to review contracts.

38. Decreto 89 (1981)(Reglas Procedimiento del Arbitraje Estatal), Art. 8(c), *Gaceta Oficial,* June 8, 1981.

39. Decreto-Ley No. 36 (1980)(Sobre la Disciplina de los Dirigentes y Funcionarios Administrativos Estatales), Art. 4.

40. Decreto No. 60 (1979) (Reglamento Orgánico de los Organos del Sistema de Arbitraje Estatal), Art. 10(j), *Gaceta Oficial,* December 29, 1979.

41. Ibid., Art. 10(k).

42. Interview with Dr. Benito Besada.

43. Osvaldo Dórticos, "Discurso," *Boletín Informativo,* No. 1 (OAE, 1982), pp. 4–6. This speech, which was published by the OAE in its first volume of the *Boletín*

Informativo, was given on November 17, 1980, at the inauguration of the jurisdictional activity of the OAE. Dórticos was the vice president of the Council of State at the time.

44. Ibid.

45. Second Congress of the Communist Party of Cuba, Documents and Speeches (Havana, 1981), p. 35.

46. Interview with Narciso Cobo, Havana, Cuba, October 7, 1992.

47. Interview with Miguel Reyes Salia, Principal Arbitrator OAEN, Havana, Cuba, May 23, 1984.

48. Decreto-Ley No. 129 (1991)(De Extinción del Sistema de Arbitraje Estatal), *Gaceta Oficial Ext.,* August 19, 1991.

49. Ibid., preamble.

50. Instrucción No. 141 (Tribunal Supremo), *Gaceta Oficial,* September 30, 1991.

51. Ibid.

52. Decreto-Ley No. 129 (1991), Art. 6.

53. Decreto-Ley No. 50 (Sobre Asociación Económica entre Entidades Cubanas y Estranjeras), *Gaceta Oficial Ext.,* February 15, 1982.

54. Carranza Valdés, pp. 155–156. For a complete description of the law and its provisions, see Jean G. Zorn and Harold A. Mayerson, "Cuba's Joint Venture Law: New Rules for Foreign Investment," *Columbia Journal of Transnational Law,* Vol. 21 (1983), p. 273.

55. Ibid.

56. Constitución (1992), Art. 23.

57. Ibid.

58. Decreto-Ley No. 50 (1982), Art. 1; Executive Committee of the Council of Ministers, *Possibility of Joint Ventures in Cuba* (Havana: Council of Ministers, 1991), pp. 1–2 [hereinafter cited as *Possibility of Joint Ventures*].

59. Decreto-Ley No. 50 (1982), Art. 8.

60. *Possibility of Joint Ventures,* p. 2.

61. Decreto-Ley No. 50 (1982), Art. 43.

62. Ibid., Art. 44.

63. Mexican investors in Cuba, obtained 55 percent interest in a joint venture for textile manufacture, and other Mexican investors have obtained 50 percent interest in hotel ventures where the Cuban government made arrangements with the Mexican government for the swap of Cuban debt for equity interest in the hotels. "Cuba: Trade Opportunities," *Los Angeles Times,* December 21, 1992, p. D2.

64. Decreto-Ley No. 50 (1982), Art. 25.

65. Ibid., Art. 26.

66. Ibid.

67. Ibid., Art. 31.

68. Ibid., Art. 32.

69. Ibid., Arts. 36–38.

70. Decreto-Ley No. 50 (1982), Art. 41.

71. Ibid., Art. 42.

About the Book
and Author

This book presents a comprehensive analysis of the development of law, legal institutions, and the legal profession in socialist Cuba since the 1959 revolution and evaluates their impacts on contemporary Cuban society. Slow to find footing on the unfamiliar terrain of socialism, the Cuban legal profession and institutions began to mature in the 1980s, making important advances toward the creation of a modern legal system. The new generation of lawyers is more skilled and dynamic, and Cuba's legal institutions have undertaken significant reforms.

Debra Evenson focuses on recent developments, including the 1992 modifications to the Cuban Constitution, changes in economic law compelled by the disappearance of the socialist market, and the modernization of both the criminal justice and the judicial system. She also analyzes developments in substantive areas of law, including law and equality, family law, criminal justice, property law, and economic law.

Debra Evenson is associate professor of law at DePaul University College of Law. Professor Evenson is the country's leading expert on the Cuban legal system. She began her research on Cuba in 1982 and has published and lectured widely on the subject. In 1993 she was awarded a grant from the John D. and Catherine T. MacArthur Foundation to study the role of the legal profession in Cuba during the current period of transition and reform.

Index